THE MISSILE DEFENSE CONTROVERSY

THE MISSILE DEFENSE CONTROVERSY

TECHNOLOGY IN SEARCH OF A MISSION

ERNEST J. YANARELLA

THE UNIVERSITY PRESS OF KENTUCKY

Publication of this volume was made possible in part by a grant
from the National Endowment for the Humanities.

Editorial and Sales Offices: The University Press of Kentucky
663 South Limestone Street, Lexington, Kentucky 40508-4008

02 03 04 05 06   5 4 3 2 1

Cataloging-in-Publication data available
from the Library of Congress

0-8131-9032-0 (pbk.: alk. paper)

This book is printed on acid-free recycled paper meeting
the requirements of the American National Standard
for Permanence in Paper for Printed Library Materials.

Manufactured in the United States of America.

To the members of the
Central Kentucky Council
for Peace and Justice

CONTENTS

PREFACE

It was a pleasure to be given the opportunity by the University Press of Kentucky to update and expand the study of the antiballistic missile dispute in the United States from its original focus on the politics of ABM development from roughly 1955 to 1972. Their invitation to revise this work in late March 2001 was quite unexpected but intriguing, given the declared intent of president George W. Bush to forge ahead with a missile defense plan in his new administration. The major risk of this enterprise, though, was that the second edition would be subject to the vicissitudes of rapidly changing developments that might cause the analysis and conclusions reached by September 2001 to be overtaken by subsequent events. Judging contemporary events also risks something I have long warned graduate students against—"serving history up hot." While I have tried not to take the bait, I leave it to the reader—and future book reviewers—to determine to what extent I have succeeded in avoiding these pitfalls.

In undertaking this effort, I found it both sobering and exhilarating to confront a work that gestated as a dissertation project during my last year of graduate school at the University of North Carolina at Chapel Hill and first year of teaching at the University of Kentucky in 1969 to 1970. Subsequently, the analysis and argumentation were revised and completed in 1975 as I was preparing to be reviewed for tenure and promotion to the associate professor rank. I can still see some of the naive political hopes and young scholarly dreams embedded in the writing that appear a bit shopworn as I now find myself well-ensconced in the duties and responsibilities of full professorship. While the professional goals and orientations of many scholars affiliated with research universities have changed somewhat over these nearly three decades and the structure of the political world has undergone even more dramatic modification, it is comforting to recognize that the animating spirit of the sixties that shaped my professional-political identity still reverberates here and there in my scholarly work, including this one.

I want to thank to Raymond H. Dawson, who directed the dissertation that served as the basis for the first edition and whose intellectual standards continue to inform this second, expanded edition. I have learned from his example that one of the intrinsic joys of a teaching career is touching the minds and lives of one's students in ways that are at once gratifying and unpredictable. He never asked of students that they hew some political line but expected students to strive to meet the rigorous standards of independent scholarship wherever those best lights led. I also express my gratitude to Frances FitzGerald, whose grasp of American political culture and defense policy played an important role in shaping my interpretation of the second phase of the missile defense debate. No less important was the recent book by Gordon Mitchell on strategic deception in various missile controversies, including BMD. I hope he appreciates my attempt to repay him in kind for his extensive footnotes to the first edition of this book in his penetrating volume.

I would be negligent if I did not express my debt to my family—my wife Elizabeth and children John, Rachael, and Walker—for their patience and forbearance these past six months when I hid away at Cosmo's, Lexington's great good place for coffee, conversation, and good food, and composed most of the revisions and additions to this latest edition. To Arnold Ludwig, friend, scholar, and fellow wordsmith, I express my sincere appreciation for his role as catalyst of the invitation from the University Press to bring out a new edition of the book. Thanks too to the gang at Cosmo's—especially David Baynham, Paul McAuley, Al Smith, Jim Gray, Tony Fernandez, and Lawrence Williams—for their comradeship, encouragement, and diversions when each was most needed in this enterprise. Not least of all, I want to offer deep appreciation to John "zig" Zeigler for his skillful shepherding of this second edition from conception to completion of the production process. Special thanks are in order for David Cobb, who attended to all the necessary editing tasks associated with this book's production. I also wish to express my gratitude to Claus Martel, Redstone Arsenal military historian, for granting permission to allow the press to use the cover image of the Nike missile family.

In the first edition, I expressed the hope that this study would "provoke further efforts on the part of students of war and peace in the United States to forge a native tradition of critical peace research." In dedicating this expanded work to the Central Kentucky Council for Peace and Justice, I wish to honor a coalition of representatives from peace and justice groups throughout the Bluegrass for whom I served as first co-chair at its birth and whose organization life span mirrors almost exactly the longevity of this work. In honoring this organization, I wish to express my thanks for their tireless efforts to keep the causes of peace and social justice on the public agenda in hopeful times and dark ones, too. Its generations of members know as well as do I that the work of peacemaking is never finished.

INTRODUCTION

The decision by the George W. Bush administration in early 2001 to proceed with alacrity toward developing and deploying a ballistic missile defense was the culmination of a defense decision-making process rooted in the 1950s at the height of the cold war. Yet few are now aware of the first controversy from 1955 to 1972 and how it set the stage for the second public debate, which was triggered by Ronald Reagan's famous "Star Wars" speech on March 23, 1983. This ignorance is hardly surprising to American historians or cultural critics. That Americans as a people seem particularly prone to a kind of historical and cultural amnesia has been observed at least since Alexis de Tocqueville mused on America's political foundations and peculiar cultural conventions.[1]

This work seeks to restore an understanding of these "missing" chapters in the early antiballistic missile (ABM) debate. It also seeks to explore both the continuities and differences between the first debate, from the onset of interservice rivalry over control of that weapon system to its conclusion by the U.S.-Soviet ABM Treaty reached in 1972, and the second public dispute, from the Reagan program in the early eighties through the Bush-Rumsfeld decisions in 2001 to abrogate the arms accord and develop an ABM defense against so-called rogue nations.

Although the first debate largely remained confined to executive and Pentagon conference rooms, legislative chambers, and congressional hearings, it eventually spilled over into wider political settings. By the 1960s, a significant segment of the American public had come to doubt the technical estimates and strategic judgments of its civilian and military leaders in the Pentagon. This shift in public opinion was evidenced in the news media and expressed, both inside Congress and without, through broadly based campaigns against weapons systems and military hardware like the

C-5A, ABM, MIRV, and the other frightening acronyms of strategic weapons development and the arms race.

While much of the debate focused on the excesses of defense spending and the taint of corruption in the financially well-lubricated links between the corporate and military sectors of American society, more than just the staple political issues of waste and collusion were being illuminated. Former sacrosanct beliefs and unchallenged shibboleths that had been the foundation of American military and defense policy in the postwar decade were put into question. This renewal of political activity signaled a dramatic—though not decisive—erosion of public faith in the cold war assumptions and military judgments that for nearly twenty-five years had informed executive decisions and legislative action in the area of U.S. national security.

While the massive involvement of the United States in the Vietnam War and scandals about exorbitant weapons costs played a large part in the ebbing loyalty to these beliefs, the major factor that precipitated this shift was the elevation of the question of deploying an antiballistic missile system to national attention and public dispute. Around this issue rallied a multitude of vocal citizens, former scientific advisers to the military establishment, economy-minded congress people, and others, a political coalition that nearly overturned the reigning hierarchy of national priorities guiding the nation's budgetary allocations.

The basic objectives of this work are threefold. First, I have attempted to provide a general historical narrative of the most important events in the evolution of the missile defense controversy between 1955 and 1972 and then between roughly 1982 and the virtual present. One reason for this overview is to recover a fuller appreciation of the historical events and political elements shaping the two phases of this public dispute. Moreover, except for a few rare analyses of ballistic missile defense (BMD) by such students of national security policy and strategic affairs as Dawson, Adams, and York, little effort has been expended in trying to clarify how BMD was transformed into a major national political issue.[2]

Another basic objective is to analyze the five most salient decisions to deploy an active defense against intercontinental ballistic missiles (ICBMs) in the first controversy and then to elucidate the contours and contributing factors of the second national debate, spawned in the Reagan administration and unfolding over the succeeding Bush, Clinton, and George W. Bush presidencies. Drawing upon the methodological insights of proponents of the decision-making approach in the study of international affairs and defense policy, I will attempt to explain the following five decisions in the early history of ABM: the McElroy decision of January 1958 in effect to grant the army sole rights to ABM development; the McNamara decision in April 1961 to defer production and deployment of the army's Nike-Zeus system; the McNamara decision of January 1963 to phase out Nike-Zeus and to initiate research and development of a more advanced system, Nike-X; the Johnson decision on September 18, 1967, to deploy the Sentinel ABM system; and the Nixon decision in March 1969 to deploy a hard-point ABM system known as Safeguard.

In each case, the basis of the executive decision will be studied in the context of the relationships that characterized the differing styles of defense decision-making of the McElroy-Gates and McNamara eras. In so doing, the bureaucratic, organizational, and political dimensions of these decisions will be clarified and their influence in each instance explored in depth. From Snyder, Bruck, and Sapin to Allison, national security analysts and foreign policy specialists have been preoccupied with the politics of the Defense Department as a complex organization and with the links between domestic and defense and foreign policy. I will attempt to give due emphasis to these facets of the major decisions affecting the development and fate of BMD in the United States.

My third objective, rather than simply trying to delineate the various factors (strategic, technological, political, organizational, economic) affecting each of these decisions, is to weigh their impact upon the history of the first phase of ABM dispute from 1955 to 1972. I shall thereby attempt to show how a peculiar combination of strategic and technological elements came to exert such a heavy influence on decisions affecting BMD that a kind of internal logic to American ABM development crystallized and predominated defense decisions concerning weapons innovations. This logic, although obvious in retrospect, was perceived and understood only half-consciously by major political actors and key decision-makers. This pattern will be defined in terms of the operation of a "technological imperative" in defense decision-making.

Two major themes occupy this work: the problem of technology and its relationship to the dynamics of the arms race; and the implication and influence of cultural values and streams of thought on national decision-making, relating in this case to the ream of national defense and technological innovation. During recent years in popular reflections on the nuclear arms spiral, the picture of military technology as a virtually uncontrolled and uncontrollable juggernaut has received wide currency. Indeed, even close students and active participants in the arms race have given credibility to this image in their analyses and writings. T.C. Schelling, for example, has written of the unbridled nature of modern weapons technology, as each generation of strategic and other military weapons systems becomes obsolete only a few years after its deployment. Even Herbert York, a scientist who was intimately involved in the decision-making process surrounding advanced strategic weapons development in the 1960s, asserted that "the technological side of the arms race has a life of its own, almost independent of policy and politics." Finally, a longtime publicist of the ramifications of science and technology upon modern society, Ralph Lapp, has suggested that a "technological imperative" operates in the development of military weapons—an imperative whose logic dictates that "if a weapons system could be made, then it would be made."[3]

Whatever political value they may have in mobilizing public concern, these writings do little to illuminate the deeper meaning and historical roots of this phenomenon. What literature exists on this subject merely nourishes the overdrawn portrait of military technology in the public mind rather than elucidating its substantive core. Moreover, critics of the technological imperative concept rightfully point to numerous instances (especially in the McNamara Defense Department) where costly but politically attractive weapons programs like the B-70, the Skybolt, and the nuclear-powered airplane were canceled on the basis of rational-economic analysis.[4] While the specter of technological domination in the strategic arms race is unquestionably overstated in most popular writings and in some scholarly quarters, serious consideration of these matters is nevertheless needed.

In trying to understand and make concrete the operation of a technological imperative in defense decision-making, I will challenge those who endow it with an objective cast and a deterministic logic that would hinder efforts to establish genuine democratic control over weapons technology and the strategic arms race. By uncovering the underlying assumptions and institutional foundations of research and development (R&D) in offensive and defensive weapons technology, I strive to render the purported technological imperative into its human elements and social forms.

The technical facet of technology (*techne* in its narrowest sense) is only a small part of what is meant by technology in its social context. As Herb Gintis has observed: "It is wrong to think of technology as a single unidimensional force which an economy can only have 'more' or 'less,' but whose substance and form are essentially independent of social decision. What 'technology' is at a point in time is the sum total of the past decisions made as to what forms of research are embodied in actual production in factory and office."[5] Thus, what constitutes technology and technological development are such things as the ideational basis of past and present technological planning, the particular institutional setting and organization of technological planning, and the socioeconomic context of the technological planning enterprise.

I concede that the condition of the cold war, with its climate of high risk and uncertainty, affected the shape of decision-making in strategic weapons development and deployment as well as the pace of weapons innovation at the strategic level. Yet within this context certain controlling assumptions about nuclear strategy, technological planning, and executive administration brought into the Department of Defense by Neil McElroy and Robert S. McNamara and integrated into American strategic weapon planning and programming had important consequences for the character, direction, and speed of technological development of U.S. strategic weapons. As will be shown, McElroy forged the institutional foundations of the technological imperative by centralizing military research and development in the Office of the Secretary of Defense (OSD) in 1958, and McNamara furthered those trends by systematically interconnecting the offensive and defensive realms of R&D in weapons technology.

I intend to show that a major impetus to the acceleration of the strategic arms race in the 1960s resided in the unrestrained dynamism of American offensive weapons technology and its connection with development in American defensive weapons technology. That is, I shall demonstrate how the technological planning process in strategic weaponry aggravated the course and pace of the strategic arms race and took on key features of a closed system increasingly indifferent to such external data as the nature of the Soviet threat, the character of Soviet strategic policy, and Soviet views on particular weapons programs.

American efforts to create a defense against missiles may be traced back to the fall of 1944, when Germany began launching its V-2 rockets against cities in France and Great Britain. But the first serious attempts to develop an ABM system began in November 1955 with the army's decision to undertake feasibility studies into the technical problems and practical possibilities of missile defense. As the design of missile defense systems evolved over time, at least five functions were recognized as necessary to the operation of an active defense against ballistic missiles:[6] acquisition: the detection of the threatening enemy warhead or reentry vehicle (RV); target track: the tracking of the incoming RV and its predicted trajectory; discrimination: the process of screening and sorting out the real RVs from the parts of the missile booster, chaff, decoys, and other penetration aids (penaids); missile track and guidance: the tracking and guiding of the interceptor missile to reach its target, the incoming RV; and interception: the destruction of the hostile RV by the release of X-rays and electromagnetic pulse (EMP) produced by the detonation of the interceptor nuclear warhead.

Scientists and engineers working on BMD in military and industrial laboratories in the 1950s put together the basic component parts of an ABM system. When the army was assigned the responsibility of developing BMD in 1958, the main components of an ABM were determined: radars to seek and track the enemy warhead; high-speed computers to process radar information in order to track incoming objects and their trajectories, discriminate real targets from decoys and other penaids, and target and guide interceptors to the enemy warhead; missile interceptors tipped with a nuclear weapon to destroy or otherwise neutralize the incoming nuclear reentry vehicle; and an interlocking command, control, and communications system to integrate the individual elements. In the following years the technology of each of these individual components was advanced in an effort to keep pace with improvements in offensive weapons technology and penetration aids. No distinctively new components, however, would be developed and added to the original Nike-Zeus system by the army.

Aside from the early ABM programs, which focused on land-based BMD systems, other concepts have been explored with varying degrees of interest and promise. A seaborne antiballistic missile system (SABMIS) was considered by the navy as an alternative to the army's land-based systems. In addition, research and development on outer-space (exoatmospheric) BMD systems using a network of satellites have been sponsored at various times by the air force and the Defense Department's Advanced Research Projects Agency (ARPA). And the latter agency, under the auspices of its original founding act, surveyed a wide spectrum of the most esoteric concepts of ABM systems, from the scattering of needles in space to the use of laser beams and plasma as target interceptors.[7]

By the time the internal debate over BMD spilled over into the public arena in the late 1960s, four basic interpretations concerning the role of ABM were discernible. Before McNamara announced the presidential decision to deploy an ABM system (known as the Sentinel) in September 1967, the most actively contested rationale for ABM conceived of it as a genuine defense against the offensive might of the USSR and China. In this view the ABM system needed to serve as an area defense (i.e., affording protection for thousands of square miles) as well as offer terminal defense protection (i.e., permitting coverage for a few hundred square miles). Among the staunchest advocates of this view during the heated public furor over ABM between 1966 and 1967 were the army, most (sometimes all) of the Joint Chiefs of Staff, and several powerful chairs of congressional subcommittees that oversaw the defense budget.

A second interpretation was actively disputed during this period and became the subject of more intense review in the 1969–1970 round: ABM as protector of America's strategic offensive forces. Patterned after the terminal defense concept, this view argued for the deployment of a network of ABM systems around U.S. land-based Minuteman ICBMs. Subsequent to Nixon's decision in March 1969 to deploy the Safeguard ABM system, this view found widespread support among many noted scientists connected with the "infinite containment" school of thought on American nuclear policy.[8] Even before the announcement of this decision, key persons within the OSD were sympathetic to this stance.

The view of ABM as the symbol of the arms race was yet a third interpretation of the ABM issue. Rather than acting as a rationale for deployment, this fundamental view of ABM served as a key tenet underlying the policy of postponement that the Johnson administration maintained until late 1967. Like its other proponents, McNamara came to identify the fight to deploy an ABM in the mid-1960s with the insane logic of the arms race; that is, the prevention of an ABM system came to be thought of as tantamount to putting brakes on the seemingly ceaseless momentum of the nuclear arms race.[9] From 1964 onward, this view of BMD was promoted and shared by another distinguishable group within the scientific community, namely, the "finite containment" school, which included such eminent scientists as Herbert York, Jerome Wiesner, and George Kistiakowsky (all vocal critics of Sentinel and Safeguard later).

A final interpretation of ABM systems was aired during the dispute: ABM as an alternate avenue to arms control and disarmament. Few major figures in the extended public controversy over ABM embraced this view in its unqualified form. Typically, exponents of the second view noted the extra benefits in arms control that might come from deployment of a terminal defense system. Or critics of BMD, such as Jerome Wiesner, sometimes granted the ABM limited potential value as a protective barrier during negotiated reductions of strategic offensive weapons.[10] Without doubt, the most articulate protagonist of this rationale was Donald Brennan, a mathematician and former president of the Hudson Institute. In numerous scholarly articles and on many occasions before congressional subcommittees, he defended ABM deployment and the strategy of defense as an alternative to the continuing prospect of "mutual assured destruction" between the two superpowers by retaining strategic deterrence as the cornerstone of American national security policy.[11]

Allusion to nuclear deterrence and its central place in the postwar history of U.S. nuclear strategy anticipates the overriding issue in resolving the controversy over BMD: the strategic dimension. The ultimate issue was whether the strategy of deterrence should be retained and the United States accept the sufficiency of the offense or whether the strategy of defense should be embraced and the United States opt for a significant damage-limiting capability. Continuation of the former would have meant relying on strategic offensive weaponry as a means of deterring general nuclear war, while renouncing the hope of limiting the amount of destruction in the event deterrence failed. On the other hand, the alternative approach would have held out the promise of providing a damage-limiting capability, but it was fraught with the peril of stimulating at worst a new and complex arms race occurring both offensively and defensively. The likely result would be a breakdown of controls and tacit conventions extant in the international system for settling disputes and the emergence of an environment of great uncertainty, widespread fear, and incalculable risk. In this work, I will attempt to set out the peculiar merits and liabilities of the case for retaining the strategy of deterrence as opposed to promoting innovation at the strategic level.

Because of McNamara's deep involvement in the BMD decisional process and because of his unyielding opposition to ABM deployment and eventual success in preventing it from becoming more than an ancillary part of the U.S. strategic arsenal, an analysis and an assessment of his evolving policy on ABM development and its relation to American national security will be offered. This inquiry will issue in a broad-ranging critique of McNamara's ABM policy and a point-by-point refutation of the assumptions underlying his argument concerning the role of the "action-reaction" phenomenon as the prime stimulant of the arms race. With regard to the former, I will be concerned to dispute McNamara's reluctance to accept anything but a strictly secondary (damage-limiting) role for ABM systems, despite his professed willingness until 1967 to entertain other functions and a different priority for active defenses. In addition, I will disclose how far McNamara was willing to go in multiplying the offensive destructive potential of the American strategic arsenal and in exacerbating the strategic arms race to avoid a serious consideration of BMDs as an alternative to offensive arms buildups. Concerning the latter, I will contrast the presuppositions that informed McNamara's interpretation of the major factor perpetuating the nuclear arms race with what I consider the more empirical supports to my interpretation of arms race dynamics derived from the strategic, organizational, and economic underpinnings of the American weapons planning process.

This work's central thesis concerning the source of the dynamics of the arms race will be fortified by contrasting the general approach to strategic weapons development, innovation, and deployment by the United States (called the technological breakthrough approach) with that of the Soviet Union (called the strategy of technological incrementalism). Without replacing the strategic and political elements of defense decision-making on BMD innovation with a technological determinism, I seek to show how the increasing American commitment to continuous qualitative innovation in strategic weaponry during the McNamara years did much to transform rational decision-making into a seemingly autonomous process ruled by a technological imperative.

A second theme offered is the sometimes evanescent, sometimes weighty, role that culture plays in public affairs. This theme will be explored in the context of the second national debate over developing and deploying a ballistic missile defense. Here I seek an answer to two key questions: How could a defense against the dubious threat of offensive ballistic missiles be revived and given the go-ahead nearly forty years after being politically interred? How did this technology find such a mission in an international environment overwhelmingly hostile to its deployment?

The United States has been long considered a unique nation among Western industrial democracies and capitalist countries. Whether seen as the first new nation, a virgin land, a people of plenty, or a country whose society and politics have been mired in the consequences of the peculiar institution of slavery,[12] the cultural heritage and religious traditions of the past have weighed heavily in shaping its political landscape and animating its loftiest dreams and most harrowing nightmares. As numerous historical chroniclers have pointed out, America's largely Calvinist heritage helped spawn a vision of the United States as a redemptive force with a God-given responsibility to root out evil and spread goodness throughout the world either by shining moral example or, when necessary, by the swift and sure military sword of justice.[13]

How this strain in American culture influenced the course and substance of the second phase of the missile defense controversy will be the burden of this book's final chapters. Having offered as a prelude an overview of the politics of ballistic missile defense from Ronald Reagan to George W. Bush, this analysis will show how, in the context of an America triumphant and an administration orienting its foreign and military policies toward what Charles and Mary Beard once called "isolationist unilateralism,"[14] the 2001 decision to dismantle the ABM accords and to move rapidly to deploy a national missile defense (NMD) is explicable in terms of the reactivation of this ideological imperative buried deep in America's religious history and cultural foundations. Ultimately, this analysis seeks to elucidate how, in transit from the first to the second controversy over ballistic missile defense, a technological imperative was supplanted by a political—or better—cultural imperative. And in the process, I argue, the McNamara legacy was overturned, along with its most revered achievement—the ABM Treaty.

1

DEFENSE POLITICS IN THE
EISENHOWER YEARS

GOVERNMENTAL decision-making does not occur in a political
or institutional vacuum. Besides the constitutional limitations
imposed upon public decision-makers, a vast range of constraints operate to circumscribe the latitude of choice available
to officials. Among these limiting features are included the
force of tradition, the sanctions of bureaucratic rules and
procedures, the norms generated by the institutional subcul-
ture, as well as the guiding principles and policies of the
electoral process. Defense decision-making on military strategy
and weapons programs in the United States is no exception.

While the Defense Department has been relatively immune from traditional limits and constitutional restraints, the
defense budget and its various programs each year by the central civilian and military policymakers in the executive branch
take place within the norms, conventions, traditions, and
structural relationships that have developed over time and are
capable of periodic alteration. Historically, these changes have
found impetus from such things as the prerogatives of central
management in the civilian OSD (oftentimes accompanied or
assisted by congressional reform or statutory mandate) and
the translation of public restiveness into political influence by
members of the various formal institutions or informal lobbying organizations linked to the Department of Defense.

During the 1950s, a discernible style of defense decision-
making and pattern of defense politics gradually became apparent. An understanding of the first key decision in the
history of the ABM controversy in the United States (i.e., Neil
McElroy's decision to resolve tentatively the army-air force
squabble over development and operational control of an

ABM system) involves an understanding of the basic elements of this style of defense policymaking in the 1950s. The McElroy decision can then be related to the more general patterns and characteristics of defense politics which evolved over the course of the Eisenhower years and held sway (despite energetic efforts in Congress to promote organizational innovation) until virtually the end of the first year of the Kennedy administration.

A useful guide for comprehending the style and form of the politics of American defense policymaking during the Eisenhower era is the insightful work of Philip Selznick in organizational theory, especially his pioneering work *TVA and the Grassroots*. In the context of a case study of the early history of the Tennessee Valley Authority, Selznick seeks certain characteristics and tendencies common to the institutionalization and operation of complex organizations.[1] Many of the shared patterns and tendencies that he perceives in the operation of the TVA are useful in illuminating the context of defense decision-making during this period, particularly his characterization of the "paradox of delegation." According to Selznick, any complex organization by its very nature is endangered by inherent entropic tendencies. On the one hand, although it may be created for some specific goal, this strategic objective must be put into operation; and typically this translation from general to specific terms cannot be accomplished in a clear and straightforward manner. Thus, for example, the overall goal for the Defense Department is that of providing military security for the nation. But how this objective of maintaining national security is to be defined precisely in terms of military strategy and supporting programs is never self-evident. Indeed, in recent years even the historical connection between increases in armaments and an increase in national security has been questioned–if not completely refuted–by the unique characteristics of modern weaponry.

Additionally, the implementation of this general goal requires the delegation of specialized tasks to substructures of the organization in order to promote efficiency. In the Defense Department these substructures are the army, air force, navy, and marine corps, whose basic responsibility is to serve as instruments for realizing the goals of the department. These subdivisions over time, according to Selznick, tend to view their functional tasks as ends-in-themselves and perhaps even to reinterpret them so that they come into conflict or compete with the general goals of the larger organization. Reinterpretation occurs generally in the context of the development by each branch of a distinctive tradition, specific goals, and a desire to protect its own interests.[2]

Rather than providing here a comprehensive examination of the development of the Department of Defense into a complex bureaucracy, I will highlight the specific form that the common characteristics of complex organizations took in the case of the Defense Department in the 1950s.[3] This will be done by examining the strategic goal and directing policy, the climate of opinion, the ramifications of delegation, and the specific role played by the civilian managerial agency of the Pentagon.

The goal of the Defense Department–the promotion and maintenance of the common defense–during the 1950s was put into operation through the strategic doctrine of the New Look. The origin of the New Look lay in the Eisenhower administration's desire to establish some balance and reconciliation between foreign and domestic, military and economic goals, to commit itself to a domestic policy of fiscal responsibility, and to establish a strong economy during the transitional period brought on by the death of Stalin and the ending of the Korean War.[4]

Shaping the New Look military programs were the belief that the "threat to national security was a dual one, economic and military, and a proper balance between a strong economy and strong military forces was necessary to meet this threat" and the attitude that "once the proper balance between economic and military programs was achieved, it should be maintained."[5] Also fundamental to the New Look was the preponderant American superiority in nuclear weapons and the means of delivering them. The decision to place greater reliance upon nuclear weapons and to make strategic retaliation the keystone of defense had a decisive impact upon the scope and character of defense politics during this decade. Since aircraft were still the primary means of delivering nuclear weapons over great distances, airpower would be given the highest priority. And although the inadequacies of the New Look (particularly in its stress on massive retaliation) would lead to a revision in its basic formulation and although technology would offer missiles as a replacement for the manned aircraft, strategic bombing would remain in its position of top priority throughout the 1950s.

At least five facets of the New Look doctrine had a critical influence on the politics of defense decision-making and on the pace and direction of R&D efforts by the military services at this time: "the emphasis upon strategic retaliation, the faith in novel technology, the 'long haul' perspective, the reliance upon nuclear weapons, the depreciation of manpower and conventional capabilities." Generally, they prompted the services to fund R&D projects relating to air and missile systems and to develop rationales claiming that their programs added something distinctively new and important to the overall goal underlying strategic bombing. Specifically, it promoted programs which were "induced by haste, boldness in technology, and a relative neglect of research and development fields separate from the mainstream of large systems." [6]

The defense decision-making and bureaucratic politics in the Pentagon is surrounded generally by a mood of expectation and anticipation, hopes and fears about the international environment in the present and near future. More concretely, this mood includes estimates of the hostility and potential strength of possible adversaries; calculations about the stability of the international arena and the predictability of the potential enemies' actions in that arena; and judgments about the character of military technology and its impact upon strategic doctrine. Participants in the policy debate take that climate of opinion into account when formulating strategy or vying for operational control of a weapons system.

In the 1950s the assessment of the military environment was characterized within the executive, in Congress, and among the public by a threat to national security from a potential enemy perceived to be both hostile and aggressive in nature and capable of inflicting great damage upon the United States. A second aspect of this climate of opinion was the shared belief in the extreme unpredictability of what that potential adversary might do; and, third, there was the widespread attitude that the feverish tempo and awesome potential of military technology were such that estimates about the continued stability and security of the American posture of strategic deterrence were problematic.

In congressional committees, great deference was given to military expertise on matters of national security. The condition of perceived high risk and uncertainty had endowed the military spokesmen with a distinct power advantage over their civilian superiors in congressional debate concerning the nation's defense. In this situation, the typical query of congressmen and senators during annual legislative review of defense appropriations was not the critical question "how much is enough?" but rather the solicitous offer "do you need more?" In this situation the OSD allowed duplication of developmental efforts in strategic weapons programs to proceed for long periods before assigning individual responsibility to a single service.

The controversies over weapons and operational control in the Defense Department during the Eisenhower years were generally marked by interservice rivalry, duplicative efforts in weapons development and strategic programs, jurisdictional disputes over roles and missions, diversity of functional interests by each service, a skewed distribution of power and responsibility among the services, and adoption of role of mediator by OSD. Each of these elements will be examined briefly.

As Selznick notes, a feature typical of most complex organizations arising out of the "paradox of delegation" is the emergence of conflict and competition among subdivisions for the coveted prizes of safety, deference, and value. In the Department of Defense this took the form of interservice rivalry. For, as the Defense Department increased its power and financial support during the period of the cold war, it became a battleground in which its three major services entered into unending combat in pursuit of the limited, but highly valued, economic, status, and security rewards of organizational politics.

The impact of interservice competition on civil-military relations in the 1950s was both direct and striking, resulting in the suppression of potential conflict between civilian and military agencies within the Pentagon and its deflection into contention among the military services.[7] The civilian OSD, therefore, did not have to confront on any major issue of strategic importance a united military establishment. As a consequence, the civilian agency of the Defense Department could exploit to the maximum degree the flexibility and latitude springing from military disunity by mediating service disputes over jurisdictional issues.

By the middle 1950s strategic consensus among the services and others was evident in agreement concerning the requirements for strategic deterrence and the functional programs necessary to meet these requisites. As a result, interservice haggling moved from dispute over strategic issues to contest over proprietary matters. Thus, basic questions like strategic alternatives (deterrence vs. disarmament vs. preemptive war) and the fundamental existence of the services (functional division vs. unification) were suspended and the lines of struggle were redrawn to include more marginal issues concerning budgetary funding, jurisdiction over roles and missions, and the allocation of responsibility for a single program or activity. Issues like the relative percentage of the overall defense budget, rights to a particular military role, and developmental or operational responsibility for a specific program became the basic fuel igniting interservice competition. Overall, then, mere strategic consensus of fundamentals did not preclude interservice squabbling over priorities and relevancies.

A second notable element of the politics of defense in the Eisenhower administration was the increase in duplicative efforts in R&D on weapons and delivery systems, as well as in functional programs. One factor encouraging duplication was surely the climate of opinion suffusing the decision-making apparatus in defense. The fears of war breaking out at any moment, the perception of a hostile and potentially aggressive enemy capable of inducing heavy loss upon North America, and the belief in the vast potency of a military technology capable of rendering obsolete whole weapons systems–all these attitudes promoted duplication as a lesser evil to the possibility of unpreparedness.

In addition, duplication tended to be rationalized on the grounds that it maximized the learning process in weapons developments. As Michael Armacost observes, "by temporarily deferring choice between competitive projects, time and information may be obtained, and the flexibility to adjust the design for a finished weapons system to changing circumstances and greater technical experience sustained." [8]

The shift in the character of the issues at stake in interservice controversy–from strategic to proprietary issues–was another condition that facilitated the rise of duplication. Since strategic bombing was accorded priority in the doctrine of deterrence, the branch services tended to vie for jurisdictional rights to roles and missions within the functional needs set up by the requirements of the overall strategy. Increases in the status of formerly lower priority activities and programs also tended to foster service competition and duplication. The case of the program of counterinsurgency in the late 1950s and the early 1960s is a classic example of how rising status elicits a proliferation of closely related programs among the services only tenuously related to traditional service missions.

Finally, the characteristic role played by the OSD and, more important, the type of procedural control it typically employed in delimiting the scope of interservice conflict and in resolving issues in dispute by decision were other factors promoting duplicative projects at the developmental stage and beyond.

The broadly based agreement over the doctrine of strategic deterrence, the primacy of strategic airpower, and the general functional requisites of the guiding policy had the effect of constraining political controversy among the services to bargaining over jurisdiction of roles and missions. So, for example, in contrast to the B-36 controversy in 1949 which involved fundamental issues of unification and strategy, the Thor-Jupiter dispute between the army and air force in 1956 concerned the questions: who should construct the missiles, who should operate them, and how much should be spent on the missiles? [9]

In theory, the service whose traditional activity was relatively low in the hierarchy established by the strategic policy could pursue two political options: it could attempt to trigger policy debate over the strategy in an effort to alter the ranking of the various activities or it could try to get a piece of the action by claiming part of the priority activity. In practice, this latter alternative tended to be the sole option open to it, given the narrow boundaries imposed by general agreement on fundamentals. The substance of the ABM debate between the army and the air force in the middle 1950s and the arbitrary range restrictions forced upon army rockets–both offensive and defensive–by the secretary of defense at the same time are illustrative of these tendencies.

A fourth element conditioning the bureaucratic politics of the Defense Department during this period was diversification of functional programs within each branch of the armed forces. For example, in the 1950s, besides its traditional interest in the ground combat mission, the army also developed programs in guided missiles, BMD, and limited war capabilities; the navy and air force expanded their interests to include a broad range of functions as a hedge against the future. Thus, no one service too closely identified itself with one functional interest in the strategic programs and activities.

The diversification of function acted as a moderating force on interservice rivalry. If no service depends upon a single strategic purpose, no service need oppose intransigently changes in strategic purposes. Nor does any service have cause to resent losses in major political gambits to secure jurisdiction over an important role or mission within a high status activity (e.g., the army's loss in the Thor-Jupiter case), since defeat tends to be mitigated by the breadth of one's functional interests and the prospects of victory in one of the many other interests in the same area being pursued simultaneously. Organizational flexibility and balance thus resulted from the quest for multiple interests. Even the air force continued to seek out new strategic missions to exploit during these years, despite its large share of the budget as a consequence of its natural association with the highest status activity in the strategy of deterrence.

The breadth of functional interests pursued by each branch service and the encouragement of duplicative efforts in weapons and program development built into the strategic and institutional context did not, however, ensure equality of power in the politics of defense decision-making and interservice rivalry. A skewed distribution of political power and military responsibility between 1954 and 1961 was exhibited, as Alain Enthoven and K. Wayne Smith have observed, in the fairly constant proportion of the defense budget allocated to each of the military services–approximately 47 percent to the air force, 29 percent to the navy and marines, and 24 percent to the army.[10]

Raymond H. Dawson and William Lucas have drawn a useful distinction between status activities and normative activities in complex organizations and applied it to their analysis of the dynamics of the organizational politics of defense in the 1950s and 1960s.[11] Status activities, for them, correspond to those functions and programs that are established by the specifying of the overall objective or policy directing the organization. These activities are ranked according to the degree to which they contribute to the larger purpose of the organization. They see normative activities, on the other hand, as springing from the combination of traditions, goals, and subideologies of the substructures of that organization. These traditions, goals, and subideologies coalesce over time into unique outlooks and structure the relative hierarchy of the subdivisions' normative activities. Differential power and influence within the overall organization comes from a combination of the organization's status activities with the individual substructure's normative activities.

In defense politics during the Eisenhower years, the New Look operationally defined its objective of strategic deterrence or massive retaliation in terms of strategic bombing. Thus identified, strategic bombing became the highest status activity. This gave the air force a tremendous bargaining position over the other services in the controversies over weapons development and operational control within the Pentagon and over funding in Congress.

Eventually, each service sought to justify its existence in part in relation to this general strategic mission. And, indeed, the other two service departments did achieve a measure of success–the navy with its Polaris missile system, the army with the ABM. (Recently, Herbert York has suggested that the overriding reason for the army's acquisition of its BMD role was McElroy's decision to mollify army discontent over its exclusion from this general strategic mission.)[12] Moreover, shifts in policy elevated some of the lower status activities (e.g., the limited war mission). The air force, nevertheless, maintained its dominant position in the interservice politics and strategic controversies of the 1950s.

The 1950s witnessed two contradictory trends relating to the OSD. On the one hand, the general thrust of legislative reorganization and reform of the Defense Department from 1947 to 1958 was typified by an unwavering movement in the direction of consolidation and centralization of power in the OSD. On the other hand, in disputes within the Pentagon over the planning and development of military programs and in the resolution of jurisdictional and operational matters, the secretary of defense was regularly cast in the role of ultimate, but reluctant, adjudicator of these disputes, rather than as leader and active innovator.

One reason for this circumstance concerns the personal capabilities and shortcomings of the leading officials in the Department of Defense. The individuals who manned the OSD during the Eisenhower years possessed neither the desire nor the competence to centralize command and authority. In comparison, those men who held high positions in the military, such as James Gavin, John Medaris, and Hyman Rickover, were far better versed in, and had a great deal more zest for, the bureaucratic politicking that had come to predominate in the politics of defense.[13]

Perhaps more important than the personal factor was the lack of a distinctive outlook on military requirements. Without some criteria for evaluating them, the secretary of defense usually had to depend upon external, nonmilitary considerations–most often economic–for defending his decisions either to the services or to Congress. Typically, during the Truman and Eisenhower administrations, the president and his secretary of defense determined very early in the budgetary review process the maximum size of the defense budget considered economically and politically feasible for the upcoming fiscal year. Total government revenues were estimated on the basis of what the economy could stand in taxes; then, from this estimate, were subtracted essential domestic expenditures (fixed payments and an anticipated cost of domestic programs) and foreign aid; the remainder was then allocated to national defense. While some degree of control was achieved, OSD was continually put on the defensive in congressional debate over funding and in the executive legislation of strategic programs due to its inability to compete with the lobbying of individual branches of the military services.

A third factor making it difficult for the secretary of defense to close the gap between formal and expressed power and authority in his office involved the kinds of controls (and their limits) that this office commanded during the 1950s. Using the distinction suggested by Herbert Simon between the "politics of adequacy" and the "politics of efficiency," Dawson and Lucas have observed that the Department of Defense, until 1961, practiced the "politics of adequacy" in defense decision-making.[14] The paramount question was: is this budget adequate to meet the needs of national security? More concretely, this strategy of decision-making and executive control was expressed in the bifurcation of budgeting and planning in defense policy. The planning component tended to reside with the armed services, which typically used the traditional "requirements approach" to determine what was necessary for national defense. The budgeting component lay with the OSD, which used the normal techniques of fiscal management.

This meant, on the one hand, that the OSD was arrayed against a split, but semiautonomous, military establishment individually supported by its own associations, scientific laboratories, intelligence agencies, and favorite industrial suppliers. In this situation, each service then decided what military weapons and programs would be funded on the basis of the portion of the budget allocated to it. Only in the case of a clash over roles and missions would the secretary of defense play an active role in mediating these issues. Michael Armacost has graphically described the degree of autonomy bestowed upon the branch services by this technique of control: "In the mid-1950's a service department could pursue a developmental project on the basis of urgency inspired by independent intelligence evaluations; it could finance the program out of a service budget only loosely audited against a comprehensive strategic concept; and it could employ both early successes in test programs and political support engendered by the diffusion of development and production contracts to sustain the life of projects initiated through 'foot-in-the-door' tactics." [15]

On the other hand, a measure of civilian control was attained using this procedure. Once executive decision determined how much money would be allocated from the annual defense budget for defense spending, neither the impassioned pleas from the offices of the military services nor the polemical speeches from congressional committees could compel the OSD to spend one cent above that figure, even if Congress apportioned a sum larger than requested. Then, too, the absence of a united front among the military services permitted the secretary to extend his control over the resolution of disputes concerning jurisdictional rights and issues relating to duplication. It remained for Robert S. McNamara in 1961 to seize the opportunities provided by law to centralize command and authority in the OSD and to fashion a distinctive "defense management" ideology that could challenge the rival sub-ideologies of the services and serve as a competing basis for independent and superior judgment on military needs and the programs necessary to meet these requisites.

2

THE ARMY GETS A MISSION

ON January 16, 1958, Secretary of Defense Neil McElroy forwarded directives to the Departments of the Army and the Air Force setting forth their specific responsibilities concerning the development of an ABM system, as well as indicating the role that the newly created Advanced Research Projects Agency would play in the further progress of this weapons system. To the army, authority was given to:

> continue development effort in the Nike-Zeus program as a matter of urgency, concentrating on system development, that will demonstrate the feasibility of achieving an effective, active AICBM system in an electronic counter measure and decoy environment.
> The program will be limited at this time to work on the missile and launch system, and those acquisition, tracking, and computer components required for an integrated missile system.

To the air force, orders were sent to "continue as a matter of urgency that portion of its current development effort in the Wizard program that pertains to early warning radars, tracking and acquisition radars, communication links between early warning radars and the active defense system, SAGE, and the data processing components required to form an integrated system. These above elements are to be compatible with a missile system having design and performance characteristics as described for the Nike-Zeus weapon system. The Air Force program will be limited at this time to the work in the above areas." [1]

In addition to splitting assignments of missile delivery systems and radar and electronic components between these two services, McElroy's overall directive placed further developmental work on the missile, communication, and detection network under the guidance and control of ARPA and named the director of guided missiles interim authority until ARPA was institutionalized.

During 1944 and 1945 the army contracted three R&D programs that had a bearing on later ABM efforts from 1953 onward. In 1944 a developmental contract was issued by the army for research and development on a long-range surface-to-surface missile program, called Project Hermes. The second program established by the army, Project Thumper, was directed to the development of a high-altitude antiaircraft missile. This project examined the potential of creating an active air defense against the V-2. The third army project instituted during this two-year period, Project Nike, was to have a profound impact upon the army's future ABM development. Initiated in February 1945, this project evolved from Nike-Ajax (an antiaircraft missile) to Nike-Zeus (the army's first ABM).[2]

Until 1953, only fledgling efforts such as those of the army marked the theorizing and developmental work by the services on the problem of an ABM system. However, between 1953 and 1955, when it became evident that the Soviet Union was making strides in long-range missiles, the practical need for an ABM was first perceived. Perhaps the first army expedition into the ABM field was Project Plato. Plato, it was disclosed in 1953, was conceived as a Field Army ABM system.[3] This project, however, met a piecemeal demise when in September 1957 the study was canceled and in 1958 the entire project was terminated.

The Nike-Zeus, on the other hand, appeared to the army to be more promising as a missile defense system and more competitive with its interservice rivals, the air force's Wizard program and the navy's Talos. By 1955 the army pinned its hopes on the Nike-Zeus, the third generation of the family of Nike air-to-surface missiles.[4] The Nike family began in 1944 and was developed by the industrial team constituted by Western Electric, Bell Telephone Laboratories, and Douglas Aircraft (primary contractor, system designer, and missile engineer). By 1953 this team was successful in producing the Nike-Ajax. The development of Nike-Hercules–the next generation Nike missile–was begun shortly thereafter in 1953, spurred on by changes in the bomber threat from Russia. In 1955, with evidence of Soviet advances in the field of intercontinental ballistic rockets, the army sponsored a feasibility study on the practicality and problems of developing an active defense against ICBMs. Again backed by the subordinate members of the Nike-Ajax team, Bell Telephone Laboratories investigated the ABM problem through 1955, completing the study in 1956 under the direction of the Army Rocket and Guided Missile Agency. Zeus was finally authorized as a full-scale developmental program in 1957. Although initially conceived as a rival to the Bomarc (the air force surface-to-air missile interceptor), Zeus had now evolved into a full-fledged contender for the role of mainstay in the ABM network.

The intensity of the army's interest in obtaining exclusive developmental and operational rights to the ABM in the mid- and late-1950s must be viewed against the background of its subordinate position in the strategic realm, the effect of the Wilson Memorandum upon the army's hopes for achieving an independent role in space and missilery, and the impact of the resolution of the Thor-Jupiter controversy upon the army's pursuit of the ABM mission.

The army's position in power, prestige, and funding from 1945 onward was greatly influenced by the Key West Agreements, the Unification Act of 1947, and the New Look policy. On all the issues determined by the civilian secretary and his service representatives, the army fared poorly. At Key West and Newport, where the basic assignment of roles and missions for the late 1940s and early 1950s were hammered out, the army found itself bypassed as the overall distribution of strategic missions was divided between the air force and the navy. The ramifications of the Unification Act further compounded the army's problems. The price of unification was the institution of a separate air force and the loss of all but a limited aviation force–and these developments flowing from unification proved to be severe obstacles to the army's ascendancy in the postwar era.[5]

The promulgation of the New Look by the Eisenhower administration seemed to conspire against the goals and aspirations of the army with its focus on strategic deterrence, the natural identification of its highest status activity with the air force's highest normative activity, its opposition to a posture of balanced forces in favor of a strategy of high priorities, and its depreciation of manpower and conventional capabilities. In addition, the broad spectrum of public support threatened to isolate the army and consign it to mediocrity or, worse still, institutional atrophy.

Among the tactics of counterattack chosen by the army were pursuit and promotion of R&D in the field of rockets and missiles. Underlying the army's plan were three assumptions: "that the pursuit of novel technology would appeal to those holding the military purse strings"; that it "would assist the Army in meeting the requirements of their new doctrine for tactical nuclear warfare"; and that it "would also enable them to exploit the talents of a major Army asset–the Huntsville Arsenal Missile Engineers." The army then expanded its tactical combat zone from five to ten miles to many hundreds of miles; it also argued for a prerogative to develop firepower capable of reaching any weapons that could be employed against them in a battlefield situation.[6]

The army had little trouble in competing with the other services in the guided missile field. Chances of success in gaining operational control, however, were less certain. Two key defense decisions were to influence the army's long-term interest in large rockets, as well as its valuation of the Nike-Zeus ABM program. The first of these, Secretary of Defense Charles Wilson's November 1956 decision regarding roles and missions, was to influence the parameters and language of debate between the army and the air force concerning ABM development and operational control; the second was to have the effect of reordering the army's priorities in the area of missilery by elevating BMD to contention for one of the two top positions in the army hierarchy of missions and programs.

The continuing army-air force imbroglio over the Thor-Jupiter dispute provided the immediate occasion for decision.

But there were other, more general, issues concerning service jurisdiction, the settlement of which could no longer be deferred. The jurisdictional issues included troop-carrying responsibilities, tactical air support, continental air defense, and intermediate range ballistic missile (IRBM) development. Since the service representatives could not negotiate solutions to these matters, Wilson was compelled to intervene. On November 26, 1956, subsequent to gathering with the Joint Chiefs of Staff in July to seek revision of the Key West and Newport agreements, the secretary of defense issued a memorandum entitled "Clarification of Roles and Missions to Improve the Effectiveness of Operation of the Department of Defense." [7]

The contents of this directive were a stunning blow to the army on nearly every front. Its hopes of gaining an independent and significant role in guided missiles appeared dashed by the severe weight and distance restrictions placed upon their craft and by the assignment of sole operational responsibility for land-based IRBMs to the air force. The sections of the directive relevant to the ABM program, however, offered the army a small ray of hope. To the army was assigned responsibility for developing and operating land-based surface-to-air missiles for point defense; to the air force responsibility was given for development and control over land-based surface-to-air missiles for area defense. "Area and point defense systems," the memorandum noted, "cannot be defined with precision." [8]

This directive's ambiguity, as well as its silence concerning which service was to have ultimate operational control over whichever ABM system was developed and deployed, naturally led to perpetuation of interservice conflict. It also suggested the terms in which service arguments and rationales would be couched. Moreover, because of the inherent greater cost of an ABM system constructed for point defense, the directive also structured the positions of each of the service contestants.

In Armacost's succinct but apposite characterization, "the

Thor-Jupiter controversy is in a sense the story of the rise and demise of the Army's efforts to acquire an independent and meaningful role in the development and use of long-range ballistic missiles." [9] The army, in fierce competition with the air force, had vied for the highly coveted prize of rights to development, production, and operational control of an IRBM system. Overlapping the service division between the army and the air force were two other lines of cleavage pitting the airframe industry against other industrial aspirants and the "arsenal system" against the "weapons system manager" concept of development. Armacost's exhaustive and definitive case study succeeds in capturing both the general and the unique characteristics of this controversy.

The import of this jurisdictional dispute for the future of ABM development by the army was great. The army tried to salvage something from the decision to assign sole responsibility for IRBM operation to the air force and to transfer the Jupiter program to its archrival. Ultimately, however, the best the army could achieve was to extend funding of the Jupiter for several more months and to provoke–with the aid of the Russian launching of Sputnik–a decision by McElroy on November 27, 1957, to go into dual production of Thor and Jupiter.[10]

The army by late 1957 became preoccupied with the search for new projects that might recoup some of its lost or waning status and set itself off as distinctive. One of the alternatives chosen by the army was the BMD mission.

The growing importance of air defense development for the army was manifested in numerous ways. By 1957, the army's budget allocated 10 to 15 percent for this mission. Moreover, heavy emphasis was placed upon the deterrent value of air defense, even to the point of characterizing this role as the army's "second primary function." Indeed, optimism became so heavy that at one point in congressional testimony, General James Gavin, then head of army R&D, assured committee members that the nation's need for a fully effective air defense (to 100 percent) was attainable.[11]

The army's positive thinking was carried over to BMD. Part of its case lay in its belief in "the need for a proper balance between offensive and defensive components" for providing "an adequate atomic general war deterrent." In his testimony before the House Appropriations Subcommittee, General Maxwell Taylor argued: "It had been easy to fall back on the line of reasoning that the best defense is a good offense. But the fact is that, under a national policy of abstention from initiating an atomic attack on our enemies, we are obliged to develop an air defense capability as an indispensable component of our overall general war deterrent force. Otherwise, we will invite attack and expose our people as well as our offensive forces to destruction and to fruitless loss." Supplementing this tenet advocating an offensive-defensive balance was skepticism about the ultimate character of long-range ballistic missiles. "The Army has never subscribed to the theory," alleged Secretary of the Army Wilber Brucker, "that the ICBM is or will be the ultimate weapon." [12]

Finally, pains were taken to link BMD to traditional army doctrine, including air defense and combat responsibilities. The army's ABM program was related to its air defense mission by broadly interpreting its tasks to include "provision of anti-aircraft units including guided-missile units for the defense of the continental United States." Its association between ABM development and its battlefield responsibilities was justified on the grounds that such weapons would help "maintain the integrity and the independence of the land soldier." [13]

Like the army, the air force (then the Army Air Corps) benefited from V-2 test firings conducted as part of Project Hermes in 1945. During the same year, the GAPA (Ground-to-Air Pilotless Aircraft) project was initiated as a consequence of high priority placed upon antiaircraft missiles over long-range offensive missiles at the time. Out of this program grew two offspring: the air force's Wizard ABM program, and the Bomarc area air defense missile. The latter program, which emerged directly out of the GAPA project, was the chief competitor of the army's Nike-Hercules for responsibility for air defense in the United States. This three-year interservice conflict (1956-1959) and its ultimate resolution was to have great bearing on the army-air force struggle over ABM.

The relationship between the Wizard program and GAPA was slightly more circuitous. After 1945, in an effort to generate and refine a new method—"collision intercept"—for destroying a ballistic missile, GAPA merged with the army's Project Thumper. This revised project in turn merged with a project being conducted by the University of Michigan's Aeronautical Research Center and was renamed the Wizard program.[14]

With the kindling and expansion of serious interest by the air force in BMD, the Wizard program eventually outgrew the boundaries of the GAPA-Thumper-University of Michigan project. Wizard became the code name for the air force's ABM program—a program that included feasibility studies and component developments by three different contractor teams. Between 1955 and 1958 the Wizard program was basically comprised of R&D studies contracted to Corvair-RCA, Lockheed-Raytheon, and Bell-Douglas. Bell-Douglas was the same contractor that was working with the army on its Nike-Zeus. General Donald Putt, air force deputy chief of staff for R&D, alleged that the two were almost identical, and, moreover, that the other two proposed systems developed by Corvair-RCA and Lockheed-Raytheon "had greater promise than did the Bell-Douglas." [15]

Air force deprecation of the Nike-Zeus and the Bell-Douglas systems developmental proposals undoubtedly stemmed partly from service bias and partly from the two-year lag in its program vis-à-vis the army's. The army had an ABM missile and a systems proposal; the air force had no such integrated package. The air force was definitely a latecomer to this enterprise. Still, the air force's wariness to commit itself at this time to one design or another may have had warrant. Aside from its qualms about Zeus's effectiveness as a missile, the air force was worried about the capability of the overall Nike-Zeus ABM system (missile plus detection, tracking, and communications components) to take into account enemy advances in decoys and other penetration aids. Consider this exchange between air force Colonel Joseph Lombardo and Congressman Robert Wilson, member of the House Armed Services Committee:

Mr. Wilson: Why did the Air Force feel that the other 2 systems of this 3-system setup they were studying were superior; particularly, why were the other 2 systems better than the Nike-Zeus system that was ultimately chosen?
Colonel Lombardo: Well, one of the primary reasons was that we realized that a smart enemy will develop an ICBM [censored]. We felt that the other two contractors had put more time into the problem of [censored] than the Bell-Douglas team. In fact, it was the contract contention that the Air Force gave to Bell-Douglas, which is the Nike-Zeus study, that started them in the [censored] problem. Up until that time they had not looked at [censored] as though it was any problem. Even the ORO Army report, that is out right now on air defense, gives the Corvair-RCA proposal more credit on the [censored] problem than the Nike-Zeus.[16]

RCA was assigned the specific duties in the Corvair-RCA team to develop the acquisition radars, guidance systems, and computers.

The Wilson Memorandum and the decision on operational responsibility relating to IRBMs did little to undermine the air force's position of primacy or to shake its confidence in the status of strategic offensive capabilities in the program policies in the OSD. For the air force, "our defense is primarily our deterrent rather than our active defense to keep them from coming through"; this meant, specifically, "in logic we must be careful not to put too much money in the Maginot Line of defending and destroying stuff that is coming towards us."[17]

As the air force's stance on ABM development and deployment unfolded throughout 1957, a contradiction in its case became apparent. It voiced, on the one hand, great skepticism of point defense–or, for that matter, any defense at all–favoring instead offensive retaliation. Yet, simultaneously, it was engaged in developing its own BMD, endowing the Wizard program with highest priority in the ABM field in the fall of 1957 and contesting the army for operational control of any such system. This inconsistency between strategy and development was not resolved until 1959, when Richard Horner, assistant secretary of the air force, announced that the eventual cost of Wizard would outweigh possible benefits and that therefore the air force believed defense money could better be spent for increasing offensive capability.[18]

The most comprehensive and coherent expression of the air force's case against deployment of the army's Zeus was put before the Joint Chiefs of Staff in mid-November 1957.[19] The air force adduced five arguments explicitly against the Nike-Zeus, but implicitly against any ABM system: the basis of deterrence to general war must be the nation's strategic offensive capabilities; deployment of the army's missile would contribute to the popularization of a Maginot Line myth; the Zeus system was technically deficient, since it could be fooled and overloaded by decoys and other objects; the earliest anticipated deployment date was 1961–too late to neutralize the anticipated "missile gap"; and the Soviet Union would undoubtedly offset any protection obtained by the United States from Zeus deployment by increasing its offensive missile threat. On these arguments, the air force rested its case.

Like the army, the navy too pondered the problem of air defense before the end of World War II. While the German V-2 was the threat that piqued the army's early attention, the Japanese kamikaze was the stimulus of navy concern. Instituted to find ways of protecting carrier attack forces at sea from kamikaze and other alien projectiles, Project Bumblebee was directed by Johns Hopkins Applied Physics Laboratory under the auspices of the navy.[20] From these early research studies was generated a family of surface-to-air missiles for shipboard use–Talos, Terrier, and Tarter.

The navy had not been averse to participating in interservice rivalry over the ABM role. In fact, in 1959, it recommended the Talos missile for an ABM missile system. As a consequence of early roles and missions assignments, however, the navy did not vigorously seek out this mission as a vital part of its overall strategic programs. At the Key West and Newport meetings the navy succeeded in negotiating a partial responsibility in general war deterrence and a subordinate place in the strategic offensive mission. In return for acknowledging the air force's "dominant interest" in nuclear weapons and foreswearing the construction of a strategic air command of its own, the navy gradually gained "access to the atomic stockpile, the right to employ such weapons 'to reduce and neutralize the airfields from which enemy aircraft may be sortying to attack the fleet,' and an air force acknowledgment of their right to participating in any all-out air campaign." [21] With this bargain sewed up, the navy could be sanguine about its future prospects.

The navy's relative indifference to the ABM controversy resulted from its traditional doctrinal view that the navy was not confined to any single medium of operation (land, sea, or air) but that its mission required forces in all three areas. Consequently, the navy cultivated a broad range of capabilities which had three major ramifications for interservice politics. First, its broadly diversified forces serving a variety of functional purposes meant that "the Navy has been a satisfied service and a staunch defender of the *status quo* in interservice relationships." Second, the navy achieved a measure of immunity from drastic increases or decreases in its size or strength from shifts in policy or breakthroughs in weapons technology. Allied to the first two implications was a last consequence: the promotion of a passivity in interservice politics that avoided the scars and animosities of fierce competition and bequeathed to the navy the enviable position of having its support or neutrality courted constantly by the other two rival service departments. The case of navy defection from support of the army's Jupiter program and the easy success of the navy in promoting and obtaining the Polaris submarine missile system are two illustrations of the smoothness of the navy's sailing in the turbulent sea of interservice politics.[22]

During the skirmish between the army and the air force over the ABM from 1956 to 1958, the navy was busy rallying support in the executive and in the Congress behind the Polaris program. Regarding its attitude toward ABM developments, it took the official line that "the problems of this task force will not be complicated by ballistic missiles," so no work on, or projected interest in, ABMs was expected.

Interest in the organization and management of missile programs within the defense establishment goes back at least to 1946 when a Committee on Guided Missiles was instituted by the Joint Chiefs of Staff to oversee missile developments in the United States. Since 1947 a patchwork of committees and offices have emerged and have been merged, reorganized, dissolved, and resuscitated in efforts to obtain some central control and coordination of American missile projects.[23] The results of these organizational maneuvers have tended to provoke further confusion by adding another layer of bureaucracy—lacking specific responsibility and certain authority—onto an interservice arena characterized by a semiautonomous structure, a galloping technology, and a propensity to political dispute. A survey of these organizational changes establishes part of the backdrop to Secretary of Defense Neil McElroy's January 16, 1958, decision.

Subsequent to the passage of the National Security Act in 1947, the Committee on Guided Missiles was continued as the Research and Development Board. In 1950 the Joint Aircraft Committee was reestablished under the aegis of the Munitions Board. Its basic task was to advise the Munitions Board on military facets of industrial mobilization, particularly as it related to aircraft and missile R&D and production. In the same year, George C. Marshall, then secretary of defense, established the Office of the Director of Guided Missiles. K. T. Keller, the first director, connected the three committees by serving as consultant to the chairmen of the Munitions Board and the Research and Development Board. A major shakeup and reorganization of missile management responsibilities took place in 1953 in the Wilson Defense Department. Entitled the Wilson Reorganization Plan No. 6, the design dissolved the Office of Director of Guided Missiles, as well as the Research and Development and Munitions boards. In place of these directing agencies, Wilson located their functions in the offices of two assistant secretaries of defense: one, for research and development; the other, for applications engineering. Until criticism and ferment lodged against the missile program triggered further administrative organizational reform in 1957, the last major development in missile management occurred in 1954, when the Research and Development Coordinating Committee on Guided Missiles was initiated.

Between 1956 and 1957 an increasing wave of protest against the faulty and confused administration of American missile programs resounded in the executive. Generally, the outcry was "inspired by mounting fear of Soviet accomplishments, the upward spiral of development costs, public airing of differences between the Armed Forces, and a growing feeling that the Department of Defense was overorganized." Congressmen involved in the annual review of the military budget were especially irate over this state of affairs; and from them a number of reforms were suggested to eliminate bureaucratic irresponsibility and to halt interservice haggling. Indeed, even President Eisenhower voiced his dismay over the petty politicking in the Defense Department and the confused state of missile management.[24]

These pressures prompted Wilson in 1956 to revive the role of a director of guided missiles in the guise of the special assistant for guided missiles. A Ballistic Missiles Committee was also organized. E. V. Murphee was appointed to the former office, who in turn was succeeded by William Holaday. When Wilson resigned, Neil McElroy, his successor, reestablished the office of Director of Guided Missiles, the broad functions of which included direction of "all activities in the Department of Defense relating to research, development, engineering, production, and procurement of guided missiles." [25] (In 1959 this office was dismantled and its director, William Holaday, returned to his former post as special assistant to the secretary of defense.)

Finally, the position of director of defense research and engineering was created by the Defense Reorganization Act of 1958. From 1956 until the beginning of 1958, when the Advanced Research Projects Agency and the director of defense research and engineering were brought into existence, confusion reigned as to the locus of coordination and responsibility for ABM development. Were these the duties of a particular service or did they lie within the province of the Defense Department? In the early months of 1958 it became evident that organizational resolution of this confusing and uncertain situation had crystallized.

Despite his distinctively civilian conception of his responsibilities as secretary of defense expressed in business management terms, McElroy felt compelled to bring research and development and administrative direction of missile and space programs under the control and coordination of OSD. The costs of indecision in the Thor-Jupiter dispute, the continuing proliferation of research and development in the services in a laissez-faire environment, the demands to accelerate the rate of technological advance, and the anticipation of jurisdictional conflict in weapons programs for outer space had in combination a decisive impact upon his decision to eliminate wasteful duplication, sublimate jurisdictional controversy over future roles and missions, and centralize command and authority in advanced research programs within his office.[26] The organizational instruments which he chose to alter prevailing patterns of defense politics and decision were the Advanced Research Projects Agency and the directorate of defense research and engineering (DR&E).

In addition to serving as the secretary's principal adviser on scientific and technical matters, the director of DR&E was delegated to "supervise all research and engineering activities in the Department of Defense" and to "direct and control (including their assignment or reassignment) research and engineering activities that the Secretary deems to require central management." [27] In these capacities, the director took on the supervisory and coordinating role over ARPA.

The first public disclosure of McElroy's intent to create ARPA came on January 7, 1958, when $10 million was requested by the president from Congress in the 1958 Supplemental Appropriations bill to fund the establishment of ARPA. Then, by directive of the Defense Department, the agency was formally instituted on February 7, 1958. At its inception, ARPA was provided with a broad responsibility "to engage in such advanced projects essential to the Defense Department's responsibilities in the field of basic and applied research and development which pertain to weapons systems and military requirements as the Secretary of Defense may determine." [28] Supplementing its legislative mandate was its specific delegated authority to issue instructions and directives to the military, to terminate duplicative or ineffective programs, and to approve, alter, or reject programs and projects under development by the services.

ARPA, then, is a small management team responsible for supervising its assigned programs through the use of budgetary controls and by the application of management, surveillance, and technical direction. Supported by the Institute for Defense Analysis on technical matters, it acts as a contracting agency, placing orders with the services and private firms for the performance of internal services. Moreover, its separate budget and higher administrative status vis-à-vis the three military services frees the agency from interservice rivalries and allows it to conduct its advanced research projects without involvement in service requirements.[29]

The importance of ARPA's creation for ABM development in succeeding years, as well as the impact of its operation on decisions in this area after 1958, can hardly be overstated. At its institution, it was charged with responsibility for the unified direction of all space projects and ABM programs, including the army's Nike-Zeus. Although the army was authorized to proceed with Nike-Zeus development as a matter of urgency, further development and coordination of an ABM system was assigned to ARPA. Soon after, the agency established Project Defender, the objective of which, in the words of the first director of ARPA, was "to obtain an advanced system of defense, either supplementary to or extending beyond the present Nike-Zeus terminal intercept concept." [30]

Two primary technical reasons evidently shaped McElroy's decision to give responsibility to the army to develop further the Nike-Zeus and to assign to the air force the task of improving communications and electronic and radar components. The Nike-Zeus missile was clearly superior to the air force's missile component of an ABM system. The air force's Bomarc was an air-breather, with all its attendant limitations for missile defense; the only alternatives which the air force could offer were missile designs on the drafting boards of its three industrial teams constituting the Wizard program. The greater understanding of the air force to the problem of decoys, evasive tactics, and countermeasure devices, as well as its past experience in radar and communications resulting from BMEWS similarly made his selection of responsibilities for the air force a sound choice.

From the Key West Agreements on roles and missions in 1947 to the Thor-Jupiter controversy in 1957, the strategic and budgetary woes of the army were manifest. Given its diversification of interests, the army in the wake of its defeat in the Thor-Jupiter dispute was able to turn to a project that promised to increase the army's standing among the services. Capitalizing upon the concern over the Soviet missile threat, the army's persuasive and politically adept spokesmen, like James Gavin, John Medaris, and Maxwell Taylor, were able to stimulate interest in an active BMD program and gain political allies in Congress. Moreover, the success of the Russian Sputnik and other military technological advances put pressure upon McElroy to counter the threat of such long-range weapons controlled by a powerful adversary.

Previous decisions made in a context more typical of the defense politics of the 1950s would have predicted acquisition by the army of developmental responsibility (and perhaps operational control) of the ABM mission. McElroy, however, decided to centralize both program and managerial control in his office. For this reason, although the army was allowed to further develop the Nike-Zeus, this program was placed under the authority of ARPA and the DR&E.

Because the decision focused specifically on the jurisdictional issue of developmental assignment and the political issue of sublimating future interservice rivalry and duplication of R&D, it failed to deal with the strategic issue of how the BMD role would be incorporated into the national strategic policy and its hierarchy of priorities. Was it to be a mission strictly subordinate to the concern of maintaining a large strategic offensive capable of deterring any enemy or was it to be elevated to the status of the highest task with the role of providing blanket defense coverage against a massive ICBM assault? In the latter case, a new strategy would need to be articulated.

But, more important, the creation of DR&E and ARPA and the resolution of developmental control of ABM had a number of dramatic consequences for the planning of military technology and the tempo and character of the strategic arms race in the 1960s. Broadly speaking, the establishment of DR&E and ARPA and the resultant centralization of military R&D in the Office of the Secretary of Defense institutionalized a new source of dynamism into defense planning at the pinnacle of administration. These actions meant that the scope of concepts of mass destruction and terror that could be explored were virtually unbounded and that the number of projects which could be funded through the developmental phase were only somewhat less numerous. It also meant that only a strong defense secretary could keep control of this profusion of technological possibilities. With the liberation of R&D in weapons technology from the constraints of service interests and perceived requirements and the formal consolidation of administrative power in OSD through the Defense Reorganization Act of 1958, the way was prepared for the "technological imperative."

Finally, its formulation occurred in a period of transition between two contexts and styles of decision-making on weapons development and innovation in the Defense Department. It partook partly of the various facets of Pentagon decision-making and interservice politics in the 1950s and partly of the rules, conventions, and structural relationships that were seized upon in the late 1950s by McElroy and were exploited to the fullest by McNamara as a means of instituting his conception of policy leadership in the OSD.

3

McNAMARA'S TWIN "REVOLUTION" IN DEFENSE DECISION-MAKING

In his first two years as secretary of defense, Robert S. Mc-Namara is considered to have effected a revolution in the decision-making apparatus and strategic outlook in the Department of Defense. This revolution, it is generally claimed, was a double revolution influencing the administration and management of national defense and the conceptualization of strategic doctrine.[1] While the administrative and strategic changes brought into the Defense Department by McNamara and instituted by him over his seven-year tenure of office may have captured the imagination of many political and corporate elites on all levels of administration in succeeding years, it is inaccurate for protagonists of McNamara's actions to impute a revolutionary cast to changes in the style of defense decision-making and strategic planning which in large measure were continuous with dominant trends at the end of the 1950s. For, though a different secretary of defense with a more conventional background in business management might have acted otherwise, the seeds of the technocratic strategy and its administrative forms which were to be most fully actualized during the McNamara era had already been planted in the late 1940s and 1950s by the pattern of congressional irritation over the politics rampant in the Defense Department (revealed in interservice rivalry, project duplication, and a weak secretary of defense) and executive willingness to promote defense reorganizations since 1948 which vested ever greater authority for centralization and coordination of power in the OSD. Thus, it was simply left to McNamara or some other like-minded person to exploit these dormant, but already enacted, powers and to bring the actual power of the OSD in line with its formal power.

Besides the specific organizational steps taken to centralize command and authority in the OSD and to establish clearer lines of hierarchy over missile management through the Defense Reorganization Act of 1958, McElroy also lessened the bases of support possessed by the services by fragmenting service, industrial, and scientific loyalties that had coalesced after years of joint projects. For example, after the establishment of the civilian National Aeronautics and Space Administration (NASA), McElroy waged a long and ultimately victorious battle with the army to transfer its Ballistic Missiles Agency headed by Werner von Braun to NASA to prevent rival ambitions in space between the civilian agency and the army. The separation of Space Technologies Laboratories from air force control and its evolution into Thompson-Ramo-Wooldridge serves as another case of service resistance to dismantlement and OSD success in severing service, corporate, and research links.[2]

In his first months in office, McNamara moved to complete the organizational overhaul of the Pentagon which had been initiated by his predecessors McElroy and Gates. By breaking up alliances between the services and their favored industrial suppliers and in-house laboratories, McNamara was seeking to alter the balance of power between the OSD and the major service departments. Then, to strengthen the power base of his own office within the defense bureaucracy, he further unified the defense establishment by delegating many tasks performed individually by the service departments to new agencies in the OSD. Beginning in 1961, the following responsibilities were consolidated into the OSD: departmental purchasing and procurement services were centralized in the Defense Supply Agency; intelligence and security activities were integrated in Defense Intelligence and the National Security Agencies; common and long-line communications were established in the Defense Communications Agency; Defense Department-contractor links were formalized in the Defense Industrial

Advisory Council; auditing was centralized in the Defense Contract Audit Agency; and Pentagon-university ties were strengthened through the Defense Science Board.[3]

Through the integration and centralization of these traditional service functions under the direct control of the defense secretary, the autonomy of the army, air force, and navy was greatly eroded. The result of this organizational centralization was the undermining and partial dismantlement of the "military-industrial-scientific" complex which operated in the 1950s and 1960s.

Crucial to the success of McNamara's organizational revisions in the Department of Defense was the necessity of forging a distinctively "defense-management" ideology to complement these administrative reforms.[4] In the past, the civilian secretary was armed with only the criteria provided him by traditional business management practices; thus, he stood at a distinct bargaining disadvantage over against the military services in fashioning the annual military budget and getting it passed through Congress. In an international environment of high risk and uncertainty, few wished to oppose the knowledge and expertise of a military spokesman who laid down his requirements. The defense secretary had no legitimated basis for forming independent judgments on military needs; and, moreover, the history of congressional deference to military expertise is well known. Because the planning and budgeting components of defense administration were divided between the service departments and the OSD respectively, virtually his only control over the content of the budget was to establish limits and to force the services to determine how much of their budgets could go to their self-determined priorities. To erode the influence of the "requirements approach" used by the services, McNamara propagated a unique defense management ideology in his office. He grounded this technocratic ideology in a different type of expertise–analysis.

Undoubtedly, the generation of a unique management vision in OSD would have been delayed and perhaps have been less pronounced had a person other than McNamara, even another technocratic manager from the corporate state, occupied the position of secretary of defense. Possessed of "an inquiring and incisive mind, an unlimited capacity for work, and a personality which lacked pretense and detested it in others," he brought to his office from Harvard Business School and Ford Motor Company a faith in scientific management that was expressed in the belief that "the techniques used to administer these affairs of a large organization are very similar whether that organization be a business enterprise or a Government institution or any other large aggregation of human individuals working to a common end." [5]

Over and above his faith in the rationalizing ability of scientific administration was a perception of his role in defense decision-making that set him apart from previous occupants of his post. Departing from the business-management orientation of Wilson, McElroy, and Gates, McNamara embraced a view of his role in terms of policy leadership. "I see my position here," he asserted, "as being a leader, not a judge. I'm here to originate and stimulate new ideas and programs, not just to referee arguments and harmonize interests." [6]

Like typical groups within large organizations, the directing agencies charged with managing the overall operation tend to develop unique sets of orienting goals, normative outlooks, and grounded traditions. In the 1950s the goals, outlooks, and conventions permeating the OSD tended to spring largely from the controlling strategic assumptions of the president, the condition of the strategic environment and the decisional procedures which it encouraged, and the more traditional views of governmental administration held by public officials whose backgrounds lay primarily in business and finance. In the 1960s, McNamara altered each one of the guiding definitions of these elements in OSD in his renovation of the decision-making process in the Defense Department.

For civilian control over the budget and mediation over jurisdictional conflict, McNamara strove to establish a type of control that fused planning and budgeting. In place of the "requirements approach," he opted for an efficiency approach which imposed an entirely new measuring rod by which to judge the worth of new military programs and which insisted upon the necessity of subjecting all proposals to this analysis. He appropriated analytic tools from a tradition of management stemming from operations research and systems analysis— techniques that originated during World War II and were first advanced by practitioners in physics, engineering, mathematics, and biology. What was distinctive to the McNamara "revolution" in defense decision-making then was his willingness to go outside of the traditional kinds of business management (delegation of authority, separation of planning and budgeting, assignment of a mediator role to central administrative agency) and to adopt the latest analytical and management techniques being taught at Harvard Business School and being developed at Rand by people such as Charles Hitch and Alain Enthoven. Thus McNamara was able to ensure managerial primacy in the Defense Department and to create a centralized decision-making and planning model for other federal, state, and local governmental agencies, as well as for corporate, educational, and health organizations infused by the technocratic quest for administration and control.[7]

Many social scientists have noted the kinship between strategy and economics; and, indeed, some have explored the degree to which economic analysis can clarify and possibly help resolve complex issues of military strategy.[8] Since both forms of inquiry share the values of efficiency, control, and comparison, the fruitfulness of probing such possibilities seems wholly justified.

The basis of defense management propounded by McNamara and the analytic counterweight to military expertise which he fashioned was the "technique of analysis"[9] that he quickly instituted in the defense planning and budgeting system. The proximate source of this new technique was the work of the Rand Corporation and some university-affiliated research institutes in applying systematic quantitative analysis to problems of organizational management and strategic decision-making. The invention of various statistical and computer operations and analytic methods, such as linear programming, systems analysis, and game theory, had as their purpose the formulation and breaking down of problems, the distinguishing of alternatives, the establishment of quantitative measures and indexes, the comparison of likely results of different choices, and the selection of the optimal choice in circumstances characterized by multiple variables.

One of the prime exponents of this new decision-making approach in the 1950s, Charles Hitch, was brought into the Defense Department by the new secretary to install the comprehensive Planning-Programming-Budgeting System (PPBS) to put these methods into effect in defense policymaking. Although this method is highly complex, PPBS may be most easily elucidated by focusing on three of its essential features: operations analysis, cost effectiveness analysis, and systems analysis. Operations analysis devises means for testing and comparing how different types of weapons, aircraft, and missile designs stand up under combat conditions and provides technical information for making decisions on alternative programs and designs.[10]

Underlying the cost effectiveness component of PPBS is the demand that costs be considered in the formulation of military programs. To achieve the most effective use of scarce resources with minimum waste, this technique dictates that "each unit of input–human, material, or monetary–must produce the maximum unit of military output." [11] Thus, the value maximized by this technique is efficiency and the data relayed to the decision-maker is primarily economic.

A third cardinal feature of PPBS is its systemic character. Generally, this is expressed in a twofold manner: its overall framework is designed to join its essential parts and functions into an integrated process; and it attempts to relate systematically the weapons or forces it is analyzing to overall strategic or military needs. Elaborating upon the latter point as it applies to weapons systems, Bernard Brodie has argued: "The central idea is that no weapon can be considered independently of the other weapons and commodities that are used with it, that all endure through some period of time and require men to service them and to be trained in their use, that all these items involve costs, and that therefore relative costs of differentiated systems, as considered against some common standard of function, are basic to the problem of choice between systems." [12] Through this dual process of integration, the systemic function promotes the value of control and dispenses organizational information to the decision-maker.

In sum, then, the integration of the PPBS and all the procedures of policymaking associated with it allowed OSD to exert enormous initiative and influence in rationalizing many facets of defense planning and fostering greater consistency between planning and budgetary support.

The second "revolution" over which McNamara is considered to have presided was a revolution in global military strategy. Here, too, the image of change on this dimension may be challenged, since the alterations he brought about appeared to have come full circle and returned to the strategy of minimum deterrence promoted by the Eisenhower administration. His reformulations, however, did carry with them their own unique contributions to a vision of the common defense and had a decisive influence upon the development of strategic weapons technology and the character of the arms race in the 1960s. Moreover, the evolution of his strategic outlook had a hidden telos which sprang partly from the strategic legacy of the doctrine of the New Look and its deterrent strategy and partly from the bias of his defense-management ideology. It was this strategic vision and its underlying thrust which was to give the technological imperative its awesome potential and dynamism in fueling the strategic arms race in the 1960s. The telos of his strategic thinking can be illuminated by examining the following progression of concepts that guided his general outlook on strategic doctrine: counterforce strategy (1962); damage limitation (1964); assured destruction/ damage limitation (1965); and assured destruction (1967).

A nation's strategic doctrine, like any overarching design in a large undertaking, defines boundaries to present military needs and sets a direction to future requirements. In the 1950s, the strategy of deterrence established the mission of the strategic nuclear offensive as the highest status activity and relegated the task of various forms of defense (antibomber, antimissile, fallout shelters) to a strictly ancillary role in the nation's overall defense plan. For a number of reasons, it was believed that bombers must always get through if America's national security were to be maintained. The nation's security by the end of the 1950s seemed to depend less on the belief that the lives and treasure of the country could be protected from the effects of an all-out nuclear attack than on the threat that the United States could pose to any would-be enemy—that, in the event of a first-strike, full-scale assault, it could retaliate with its remaining weapons with sufficient strength effectively to destroy the adversary. Deterrence, rather than war-winning or defense, had become the keystone of national security.

Robert McNamara became secretary of defense at a time when the United States found itself with a three-to-one superiority over the Soviet Union in its intercontinental nuclear strike force as a result of the American overreaction to the illusory missile gap of the late 1950s. American strategic doctrine took on an increasingly systematic and quantitative character as planning, programming, and budgeting were integrated and as the offensive and defensive components of strategic planning were joined in order to foster the most efficient mix. For whatever reasons, with the assent of President Kennedy, McNamara programmed strategic capabilities for the next few years so that by the mid-1960s the United States had attained a four-to-one superiority over the Soviet Union.[13] In order to justify the fiscal expenditure of $9 billion in the administration's defense supplemental to the Eisenhower military budget and to rationalize the increase in American nuclear superiority, McNamara addressed the nation in June 1962 at Ann Arbor, Michigan. In this first definitive statement of current American doctrine, he enunciated the outlines of a counterforce strategy, including its objective, requisites, and assumptions. This strategy, he argued, would allow the United States to approach the fighting of nuclear war as if it were any other military conflagration. Military forces and installations would be the targets. Counterforce doctrine would offer the United States "a strategy designed to preserve the fabric of our societies."[14]

The major requirement of this strategy was the capacity of this nation to retain sufficient military strike power so that, even if attacked in a surprise assault, it could respond with a second-strike force capable of destroying the enemy. Thus, the opponent would have the "strongest imaginable incentive to refrain from striking our own cities." This strategic disposition presupposed a posture of nuclear superiority and was premised on the relative strength, not the absolute might, of each strategic arsenal. As a consequence of the first two assumptions, it further presupposed that quantitative increases in power by the adversary required multiple increments in U.S. strength.[15]

Beginning with the Ann Arbor speech, then, McNamara evidently began to court at the strategic level the possibility of modifying the American dependence upon deterrence for national security by adding a war-fighting component to the nation's global strategy. This seemed clearly to underlie his articulation of a counterforce strategy with its advocacy of a mutual refocus of targets away from urban centers to military forces and installations. By 1964 McNamara's thought shifted slightly. In his annual posture statement for Defense appropriations for fiscal 1965, he introduced the concept of "damage limitation"–the goal of limiting damage and destruction in the United States in the event of nuclear war.[16] In disclosing this new strategy, he sought to describe the extreme strategic alternatives that had frequently been offered in debates over defense strategy in the United States.

The strategic continuum, according to McNamara, spanned the range from the policy of finite deterrence with a "cities only" capability to a counterforce strategy with a "full first strike" capability.[17] He rejected the former because a larger strategic force would be required to achieve a sufficient margin of certainty for the "cities only" capability than was assumed by its proponents; and further force increments beyond the specific strategic force to destroy Soviet cities significantly reduced potential damage to the United States and Western Europe that would occur in a nuclear exchange. As for the latter, he regarded it as unattainable, and perhaps uneconomic, since no effective antisubmarine capability was likely in the near future and no reasonable assurance could be held out for the destruction of all or most of the Soviet Union's hardened missile sites, even if the United States were to double or triple its strategic forces.

McNamara concluded that with any force level which the United States might conceivably build, a nuclear exchange between the two superpowers would greatly damage both sides. He thus reasoned that a damage-limiting strategy would be the most effective policy. This strategy, larger than the uncertain "cities only" capability and smaller than the unrealizable "full first strike" capability, would ensure the destruction of the enemy's war-making capacities, while limiting, to the extent possible, damage to the United States and its allies. What McNamara was striving to do was to reconcile strategic force requirements with the functional missions and overall defense policy of the United States. In addition, his technique of analysis was beginning to influence the shape of his strategic policy.

In 1965, in his annual posture statement, McNamara reflected on the nuclear war problem and the most effective way of handling it in the period from 1966 to 1967.[18] Here he coined the term "assured destruction" and related it to damage limitation. For McNamara, these two concepts signified the twin strategic objectives orienting our general nuclear forces (strategic offensive forces, strategic defensive forces, and civil defense programs). The objective of assured destruction was defined by him as the "capability to destroy the aggressor as a viable society, even after a well-planned and executed attack on our forces." This idea always existed in McNamara's general statement of the strategic theory guiding U.S. defense policy, but until 1965 it had been mistakenly subsumed under the conception of counterforce and then damage-limiting strategy. He recast damage limitation in terms of a strategic goal or, in his words, the "capability to reduce the weight of an enemy attack by both offensive and defensive measures and to provide a degree of protection against the effects of nuclear detonations."[19]

McNamara then argued that if both major powers embraced the same general strategic goals–deterrence of the other and a measure of damage reduction–then the American assured-destruction problem was the Russian damage-limiting problem, and vice versa. The import of this relationship had vast implications for the interaction between the American and Soviet offensive-defensive systems, as well as for the range of defensive programs needed and the type of defensive measures that would yield the greatest protection per unit cost.

In the first place, McNamara asserted, achievement and maintenance of the capability of assured destruction is the first overriding objective for American strategic forces. Only then can damage limitation be considered. Certain ineradicable obstacles, however, qualify the extent to which damage attenuation can be attained. Regardless of how extensive the U.S. general nuclear forces might be, it would be impossible to give the American civilian population total protection. Thus, whatever the United States might do, the Soviets possess the technical and economic means to assure their capacity to inflict a high level of fatalities. Such a response by the Soviet Union would be both justifiable and necessary precisely because our increases in damage-limitation would inextricably threaten their assured-destruction capability.[20]

In the second place, because any one of the three kinds of Soviet strategic offensive forces could inflict intolerable damage on the United States, any heavy defense directed only against one form of attack would have limited value. The adversary could simply outflank the defense against manned bombers by targeting only missiles against regions solely defended by antibomber systems. For this reason, "a meaningful capability to limit the damage of a determined enemy attack . . . requires an integrated, balanced combination of strategic offensive forces, area defense forces, terminal defense forces, and passive defenses."[21]

In the third place, for any given level of offensive capability possessed by the enemy, successive increments to each of the various American strategic systems operate in accordance with the theory of marginal utility, i.e., each addition brings diminishing returns. Based on these principles, McNamara concluded that every weapons system is in rivalry with every other weapons system in determining which configuration and relative numbers would establish the highest assured destruction or damage-limiting force. This meant practically that a specific ABM system would have to compete on a cost-effective basis not only against other defensive programs but also against offensive systems, whose increases above a certain point (roughly, the level of assured destruction) also contribute to damage limitation. Additionally, these principles implied that, to prevent outflanking maneuvers by an enemy, the total cost of deploying an ABM system had to be the sum of the cost of such deployment plus the cost of fortifying bomber defenses and antisubmarine warfare forces.[22]

Although these interrelationships between assured destruction and damage-limiting capabilities and between offensive and defensive systems were only incompletely realized before 1965, they do shed light on McNamara's predisposition in 1963 and 1964 for a full-scale civil defense program, whether connected to an active defense system or standing on its own as a passive defense. Moreover, the concepts and underlying principles propounded in this statement in 1965 clearly reveal the basis for his staunch advocacy of a complete nationwide fallout-shelter system, even in the face of strong opposition in Congress and among the American public. The construction of such a system, he believed, "would provide the greatest return, in terms of lives saved, from any additional funds spent on damage-limiting measures." [23]

The evolution of McNamara's strategic thinking reached its culmination in his announcement in San Francisco of the deployment of a thin ABM system in September 1967 and in his final annual posture statement in February 1968.[24] In these places, the concept of damage limitation had been almost entirely dropped from his repertoire of strategic terms. The accent now was on assured-destruction capability. Indeed, these statements represented a virtually point-by-point repudiation of the Ann Arbor doctrine and a revival of the tarnished notion of nuclear parity or sufficiency from the Eisenhower years.

In an effort to forestall the construction of a heavy ABM system, McNamara emphasized that the continued capability of assured destruction by the United States provided this nation and its allies with the deterrent rather than the ability to limit damage to ourselves.[25] He hoped to avert a further escalation of the nuclear arms race by either the United States or the Soviet Union by halting the "action-reaction phenomenon" which he believed fueled the arms race. By showing that security rested in the mutual capability of both the United States and the USSR to destroy each other and in their respective inability to prevent such destruction, his goal was to explode the myth of security through defense.

In making his case, the defense secretary cited as earlier proponents of his position Bernard Brodie and a former secretary of the air force, Donald Quarles. Anticipating the argument essentially put forth by McNamara in late 1967, Quarles had said a decade earlier: "Beyond a certain point, this prospect (mutual nuclear deterrence) is not the result of relative strength of the two opposing forces. It is the absolute power in the hands of each, and in the substantial invulnerability of this power to interdiction." [26] Thus, for all the modifications and refinements in strategic thinking undertaken in his administration, McNamara's strategy of assured destruction was basically the strategy of deterrence inherited from the Eisenhower years.

To a degree unprecedented in the history of the Department of Defense and of the War and Navy departments, McNamara and his civilian advisers succeeded in centralizing decision-making authority in the OSD, in rationalizing the policymaking process, and in shaping strategic doctrine. These organizational achievements were accomplished, however, only at the cost of creating new strains and divisions inside the Pentagon and between the executive and the Congress. In fact, the longer McNamara reigned as civilian leader of the defense establishment, the more it seemed that a "paradox of centralization" [27] began to impose itself upon his administration over defense. This paradox tended to express the political liabilities of organizational centralization through two discernible tendencies: the increasing trend toward the displacement of the interservice conflict of the 1950s by strife between the civilian leaders in the Department of Defense and their military counterparts; and the growing antagonism of a vocal segment of Congress toward the executive branch (in large part, the OSD) for its repeated vetoing of legislative decisions in the realm of defense policy.

By 1966 and 1967, the military establishment was arrayed against McNamara on major policy issues such as the efficacy of the bombing strategy in North Vietnam and the wisdom of deploying an ABM system. Since service appropriations had been marked by abundance during the first two years of McNamara's tenure, the implications of the systems-analysis and cost-effectiveness approaches to defense planning and budgeting had not reached the military. But the slow and subtle erosion of traditional service functions and their appropriation by civilian agencies in the Pentagon, as well as the increasing substitution of new standards of military evaluation for traditional military criteria, began to be felt in later years. The demise of the nuclear-powered plane, the RS-70, and the nuclear-powered carrier, the handling of the TFX, and the policy of postponement maintained on ABM deployment all took their toll upon service prestige and affected their perception of civilian decision-making under McNamara.

Receiving what they believed was a poor hearing on issues of military policy and defense needs, the services increasingly widened the arena of policy debate and turned to traditional areas of support in Congress. As the grievances mounted and became more uniformly distributed, the military services began to unite in common alliance, particularly the Joint Chiefs of Staff, in an effort to manifest their dissent.

Executive-legislative relations, too, were influenced by the centralizing and coordinating efforts promoted by McNamara. Signs of legislative restiveness and frustration in Congress on defense matters had been apparent at least since 1959 in the Nike-Zeus case and had been manifested in a variety of forms. One indication has been the propensity of one or both of the legislative bodies to participate in defense policymaking by voting extra funds beyond administration requests for programs relating to major weapons systems like the Nike-Zeus, the RS-70, and the Nike-X. In each case, the congressional move was rebuffed by executive noncompliance. Significantly, in another expression of reassertion of constitutional prerogative, successive Congresses since 1959 have legislated new requirements for annual authorization bills to include all appropriations for the procurement of all major delivery systems and combat vehicles and all appropriations for research, development, testing, and evaluation conducted for or by the armed services. As R. H. Dawson has observed: "This situation could at some point place the Administration in a position of accepting some Congressional decisions on strategic weapons, if nothing else, as a means of forestalling further statutory enactments which could significantly diminish the area of discretionary action for Defense Department officials." [28] Whether another secretary of defense could have forged more skillfully a rational strategic edifice in the rough terrain of national politics while avoiding service confrontation and mollifying congressional discontent is conjectural. More certain is the degree to which these unintended political consequences of administrative centralization contributed to McNamara's political demise and official exit.

For much of his administration and over a wide spectrum of issues, McNamara achieved a large measure of success in molding the climate of opinion that shaped the range of viable options and informed their choice. Reacting to the climate of opinion of the Eisenhower era and its impact on weapons development and innovation, he was able to generate a new strategic consensus on doctrinal issues in the 1960s and for a time to enforce the functional needs and imperatives of that consensus in the formulation of key weapons systems. At least three features of that climate of opinion have relevance to the ABM issue and the three important decisions which he rendered.

First, Michael Armacost has observed that in trying to

relate military requirements to strategic doctrine, "the Secretary and his staff have expressed a greater Missourian skepticism toward novel weapons projects." [29] This questioning attitude, it is argued, was exhibited most often in the tendency to promote intense developmental effort only in those areas where an explicit military need could be identified. While this may have been true during the last year or two of McNamara's tenure, at least two factors militate against its force for the first five years of his administration. In the first place, the defense secretary's own ambiguity at the strategic level– including his consideration of war-fighting and then defensive capabilities as part of America's strategic posture–encouraged the examination and proliferation of exotic weapons concepts across the broadest continuum of weapons ideas. Moreover, the technological planning process which McNamara constructed and its underlying assumptions promoted a dynamism to strategic weapons technology of a qualitative kind that proved difficult to control even by an energetic administrative leader possessed of "Missourian skepticism." And, finally, even when the goal of assured destruction took on overriding importance in America's strategic design, McNamara was willing to unleash MIRV (offspring of penetration aids development), a novel weapons idea which had a most dangerous and highly destabilizing impact upon the prevailing strategic situation.

A second characteristic of the climate of opinion partly shaped by McNamara's design concerned the future of the arms race. Especially in his final years as defense secretary, McNamara increasingly tried to publicize the hazards of perpetuating the strategic arms race, the diminishing returns to security brought by its advance, and the need to manage and control its pace and direction, if not its existence. Whether it was born of the naive assumptions of a liberal society and its faith in rational control or sprang from a universal humanitarian hope, his articulation of the insanity of the arms spiral and the overriding importance of its harnessing helped to mobilize many thousands after his departure from office to attempt to realize that goal. Still to be answered is whether the substance of his arms control policy offered a genuine route to arms limitation and eventually disarmament or whether the goals and accomplishments of this policy and the bilateral negotiations it helped to precipitate were more illusory than real.

Yet, even in the end, when decisions on Vietnam, ABM, and MIRV prompted a pervasive revulsion for the men and ideas that effected those decisions and led to a significant alteration of the preparedness environment of the 1950s and 1960s, McNamara could find consolation in his third contribution to a changed climate of opinion: his legacy of analytic techniques and strategic assumptions which were later used by senators and congressmen to challenge major Pentagon spokesmen and congressional allies on further ABM deployment and on the size and scope of the military budget in the first years of the Nixon administration.[30] Undoubtedly, the general rebelliousness of a significant segment of Congress toward erosion of its constitutional prerogatives also played a role in encouraging these later reactions. But even this factor was part of McNamara's ambiguous legacy.

4

ZEUS DENIED

THROUGHOUT 1959 and 1960 the army continued to advance arguments for early deployment of its Zeus ABM system, only to be rebuffed on each occasion. In 1959 it recommended $1.3 billion for Zeus for fiscal 1960, of which $300 million would go to further R&D and $700 million would be applied to tooling, production facilities, and construction of several Nike-Zeus bases. This total budget request, in the end, was pared by the administration to $300 million.[1] The following year, the debate centered on the question of whether the system should be produced and deployed before R&D test results were known. In all these pitched battles, the army stood virtually alone in its conviction that the system would work and therefore should be deployed forthwith.

In opposition during these years was an unbeatable coalition constituted by the White House, OSD, and the air force. With a presidential election in the offing, the administration found political and economic reasons for postponing decision on Zeus deployment. With an estimated $15 billion price tag on this missile and communications package and the desire of the administration either to balance the budget or to offer a tax cut (or both) to the American electorate during the 1960 election year, the army's requests for $1.3 billion in 1959 and $2 billion in 1960 for deployment were among the military requests examined in both years with a jaundiced eye. OSD, too, was opposed to these budgetary requests. In contrast, however, the considerations of the secretary of defense and the directors of ARPA and DR&E were more narrowly technical ones relating to Zeus's lack of a workable mechanism for destroying an incoming missile and its inability to differentiate enemy warheads from chaff, reflectors, and other types of decoys. The air force questioned the technical feasibility of the Nike-Zeus and promoted in its place sole reliance on America's offensive capabilities as the bulwark of defense. Only Congress allied itself with the army, and this only to the extent of authorizing for Zeus production $137 million above the administration's defense budget request in 1959.[2]

In popular and scholarly studies of the military-industrial complex, there has been a typical pattern of behavior observed on numerous occasions by various defense analysts and critics. Typically, this network of interactions among political, military, and corporate elites occurs when efforts are under way to obtain a new weapons system or to get immediate production or deployment.[3] The beginning round of the campaign is usually kicked off with the appearance of a magazine issue of one or more of the military and trade organs devoted entirely to the prospective weapons system. Then follow the intensive personal contacts with congressmen by military officials who express the urgency of getting the program off the drawing board and onto the production lines. Finally, ringing speeches of support by the "Senator-Generals"[4] resound throughout the halls of Congress. If sufficient interest is provoked, the issue receives extensive airing in subcommittee hearings, and an occasion for executive decision arises.

The ushering in of a new administration in Washington in January 1961 provided the opportunity for the launching of such a loosely organized and broadly based campaign to compel reconsideration of the ABM matter. The apparent immediate impetus of this drive for renewed debate on ABM defense was the January 30 issue of the respected technical journal *Missiles and Rockets,* followed almost simultaneously by the February issue of *Army,* the monthly publication of the Association for the United States Army, both offering cover-to-cover articles applauding the Nike-Zeus. And the subsequent actions that took place conformed almost exactly to the pattern of events characterizing the military-industrial complex.

After the full-issue coverages of Nike-Zeus appeared in these two magazines, an intensive lobbying effort commenced. Other military and trade journals published articles in the early months of 1961 lauding the progress of Zeus and assuring their readers of the imperative need for such a defensive system. In March, representatives of the army warned for the first time of a large-scale Soviet program to develop an ABM and told of the peril that would confront the United States if the USSR were first to achieve such a capability. In succeeding months, speeches were made on the floors of Congress on behalf of the army's program by such Zeus partisans as Congressmen Daniel Flood, George Miller, and John McCormack, and Senators Strom Thurmond and Karl Mundt. Congressional debate on the issue of Zeus production and deployment was climaxed by two events. Flood, Zeus stalwart and member of the House Defense Appropriations Subcommittee, sent an impassioned letter to President Kennedy urging him "to loose the Zeus, to put it into immediate production, to hasten the day when U.S. and allied forces at last can stand armed and ready with the ballistic boxing gloves so desperately needed for defense against the ceaseless threat of Communist world-wide nuclear aggression." When Kennedy's revamped defense budget was forwarded to Congress, it was revealed that authorization for funds to put Zeus into limited production had been once again denied. Thurmond then led the battle to induce the Senate Committee on Armed Services to add a $169 million authorization in the army's budget for this purpose. Unlike 1959, however, this move to marshal support won no victories in Congress.[5]

Whatever the long-term political, cultural, and economic factors crystallizing these informal relationships were, at least in the short run, the army's role in initiating the drive and heightening its momentum must not be underestimated. The army undoubtedly designed and promoted the February issue of its journal covering solely the Nike-Zeus. And the R&D chiefs who announced in an interview in early February the existence of a gigantic Soviet effort to develop an ABM system were military and civilian representatives of the Department of the Army. Furthermore, at least part of the responsibility for the widespread publicity in trade and commercial journals and newspapers could be assigned to the army—as was disclosed in testimony of army spokesmen before the House

Appropriations Subcommittee in late April.[6] Apparently, during two days in mid-March, twenty-nine newspapermen and magazine editors were treated to a guided tour of the Kwajalein Island missile test center in the Pacific Missile Range where Zeus testing was proceeding. Despite the army's claim of the nonpolitical nature of the visit, the dividends it reaped in the form of favorable publicity for the Nike-Zeus program made such portrayals questionable–particularly given the timing of the tour.

Leaving aside the issue of whether this campaign was really a conspiracy directed by the machinations of a military-industrial complex or largely the carefully orchestrated and skillfully led operation of the Department of the Army in the Pentagon, the energies, funds, and man-hours devoted to this attack appear to have been badly misplaced. For, as a copious analysis of the context and reasons for decision will exhibit, not the halls of Congress nor even the office of the president, but the conference rooms of OSD was the locus of decision-making on the authorization of funds for producing limited components of the Nike-Zeus ABM system from February to April 1961.

As a consequence of the changeover from the Eisenhower to the Kennedy administrations, congressional hearings on defense which normally convened in January and February of each year were postponed until April 1961. Before each one of these hearings, the new secretary of defense, Robert S. McNamara, read his first annual posture statement–a document comprised of a thorough analysis of the state of America's national security, a summary of key decisions on major military programs incorporated into the defense budget for the coming fiscal year, and a review of the arguments and rationales for these actions.[7] Within the BMD section, the secretary announced his anticipated decision on the Nike-Zeus.

McNamara indicated his general satisfaction with the progress of the Nike-Zeus ABM system. And he mentioned further that tests on various parts of the system–including components, ground radars, and the first two stages of the missiles–were currently in progress at the White Sands and

Point Magu missile ranges. By the end of 1961 the complete missile would be test-fired and in 1962 initial intercept tests against Atlas ICBMs would begin. Since some $863 million had been programmed for development, test, and evaluation for the entire system through fiscal 1961, he discussed the arguments for and against moving certain components of the Zeus system into the production phase before completion of the development, test, and evaluation phase.[8] He decided against such production. Having resolved the immediate, pressing issue of the status of Zeus, he continued:

Meanwhile, we are going ahead with other approaches to the problem of devising a defense against ballistic missile attack. In fact, we are requesting an increase of $21 million over the January budget for Project DEFENDER. This project is a series of studies designed to expand our present limited knowledge of the entire problem of detecting, tracking, intercepting, and destroying attacking ballistic missiles. These exploratory efforts, beyond the NIKE-ZEUS concept, in our judgment are essential if we are ever to solve the extremely difficult and complex problems involved in the development of an effective active defense against ballistic missile attack.[9]

In an effort to strengthen its position in policy debates in the executive and legislative branches of government in 1961, the army mounted two campaigns—one in November 1960, the other in February 1961—to promote acceleration of the Nike-Zeus program. In the first drive, initiated in the wake of the Democratic victory in the presidential election, the army asked for half a billion dollars to advance its ABM system for fiscal 1962 and called for a decision to launch a full-scale production program—one that would commit the Department of Defense to spending $5-15 billion over the following nine years.[10]

Basically, the army's proposals for acceleration and commitment to deploy were backed up by three arguments. First, the progress of Zeus development had been so rapid in the past six months that the ABM system might well be ready before bases and personnel would be prepared for it. Second, a major breakthrough in the system's ability to discriminate between warheads and decoys had been made. Finally, development of more powerful boosters had increased the missile speed to such a degree that warhead interception could be achieved at a greater distance from the warhead's intended target than in the past.

Its political campaign was hallmarked by the unusual step of forming a study committee manned by army weapons directors and by Defense and White House representatives from offices which on past occasions had blocked bigger Zeus budgets. This group, organized and headed by Richard Morse, assistant secretary of the army, was assigned the tasks of surveying and reporting on Zeus progress and then recommending whether this program was sufficiently advanced to warrant funding for production or site acquisition. In addition to the favorable report it expected from the Morse committee, the army also had the support of Overton Brooks, chairman of the House Committee on Science and Astronautics, who was pressing for executive release to the army of the extra $137 million voted by Congress in 1961 for additional research and development.[11]

Having failed in its attempt to elicit deployment of Zeus in the fiscal 1962 defense budget of the outgoing Eisenhower administration, the army prepared in February and March 1961 to participate in another round of budgetary and policy debates over its highest priority missile program. On this occasion, its request was restricted to proposing the initiation of production of long lead-time items of the overall Zeus system, making no demand for immediate or phased deployment of the system.

This cutback in the army's objective from late 1960 was matched by the perceptible decline in zeal for Zeus production within the Defense Department. Insight into the factors influencing the change in atmosphere surrounding Zeus was provided in House committee hearings on defense appropriations for fiscal 1962. While questioning Morse in April 1961, Congressman Gerald Ford noted that, in spite of a continued record of accomplishment, he sensed "in the Defense Department this year, in relation to last year, an even less (degree of) enthusiasm for going into production." And while concurring, Congressman Melvin Laird added: "I think some of the testimony from the Army is different this year from last year. This is not only in the Defense Department."[12] Despite initial halfhearted demurrers, Morse revealed the changed climate of opinion permeating the Defense Department as a result of the increasing sway of the "scientific school" there. More illuminating than the public position taken by Secretary of the Army Elvis Stahr before the Senate Committee on Armed Services, Morse's testimony disclosed some of the underlying reasons for the army's pessimistic mood toward Zeus production and its more moderate position in the 1961 budget debates.

According to Morse, during the previous two years the army was extremely enthusiastic about the Zeus program and anticipated that a positive decision on full-scale production and deployment of the system would be forthcoming in the near future. Partly as a consequence of the changeover of civilian personnel in the Department of the Army and partly as a result of the rise of a particular segment of the scientific community which was skeptical of the strategic value of an imperfect ABM system, the army took a more sober attitude toward the immediate likelihood of Nike-Zeus deployment and tactically retreated from a position deemed unattainable by the force of circumstances.[13] One of the few holdovers from the Eisenhower administration, Morse apparently was instrumental in persuading the new secretary of the army of the greater efficacy of pursuing this more modest objective.

Despite the outcome of McNamara's decision on Zeus announced on April 4, the army did have some reason to be encouraged. A complete systems test of the Nike-Zeus in a decoy environment was scheduled for later in the year in the Pacific Missile Range, pitting a Zeus fired from Kwajalein Atoll against Atlas ICBMs launched from Vandenberg Air Force Base. Yet even this prospect buoyed the spirits of the army less than might be expected. As Morse acknowledged: "We are not doing anything but thinking wishfully when we say we will run the test and suddenly have an answer to our defense. We are going to have [to have] more confidence in the system, and feel better about it. This is why I felt if we do anything it ought to be the minimum production rate. From this, we will also learn how to produce." [14] Thus, by moderating its goal and channeling its efforts into realizing the objective of limited production of Zeus components, the army was holding firm to its belief in the ultimate value of deployment of an ABM system for the United States, while admitting its underdog status in this battle.

Despite an outward show of optimism, the army's official position represented in Stahr's testimony was characterized by a defensive posture. Responding to a question concerning whether he had formed a judgment on the Zeus production, Stahr said: "I have formed an opinion yes; but my point is that I doubt that my opinion would be as valuable as the opinion of people who have greater grasp of the scientific question involved in the development of Zeus." He did, however, urge limited production of Zeus because of its status as the Free World's only ABM system. Moreover, evidence of Soviet ABM activity was an added incentive for beginning production. Finally, Stahr contended, waste would not be incurred by investment in Zeus, due to the scientific spin-off in the form of new radar and propellant technology which would match or exceed the original investment of the Nike-Zeus program.[15]

The OSD–including the secretary, ARPA, and DR&E–is not always unified on defense policy issues, either in policy formulation sessions in the Defense Department or in committee hearings in Congress. On the matter of ABM development in 1961, however, these offices (or at least the secretary and the directors of these agencies) gave univocal support to the decision solely to fund RDT&E of the Zeus program and to increase the amended budget for advanced ABM projects under the auspices of ARPA by $21 million.

In April 1961 McNamara appeared for the first time before the committees which annually hold authorizing and procuring hearings. In his statement, the secretary testified that Zeus had made sufficiently encouraging progress to warrant advanced and sophisticated testing of the whole system. Tests of the complete missile, he announced, would begin late in the year and would be followed by initial tests of the entire system against ICBMs in the Pacific Missile Range by the summer of 1962. For development, tests, and evaluation of the system, he indicated that $803 million had been programmed through fiscal 1961 and $276 million was being requested for fiscal 1962.[16]

He then cited the pros and cons of the army's request to procure production facilities and certain long lead-time parts before completion of the development, test, and evaluation phase. On the plus side, he observed: "Successful development may force an aggressor to expend additional resources to increase his ICBM force. It would also make accurate estimates of our defensive capabilities more difficult for a potential enemy and complicate the achievement of a successful attack. Furthermore, the protection that it would provide, even if for only a portion of our population, would be better than none at all."

These are some of the basic arguments that proponents of the Nike-Zeus system have marshaled in support of their case for at least a start on preproduction of certain Zeus components. Critics of this stand, McNamara continued, have also adduced strong arguments opposing any decision to begin production, claiming that: "there is still considerable uncertainty as to its technical feasibility and, even if successfully developed, there are many serious operating problems yet to be solved. The system, itself, is vulnerable to ballistic missile attack, and its effectiveness could be degraded by the use of more sophisticated ICBM's screened by multiple decoys. Saturation of the target is another possibility, as ICBM's become easier and cheaper to produce in coming years. Finally, it is a very expensive system in relation to the degree of protection that it can furnish." [17] On balance, then, McNamara concluded that continuation of Nike-Zeus R&D was preferable to the initiation of production or deployment of the system, and that an expanded effort in exploring other, more exotic approaches to BMD beyond Zeus was justified.

As to the general decision-making process through which McNamara went in forming this judgment, he emphasized that "the decisions were made by the President, based on recommendations which I made, based on long and exhaustive personal analysis and discussion with the parties concerned." Moreover, he clearly implied that the decision on Zeus was tentatively set on February 16 and 17, during his discussions with the service secretaries and the Joint Chiefs of Staff.[18]

More pertinent in elucidating the rational basis of his decision are some of McNamara's comments concerning the reasons and beliefs that informed his recommendation or decision. Costs, he asserted, played no part in his decision against ordering limited production or deployment. That the cost of an ABM system is higher than the cost of the ICBMs against which it would be directed is inconsequential in comparison to the real issue–the degree of protection that can be achieved. In an apparent contradiction, however, he maintained that, if the army's proposal had been accepted and preproduction had been initiated, the expenditure of funds for procurement of facilities and long lead-time items "may result in substantial waste because of subsequent changes in the design of the system during the later period of development."[19] Behind this inconsistency lay deeper reasons for McNamara's resistance to preproduction.

In response to Congressman Phil Weaver's question whether Soviet deployment would compel McNamara to alter his position against U.S. deployment, the secretary said, "I do not believe it would affect my recommendations in any way because I have assumed that we must take account of the possibility that they will have such a system." Under earlier questioning from Congressman Daniel Flood, McNamara indicated that the United States might make a multiple increase in its Minuteman force. He did, however, refuse to assign relative priorities to offensive and defensive missile systems, although his choice was implicit:

Mr. Flood: Which comes first, the chicken or the egg? Which comes first, Minuteman because he may develop a good Zeus, or our own Zeus?

Secretary McNamara: I don't believe they are mutually exclusive actions.

Mr. Flood: Of course not. I agree.

Secretary McNamara: I would say neither comes first. I would carry on each simultaneously with the maximum rate of activity that each could benefit from.[20]

The fact that one does not make a conscious decision does not mean that a choice has not been made. In this instance, this appears to have been the case, as additional decisions on the ABM and further crystallization of McNamara's strategic outlook unfolded.

Perhaps the most astute analyst of McNamara's thought on ABM was Zeus stalwart Flood. For Flood, the decision not to go into limited production indicated a basic unwillingness in the Defense Department perhaps ever to deploy Zeus: "I do not care what the Secretary of Defense says, or Dr. York, or any more of these long-haired flat-heeled jokers in science say, you cannot go from development into deployment unless you have production in these things." Confronting McNamara on this issue, Flood chided the defense secretary for not going into production of Zeus, at least on a limited basis. "I thought we had broken through this problem in this country," he stated, "of wanting things to be *perfect* before we sent them to the troops." While the discrimination problem disturbed him, he argued that it was not insurmountable, and that, in any case, the overriding fact was that "I have an enemy who can kill me and I cannot defend myself against him, and I say I should hazard all risks, within the rule of reason, to advance this by 2 or 3 years."[21]

Responding, McNamara argued that in its present state of development the Zeus system failed to meet all the necessary requisites of a successful ABM system. Future alterations of the Nike-Zeus might change that condition, he continued, but "it would be an error . . . to procure it and a great waste of resources." Flood emphasized that the specter of nuclear proliferation demanded the purchase of some protection. Committee debate between these two strong-willed public officials on this matter closed with these two parting salvoes:

Secretary McNamara: We are spending hundreds of millions of dollars, not to stop things but to accelerate the development of an anti-ICBM system–$276 million for the Zeus, and an additional $21 million for Defender project. I think this is evidence of (a) our recognition of the requirement for an anti-ICBM system and (b) the extent of our application to the satisfaction of that requirement. I do not believe it would be wise for us to recommend the procurement of a system which might not be an effective anti-ICBM device. That is exactly the state in which we believe the Zeus rests today.

Mr. Flood: I am probing your kind of reasoning. This is curious. You may not be aware of it, but you have just about destroyed the Nike-Zeus. That last paragraph did that. That is very interesting. I hope you and I will be around a while. We have to find out what makes you fellows work, and we begin to see it. It is very strange and very interesting.[22]

In later years, Flood could reflect on the perceptiveness of his analysis and the accuracy of his prediction.

Renewed controversy over Nike-Zeus in 1961 brought continued resistance from the office of DR&E to a production decision before the worth of Zeus had been proved. This opposition had been an important factor in the army's decision to modify its overarching goal in budgetary debates over its ABM program. Part of this inclination, no doubt, stemmed from the institutional perspective of DR&E on weapons programs; its responsibility was to supervise all research and engineering activities assigned to it by the secretary of defense. In the case of Zeus, given the fact that a two-year comprehensive test and evaluation program had commenced in 1960 to determine the operational feasibility of the complete Nike-Zeus system, it would appear only natural to expect the director of Defense Research and Engineering adamantly to oppose a decision to produce–even on a limited basis–prior to full-scale testing and technical evaluation.[23] Moreover, in the changeover of administrations it was to be anticipated that the continuity in the Zeus testing program under the aegis of DR&E would be a political advantage to Zeus opponents, since it would incline the new Kennedy administration against early decision.

Speaking before the subcommittee of the House Committee on Appropriations in April 1961, Herbert York, the director of DR&E since its inception in 1959, discussed the general position of his office. Generally, York stated, it recognized the development program of the Nike-Zeus as being of the highest priority in the effort of securing an effective active defense against incoming ballistic missiles; and substantial technical progress had been made during the preceding year. However, he said, concurring with the defense secretary, it was the official position of DR&E that no decision on production of the entire Zeus system or preproduction of limited parts and production facilities be taken before all the results of the two-year testing program were assessed.[24]

With respect to the effectiveness of the system against a "low-quantity and low-quality" attack, the consensus of the technical and scientific community was that the Nike-Zeus system would work in a circumscribed sense of that term. Therefore, the Zeus missile and its accompanying communications and radar systems were technically feasible.

Outweighing this pervasively shared conviction, however, were three other strong beliefs. First, due to the limited range covered by each Nike-Zeus battery, the cost of defending even a relatively small part of the United States would be exorbitant —upwards of $15 billion. Second, the Zeus was highly vulnerable to being degraded or neutralized by enemy use of various penetration techniques (decoys, electronic jamming, chaff). Overshadowing the first two beliefs was the deeply rooted and basic assumption concerning the relative advantages of offense and defense. Expressing a view shared by most of the civilian members of OSD, York remarked: "The problem here is the usual problem between defense and offense, measures, countermeasures, counter-counter measures, et cetera, in which it has been my judgment and still is that the battle is so heavily weighted in favor of the offense that it is hopeless against a determined offense and that incidentally applies to our position with regard to an anti-missile that they might build. I am convinced that we can continue to have a missile system that can penetrate any Soviet defense." [25] Unreflected upon by York was the question whether this avowed belief was a purely empirical judgment subject to refutation by further evidence or whether it was an implicit normative or political judgment structured into the preexisting stance of OSD by the imperatives of the strategy of nuclear deterrence.

Representing the official views of ARPA in the 1961 controversy over ABM production and deployment was its director, J. P. Ruina. In congressional testimony, Ruina revealed the scope of ARPA activity in BMD, the general level of funding requested for the 1962 amended budget, and some of the specific advanced ABM studies which it was supporting. [26]

According to its director, ARPA was a line agency which directed projects assigned either by the secretary of defense or the director of DR&E. During 1961, it had jurisdiction over all research on advanced BMD and was currently devoting about half of its program to this area. Fundamentally, its overall BMD program could be categorized into three broad subdivisions: ballistic missile phenomenology, i.e., "study of the environment through which a ballistic missile will pass during the various phases of its trajectory and the investigation of the behavior of a missile in that environment"; advanced techniques, i.e., "the development of instruments and techniques . . . needed to collect experimental data and to prepare the way for the design and development of similar instruments and techniques which may be required ultimately in missile defense systems"; and systems concepts, i.e., the study of categories which provide a "framework for the total research effort." [27]

For fiscal 1962, some $104 million of the ARPA budget was earmarked for BMD research. While this sum was still $24 million less than the amount appropriated to ARPA, much of the expenditure the year before was related to programs like the ABM test at Kwajalein Atoll that were continuing through 1961. [28]

There was a plethora of studies and investigations on sophisticated and esoteric ABM projects being funded by ARPA. Only the year before, its Project Defender released the results of Glipar "blue sky" program.[29] Coordinated by twelve firms, Glipar examined and tested the potential of many ideas for BMD. Among the ideas and schemes suggested were anti-missile defenses involving plasmas, lasers and other "death rays," fields, cold gases, X-rays released from H-bomb explosions in space, solid material impact, and the employment of large nuclear weapons above the atmosphere to obliterate all incoming objects, including warheads, missile parts, and decoys. Unfortunately, the Glipar program concluded that, within the bounds of existing scientific knowledge, no promising solution to the problem of ICBM defense seemed likely through the 1970-1980 period. An interesting sidelight to the results of Project Glipar was that, at least with respect to the lethality of X-rays in outer space, the program conclusions were in error. In fact, the efficacy of the Spartan longer-range interceptors of the Nike-X ABM system developed four years later was based on the capacity of X-rays to destroy or neutralize enemy warheads at an early stage in their trajectory.

During 1961, however, ARPA was providing funds for a wide range of exploratory studies contracted out to industry and to the services. In early April one of the technical journals disclosed that ARPAT (ARPA Terminal Defense), a new terminal defense against ICBMs, was being evaluated as a possible step beyond the Zeus system.[30] ARPAT was supposed to detect and identify automatically enemy ICBMs after their launching and then direct a dart-shaped platform into the atmosphere from which would be dispensed a host of hypersonic projectiles in random patterns against the threatening warheads. Its superiority to Nike-Zeus was manifold, including its theoretical ability to fire large numbers of defensive missiles from a single launch vehicle.

The military services, too, participated in these explorations of missile defense systems of an advanced type. In 1961 the following service projects received support from ARPA: BAMBI (air force), Typhoon (navy), Saint (army), and

FABMDS (army).[31] Only the BAMBI program was a serious competitor to the Nike-Zeus. The proliferation of these studies could hardly be interpreted as duplicative efforts, since they were minor in nature. At most, these projects were a collection of systems studies and certain applied research investigations.

While the army was mounting its campaign in early 1961 to trigger long lead-time component production of Zeus, the air force remained staunchly opposed to any such decision, although it did favor continued R&D funding of the army's project. The air force objected to Zeus production or deployment because of its high cost, its vulnerability to penetration, and its subordinate place in the race between offense and defense.[32]

The air force received funding from ARPA to study the possibility of intercepting an ICBM via space interceptors. This program, known as BAMBI, involved various competitive approaches to satellite-borne defense systems. The underlying principle was the idea that, since the accuracy of a ballistic missile is closely related to the cut-off velocity achieved during its boost phase, interruption or termination of missile engine-burning early in this initial launch phase would cause the missile to deviate substantially from its programmed course or abort altogether. Despite its rival standing to Nike-Zeus, the army made no objections to the air force's BAMBI. This apparent magnanimity stemmed from the fact that the earliest possible operational date was estimated to be 1975. However, like most BMD paper studies carried out under the auspices of ARPA, BAMBI never even reached the drawing boards.[33]

McNamara's new managerial style and the altered distribution of power and influence within the Defense Department were already making their imprint upon the ABM issue even in the first months of the Kennedy administration. So also were latent tensions and strains between OSD and Congress and between OSD and the military that would become more intense in succeeding years. With regard to the decision of spring 1961, the technical and cost-effectiveness considerations avowed by the various offices and agencies of OSD as the controlling reasons for postponement of Zeus deployment have been enumerated. Concealed by this veil of technical and economic arguments, however, was a deeper rationale–one vaguely sensed by Daniel Flood in his interrogation of Mc-Namara. This more subterranean logic can best be viewed against the background of the guiding rationality of defense policy and weapons innovation that reigned during the 1950s.

Permeated by a climate of opinion characterized by perceived high risk and uncertainty, defense decision-making on weapons innovation was guided by the following logic:

ASSUMPTIONS AND BELIEFS

A_1–The development of nuclear weapons has basically altered the character of general war as a political option.

A_2–The United States is challenged by a determined adversary with a dynamic technology in military weaponry.

A_3–Historically, the offense has always gotten through.

INFERENCES

I_1–National security should be defined above all by the strategy of nuclear deterrence, i.e., deterrence, not war-winning, is the strategic objective.

I_2–The offense must always get through.

I_3–Technological momentum in offensive military capabilities must continue unimpeded.[34]

Despite the rational force of this logic, the impact of the political context of defense decision-making and the political response by the leading authoritative decision-maker (Neil McElroy) to that situation elevated the priority of defense programs to a high, but ambiguous, status during the transition from one style of decision-making to another. In establishing a sharply different context for defense policymaking in the 1960s, OSD reacted equivocably to the prospect of active ABM defenses. On the one hand, OSD generally acknowledged that the opening of the dimension of defensive capabilities at the strategic level immeasurably complicated the issue of national security–both its foundation and maintenance. Consequently, McNamara experimented with the idea of damage-limitation as a component of the nation's strategic mission and encouraged the investigation of the most esoteric BMD ideas in the research and engineering agencies of his office. Yet, on the other hand, in putting the fate of Nike-Zeus (and other ABM designs) into the hands of ARPA and DR&E, he instructed these agencies to pursue the solution to an effective active defense against ICBMs as a purely technical matter. In so doing, he obscured the fact that strategic and political factors were inextricable aspects of any rational choice.

The major consequence of OSD's perspectives on BMD and weapons innovation was a logic of decision that, in the spring 1961 case, unfolded in the following manner:

ASSUMPTIONS AND BELIEFS

A'_1, A'_2, A'_3–From the logic of the 1950s, I_1, I_2, and I_3 were implicitly accepted as assumptions.

A'_4–Borrowed from the preceding logic, A_3 was widely and explicitly acknowledged.

A'_5–Based on A_2, it was believed that the United States must assume that the USSR is advancing its ABM technology as vigorously as the United States.

A'_6–Similarly, based on A_2, it was felt that the United States must assume that Soviet efforts to frustrate any defense and protect its deterrent capability are of equally high priority.[35]

INFERENCES

I'_1–Insofar as assumption A'_4 (A_3) was affirmed and held sway over decisions, the problem of ABM was interpreted as a technical problem and given highest priority in the technical (R&D) area.

I'_2–Based on A'_5 and A'_3 (I_3), technology in penetration aids must proceed with all deliberate speed and urgency in order to protect the mainstay of America's national security–its deterrent capability.

CONCLUSION

No production or deployment of an ABM system is permissible until it reaches a state of technical perfection.

As the testimony and other supporting material indicates, OSD dissimulated in congressional hearings on the issue of the relative priority of offense and defense. However, despite McNamara's proclaimed willingness to explore without prejudice the comparative advantages of offense and defense, it is clear that the resistance on his part and his scientific and engineering staff to accelerate or to deploy the Nike-Zeus was in large measure influenced by the insinuation of the strategic constant ("the offense must always get through") of the policy of deterrence inherited from the 1950s. Flood's suspicions and accusations then were more accurate than McNamara's feigned openness to BMD.

So, too, was Flood's prediction of Zeus's ultimate demise. Given the strategic biases of deterrence strategy and the way they were structured into the developmental programs of the agencies pursuing strategic weapons technology, the planners and engineers working on BMD were saddled with an impossible task, namely, the building of a technically perfect system. What made this quest utopian lay in the fact that uncertainties of a technical sort are ineradicable after a certain point, particularly as the complexity of a developmental project increases. Beyond this point, political judgment about adequacy (i.e., is the system effective enough?) must come into play and legislate decision.

5

EXIT ZEUS, ENTER NIKE-X

In his annual posture statement for fiscal 1964, Robert Mc-Namara disclosed that several major decisions relating to Zeus and the ABM issue had been determined. A thorough technical review conducted by OSD during the preceding year had led to the conclusion that the Nike-Zeus system in its present state would not be able to deal effectively with the sophisticated Soviet threat anticipated in the late 1960s and early 1970s. As a consequence, four major improvements which could be incorporated into the present Zeus design were suggested: use of the Zeus discrimination radar as a high-volume, lower-accuracy target tracker; alteration of the Zeus missile to reduce the minimum altitude at which an advancing warhead could be intercepted; development of a new high acceleration missile (called Sprint) which, due to its greater acceleration, would increase the time available for discrimination of targets; and development of a new advanced radar which could efficiently receive, assess, and track a large number of objects simultaneously.[1]

In the final determination of which program to propose, three basic alternatives were considered:

(a) The first alternative envisioned the continued development and test of the present Nike-Zeus system and a separate limited development of the new advanced radar.
(b) The second alternative called for proceeding with all four major improvements with initial deployment of a system incorporating initially only the first two improvements.
(c) The third alternative envisioned skipping the first two improvements and proceeding on an urgent basis with the development of the more advanced system (Nike-X), incorporating the Sprint missile and advanced radars, and deferring decision to deploy the system.

After evaluating each alternative, McNamara proposed to proceed with the greatest urgency along the lines of the third alternative on a developmental basis, leaving open the option eventually to produce and deploy the new system under favorable circumstances sometime in the future. In an effort to illustrate the importance attached to this Nike-X system, McNamara announced that he was requesting over $450 million for the fiscal 1964 budget–$246 million to initiate the Nike-X ABM program, $89 million to test and evaluate the Nike-Zeus project, and the rest for work relating to Project Defender.[2]

Finally, McNamara stressed the vital importance of an adequate fallout shelter program to the effectiveness of an active BMD system. In its absence, he argued, an active ICBM defense might not significantly increase the proportion of the civilian population surviving an all-out nuclear attack. Therefore, he recommended that the president's "very austere civil defense program" should be given priority over any fundamental additions to active defenses.[3]

Why did the OSD phase out the army's Zeus system? Why did it initiate the Nike-X program? Why was higher priority assigned to passive defense measures over ABM deployment?

As 1962 began, the army had reason to be buoyed by the upcoming Zeus test series in the Pacific Missile Range during midsummer, especially since it was expected that a live Zeus missile would be matched against a nuclear-tipped Atlas ICBM. Confidence in this likelihood was heightened by the fact that the American series of atomic tests–triggered in response to the Soviet nuclear test series which broke the earlier two-year test moratorium in 1961–was to coincide in time and geography with the Zeus test and evaluation program.[4] Any reason for enthusiasm and anticipation, however, was quickly dashed by a number of OSD directives, pronouncements, and decisions.

The Department of Defense issued a directive restricting the publication of information regarding the outcome of the Zeus test.[5] This action was taken to avoid references which could be interpreted as degrading the performance of either the Nike-Zeus missile or the target vehicle, the Atlas, because such information would be considered detrimental to national interest and security. This cautious attitude was extended to include designation of ballistic missile targets as target vehicles rather than as operational ICBMs and to present intercept exercises as developmental tests to determine the capabilities of the Nike-Zeus missile rather than as contests between Zeus missiles and operational ICBMs.

Whether or not a clandestine purpose behind this directive existed, the army's hopes of verifying the technical feasibility of its ABM system through these tests were all but shattered by McNamara's testimony on the defense budget for fiscal 1962, in which he voiced grave doubts over the practicality of the Nike-Zeus system. Moreover, when Congressman Gerald Ford queried him on the effect of the forthcoming tests on a possible production date decision for the Nike-Zeus, McNamara replied: "No. I think the tests by themselves will have little effect on the decision as to whether we will or will not proceed into production. I fear that we may have left a misimpression in the minds of the public on this issue through statements made over a period of years." He defended this statement by referring to a number of technical problems which could not be solved by the tests. Indeed, the strongest warrant for continuing the testing program and the development program of Nike-Zeus that McNamara could suggest was their capacity to advance knowledge on reentry phenomena and penetration capabilities.[6]

Evidence of the changed status of the Zeus was reinforced by other information reported in the April 2, 1962, issue of *Missiles and Rockets*. According to this source, Defense decisions had apparently doomed the Nike-Zeus program to a purely R&D program designed to acquire data on warhead and decoy signatures, as well as to generate information valuable to future ABM development. Thus, the army's program appeared fated for termination in 1964 upon completion of its developmental phase. Surprisingly, except for the vocal opposition of Flood and Lieutenant General Arthur Trudeau, OSD's "silent" decision on Zeus met with little resistance. In fact, the decision to phase out the Nike-Zeus program was not even announced in 1962, although the army began to reevaluate its role in the Zeus program and to consider new BMD steps beyond Zeus. "We can continue thé program," argued an army spokesman, "but we are really not interested in a purely Ballistic Missile Research Program. We want a weapons system." [7]

Vehemently rejecting McNamara's assessment of the Zeus, the army chief of research and development, General Trudeau, expressed great confidence in the system. In addition, he revealed that the army was working on two major improvements in the system that would extend its overall capabilities. The first, known as the Sprint missile, was to be a "high-acceleration, quick-reaction" missile; the second, called ZMAR, was to be a multiple-array radar, capable of searching large areas of space while detecting and tracking enemy ballistic missile warheads and guiding an ABM to the incoming missile. Both of these systems modifications, he felt, would endow the Nike-Zeus with sufficient potential to handle any likely future enemy threat.[8]

A major technical triumph, unaccompanied by political dividends, was won by the army when, during mid-July, a Nike-Zeus missile successfully engaged and intercepted an Atlas target vehicle. This was followed by two more scores (one occurring in a decoy environment) before the end of the year. These hits confirmed the judgments of the army, as well as the estimations of such Zeus skeptics as Herbert York. OSD reaction was laudatory, but restrained; and no executive move was taken to sanction production and deployment. Instead, Department of Defense thinking began to turn to alternative approaches to BMD.[9]

According to journalist James Trainor, a host of factors, including test data from the Pacific Zeus test, design improvement in the Nike-Zeus system, and better definition of the possible Soviet threat, combined with revealing research and systems studies from Project Defender, had stimulated a major shift in strategic thinking in the Defense Department concerning the technical feasibility and doctrinal utility of an ICBM defense under certain conditions. Clarification of the BMD problem from these various studies, tests, and evaluations had been so great, Trainor alleged, that a new operational concept had evolved. The basic components of this new concept involved two BMD systems: a Hard Point Defense (HPD) system for the protection of ICBM bases and command and control posts and an Urban Defense System designed for the protection of urban population centers.[10]

As Raymond H. Dawson has emphasized, " 'the decision' to deploy the ABM, like 'the decision' to 'go nuclear,' would not consist of one choice in time but would involve a series of inter-related political, economic, and strategic choices over time." Apparently, within the Defense Department (probably in ARPA or DR&E), civilian planners had begun to sift out these factors and to relate more consciously the technical, economic, and political issues to strategic doctrine. The keystone of American defense strategy for these planners was to remain the policy of stable deterrence, i.e., the maintenance of a credible second-strike capability without stimulating further destabilizing advances up the arms spiral. Insofar as possible, the United States would endeavor to sustain this posture and to elicit a mutual Soviet pose through public and private communication.[11]

Among the nontechnical considerations for these planners were the size of the anticipated military threat, the capability—both technical and economic—of the USSR to construct an effective ABM system, and the possible impact on the Soviet Union if the United States elected to build an ABM system. Despite the administration's desire not to prompt another destabilizing arms race, it was, according to Trainor, hedging its bets with this policy by developing the technology necessary for ABM and other offensive weapons (including fractional orbital bombs, which it regarded as equally provocative) in the event that the Soviets chose to develop and deploy them.[12]

The mix of technical, political, economic, and strategic considerations affecting any decision to advance beyond the developmental stage to production and deployment of an ABM system was manifested in the reasoning behind the choice of the HPD system by these planners as the most likely candidate for any future operational BMD assignment.[13] The rationale for this selection centered on its lower expense, its lesser degree of complexity, and its basic contribution to the policy of a stable deterrent. By virtue of the nature of the target it is protecting and the smaller area it is defending, an HPD antiballistic missile system requires fewer defense missiles. In addition, since the attack corridor would be extremely narrow and since the target to be defended would be hardened, this design had a number of other technical and economic advantages: the acquisition and discrimination problem would be reduced, thereby easing data-processing requirements; lower detonation of the defensive warhead would be possible; and longer time-delay before launching would allow the atmosphere to function as a screen to filter out decoys. Finally, in the strategic realm, an HPD system would contribute to the stability of the deterrent, since a first-strike counterforce assault by the adversary would decrease the reliability of his missile force and require him to enlarge considerably the number of missiles in the attack force. It would also enhance the security of the American retaliatory force.

Noticeably less enthusiasm and confidence in the Urban Defense System was voiced. Potentially, it was extremely expensive, subject to neutralization by cheap countermeasures, and likely to destabilize any preexisting Soviet-American strategic equilibrium. Only if the second shortcoming were remedied, Trainor reported, would these planners find deployment justified under special circumstances.[14]

By 1962 this position had come to dominate the thinking of certain key officials in the planning and engineering office of OSD. But aside from this article, no public disclosure of the general lines of this report nor any but the most sketchy accounts of the new operational concept and its components appeared. Certainly, the key members of the executive–from the president to the various civilian advisers to the secretary of defense–made no attempt to edify Congress, much less the general public, of any change in attitude toward BMD's role in national strategic policy. And in succeeding years these two concepts would vie with other ABM designs for consideration. Apparently oblivious to any modifications in defense planning with regard to BMD, as 1962 closed, the army anticipated approval for production and deployment of a modified Zeus system.[15]

Perhaps in an effort to provide the setting for the 1963 ABM decision, McNamara opened his discussion of strategic retaliatory forces by underscoring the complexity in trying to program these forces to maintain their effectiveness in the future. He defined their foremost mission as the ability "to deter war by their capability to destroy the enemy's war-making potential, including not only his nuclear strike forces and military installations, but also his urban society if necessary." It was a complex task to determine the proper mix and numbers of weapons delivery systems required to fulfill the strategic force's mission in the context of significant but bounded uncertainty. Uncertainty over the size and character of the Soviet Union's strategic forces and defensive systems now and in the future, coupled with the long lead-times involved in making such weapons systems operational, entailed planning at least five years in advance and projecting estimates of enemy forces for a similar period, which is highly conjectural.[16]

McNamara explained the reasoning behind the decision to postpone deployment of an ABM system. Two benefits, he said, would accrue from deploying immediately an ABM system like the Zeus: it might reduce U.S. casualties in the case of a light or medium Soviet assault on the urban centers and it would complicate the design of and tactics for the attacker's offensive weapons. But, he continued, even better reasons existed for not proceeding with actual deployment: A great deal needed to be learned about reentry phenomena and techniques for discriminating between real warheads and decoys and "about the effects of a nuclear detonation from one of our intercepting missiles on other elements of the defensive system." [17] Thus a favorable decision to deploy any system, especially an interim one with limited capabilities, would be premature. He then announced the decision to phase out the Nike-Zeus and to proceed immediately to initiate the next generation in the Nike series–Nike-X.

Once again, as in the past, the members of the House Subcommittee on Appropriations showed great interest in the BMD issue, forcing McNamara to justify his decision not to deploy the Nike-Zeus. He grounded his case against Zeus on the argument that if it had been configured several years previously the United States would have been saddled with a defensive system that would have been useless against the Soviet threat which Defense Department planners saw developing in the period from 1964 to 1968.[18]

When further pressed, the secretary of defense resorted to a device that would hold him in good stead for the next few years by providing a compelling case against deployment. As Benson Adams, a perceptive student and critic of McNamara's ABM policy, characterized it:

Arguing from his assumption and his hypothetical alternatives, he was able to rationalize his favored choice, i.e., to continue the development of Nike-X but not produce it. While the committee was considering the system's growth potential, McNamara summed up his argument by saying that the committee should address itself to the degree of protection that either the Nike-X or the Nike-Zeus could give. By postulating a variety of Soviet missile threat levels and making certain assumptions about decoys and Soviet targeting doctrine, he showed the degree to which Nike-Zeus or Nike-X might protect the country. In his opinion, his examples provided insufficient evidence of the Nike-X's effectiveness under the stated circumstance to warrant its deployment.[19]

The years of its success were to mark the high tide of McNamara's alternative basis of expertise.

In describing the relationship of a fallout shelter program to any ABM effort, McNamara stressed the inextricable link between the two. Countering Congressman Harold Ostertag's claim that many committee members were inclined to favor deployment because of its capability of saving some people, even if only a relatively few million, McNamara made an unqualified pitch for passive defenses. Arguing in terms of cost-effectiveness analysis, he contended that the quickest and least expensive means of saving human lives under the circumstances was to promote the civil defense program advocated by the president. Furthermore, he asserted, all the active BMD systems under serious review or active development demanded a complementary civil defense system, since a huge amount of fallout would be generated by ABM warheads and by incoming warheads. Without fallout shelter protection, he said, the Soviets could simply burst nuclear weapons upwind beyond the range of the anti-ICBM systems and allow the wind currents to saturate civilian population centers with highly radioactive fog.[20]

For these reasons, McNamara argued that it would be foolhardy to spend $10-15 billion for an active defense against ICBMs without integrating it into a civil defense program. Then, apparently pinning the fate of Nike-X on congressional decision on civil defense, McNamara declared: "I personally will never recommend an anti-ICBM program unless a fallout program does accompany it. I believe that even if we do not have an anti-ICBM program, we nonetheless should proceed with the fallout shelter program." In succeeding years, he related this argument more closely to his strategic conception of assured destruction/damage limitation. Only after repeated failure to gain legislative assent for a national fallout shelter program did he draw the inference that "it is wise, instead of wasting our time continuing to press for something we cannot accomplish, to spend our resources on other more fruitful areas of activity." This grain of wisdom, however, would take over three years to mature.[21]

McNamara tried to reassure the Appropriations Subcommittee that the continuing policy of postponement of the ABM did not mean ABM development would not be advanced on the highest priority basis. Still, he equivocated on the prospect of an ABM system's ever being produced and deployed, however sophisticated it might be. Congressman Ostertag wondered if the progress of offensive weapons technology in the past few years had not irrevocably altered the possibility of deploying a BMD. "It seems to me," he reflected, "that time is running out on the question of whether or not we could ever successfully, and to any avail, use an antimissile missile. In other words, no enemy is going to wait for us to develop or deploy this system." [22] To what extent this despairing circumstance was grounded in reasonable estimates of the evolving Soviet strategic threat and to what extent it was the creation of self-propelling dynamism of our own two-pronged offensive-defensive developmental programs remained unilluminated.

Harold Brown, the new director of DR&E, helped clarify the interrelationship of strategic forces. Summarizing the basic connections, he argued that at least three major contests seemed to be taking place: one pitting penetration aids against BMD, one matching antisubmarine efforts with efforts to protect Polaris-type submarines from detection or attack before their missiles can be launched, and one pitting improvements in missile hardening against advances in missile accuracy. [23]

Most significant in terms of current research and development studies and characterized by the greatest potential for altering the strategic equation, according to Brown, was the raging battle between the American ABM capability and the Soviet penetration aid capability. It was the relative advantages of the latter capability that prompted OSD to refrain from deploying the Zeus. As Brown testified to the Senate Foreign Relations Committee during the nuclear test ban treaty hearings: "The United States decided not to deploy the Nike-Zeus because its effectiveness was inadequate against U.S. penetration aids programmed for entry into the U.S. inventory before a Nike-Zeus system could be deployed, and we assume the same would be true of Soviet penetration aid capability." Not the penetration aid technology of the Soviet Union, then, but the counter ABM technology of the United States was the primary source of criteria for determining the effectiveness of the ABM systems. [24]

This salient point admitted, the comparable advantages of the offense over the defense still had to be conceded. First, the cost ratio of defense to offense still favored the offense. The cost of deploying an ABM system was inordinate compared to the cost of neutralizing any system with a variety of inexpensive penetration devices. Second, the time necessary for developing and deploying operational penetration aids was much shorter than the lead-time needed to develop and deploy an anti-ICBM system. Finally, barring a technological breakthrough, Brown could find no sign to encourage hope of a fundamental shift in the direction of the defense. Based on existing knowledge and research studies, DR&E was convinced that "in the long run it will be easier to develop penetration aids than to improve the defenses to match these developments." Again, these estimates were rooted solely in an understanding of U.S. technical capabilities in both fields.[25]

The most revealing information conveyed to Congress from the testimony of ARPA director J. R. Ruina concerned the degree to which the BMD work of this agency had changed. The agency's program had evolved in five years from the development of large hardware space projects in the McElroy era to smaller research and exploratory development projects during the McNamara epoch.[26] He praised Project Defender and spoke of its dual mission of exploring the problem of advanced BMD through research studies and limited developmental work and of assisting the secretary of defense in making an independent assessment of the ability of United States ICBMs to penetrate possible Soviet defenses.

In the early days of ballistic missile defense, ARPA had found it necessary to investigate fully all ideas concerning ABM systems that had been suggested in order to ensure against the possibility that any effective system was being overlooked. By surveying all potentially feasible systems, ARPA was able to determine in which areas research and development could best be applied. By 1963 ARPA had achieved a firm scientific foundation and was capable of making controlled laboratory experiments and full-scale field tests to investigate problems associated with measuring reentry phenomena, a matter that was essential both to the design of an effective defensive system and to the fabrication of effective reentry systems for U.S. strategic weapons.[27]

As for the search for more sophisticated, exotic ABM systems, Ruina gave the distinct impression that the focus of ARPA's antiballistic missile activity had narrowed, although research on such esoteric systems concepts involving laser beams, plasmas, and X-rays would continue. One sign of this more delimited interest was the termination of BAMBI. Leaving aside the inordinate technical demands this systems concept placed upon the designer, Ruina asserted that the estimated $50 billion price tag for implementing such a system made it economically infeasible.[28]

A second indication of its more circumscribed focus centered around the multiphased array radar. An outgrowth of developments in radar technology in Project Defender, this new radar system was to substitute for the individual radars for acquisition, discrimination, and target and missile tracking which the Nike-Zeus system employed. The twin assets of the multiphased array radar were its ability to be hardened, since the radar beam could be controlled electronically, rather than by swinging the dish mechanically, and its capacity to present a two-dimensional picture of the environment, thereby combining the individual functions of the Zeus radar cluster into one radar component. Ruina declared, "All systems presently considered, including Nike-X, [will] depend heavily on the use of phased arrays." Moreover, with the emergence of this radar, he concluded, a completely automated system could be constructed—one in which the incoming ballistic missile could be acquired, discriminated, and tracked and the defensive missile could be fired and commanded against the ICBM threat with no human assistance.[29]

While public revelation of the Nike-X did not come until February when OSD released the fourth annual posture statement of the secretary of defense, its birth might better be put at January 5, 1963.[30] On this day, the army was directed by the OSD to reorient its six-year-old Nike-Zeus development program. This new program was to consist of two elements: a project to continue the Zeus test effort at all the field test sites and a project to accelerate and put new emphasis on the development of a second generation system known as Nike-X. In divulging details of the army's new ABM program to the Appropriations Subcommittee, Lieutenant Colonel C. J. LeVan of the Office of the Chief of R&D and other army representatives expressed newfound optimism concerning the likelihood of the army's being granted operational control over a deployed ABM system in the future.

During budgetary debate in the Defense Department the army recommended that the Nike-X be carried through its developmental stage and eventually deployed and, in addition, that Nike-Zeus be deployed and then reconstructed to fit the design of the Nike-X. Although this recommendation was rejected by OSD, the army, in the words of General Dwight Beach, accepted "cheerfully" what they got. The army's request was feasible because, putting aside the communications and radar systems, the Nike-X was really Zeus plus Sprint. This meant that the Nike-X ABM system would use the Zeus missile to intercept advancing ballistic missiles at longer ranges (75-100 miles), while employing the Sprint missile against ICBMs at close ranges (20-30 miles).[31]

Two factors relating to the Nike-X gave hope to the army that it would be assigned operational responsibility for the ABM mission. First, the new ABM design would make it easier for the defense to discriminate warheads from decoys. A main conclusion of the ARPA program and the Nike-Zeus tests was that the best-known technique for warhead discrimination is by the difference in the trajectories of warheads and decoys as they reenter the atmosphere. This atmosphere filtering, however, only becomes pronounced at altitudes of less than fifty miles. With its high acceleration and low-altitude intercept capabilities, the Sprint seemed to be the perfect backup partner to the Zeus missile. Second, the army sensed a growing convergence in perspectives on ABM between itself and the OSD. In an effort to pin down this purely psychological feeling, D. Larsen said: "Whereas in discussing Nike-Zeus and its gradual changes which occurred, the army was actually arguing and opposing our authorities in the Office of the Secretary of Defense, who are highly competent people on this matter . . . [we] are agreeing at the present time. We are not arguing with them about capabilities, we are agreeing on what the capabilities are, so I think it is extremely likely that OSD will recommend deployment." [32] This perception of a "change in atmosphere" was similarly shared by other army spokesmen.

The prospect of being awarded the ABM assignment also made the army quite sanguine about the termination of the Nike-Zeus program in its developmental phase. Indeed, great virtue was attributed to the declining data-collection role of the Zeus tests. According to Colonel LeVan, continuation of the Zeus testing promised two benefits: it would provide additional information about discrimination techniques which would help to refine the Nike-X's design and it would permit the army to "tell the Air Force and Navy what their nose cones and penetration aids will look like to a defensive system . . . to improve the penetration capabilities of our long-range strategic missiles." [33] The army apparently remained ignorant of the larger strategic rationale informing OSD evaluation of ABM deployment and unaware of the dynamic interaction between offensive and defensive capabilities which was to continue to frustrate its objective.

After 1963 the attitudes and evaluations of the Joint Chiefs of Staff toward McNamara's defense policy would gain new prominence and political force in the executive branch as political division in the Defense Department began to develop along civil-military lines. And paralleling this trend would be growing reaction in Congress to executive imperialism and an increasing return to the military counsel of the traditional repositors of military expertise. But, by moving to development of a second-generation ABM system, McNamara effectively postponed a confrontation with the Joint Chiefs of Staff (JCS), who in 1963 nearly agreed to recommend deployment of the Nike-Zeus system.

While the JCS did not formally recommend a favorable decision on Zeus deployment to the secretary of defense, they were not immune to the optimism infecting the army on the potential of an ABM system. General Earle Wheeler (army chief of staff) estimated support for deployment of the Nike-Zeus as "pretty unanimous." As later testimony disclosed, the qualified nature of this assessment stemmed from the reservations of the air force chief of staff, General Curtis LeMay, who questioned the effectiveness of the system against a massive assault.[34]

The most persuasive and comprehensive rationale among the chiefs for immediate Zeus deployment was enunciated by the chairman, General Maxwell Taylor. Sharply contrasting his position with the arguments offered by the defense secretary, Taylor expressed these sentiments:

Had we crashed the Zeus program we would at least have accomplished two things. One, we would now be learning by doing. As far as my experience goes with new weapons, that is the only way you can make any great progress. It takes a considerable amount of actual employment of weapons systems to get the best out of them. The other point is that we would have had a technological triumph over the Soviets. Some day there will be a great ballyhoo that the Soviets have an antiballistic missile and we do not. The claim may be largely a sham and propaganda, but we face that possibility of a cold war defeat.

Wheeler supported this view and carried it with passion and conviction before three executive forums (the JCS, the secretary of defense, and the chief executive). Finally, the chief of naval operations, Admiral G. W. Anderson, voiced his qualified support for early deployment of the improved Nike-Zeus, contingent upon its successful performance in systems demonstration tests.[35]

Congressional efforts to elicit production of the Nike-Zeus system were brought to a climax when, on April 11, 1963, the Senate held its first secret session since 1943. The closed session was requested by Senator Strom Thurmond in order to debate the Senate Armed Service Committee's report which recommended, by a narrow 9-8 margin, that $196 million be authorized above Defense Department budget requests to initiate preproduction of Zeus components. Leading the fight to retain the funds in the military procurement bill, Thurmond buttressed his case with classified material which indicated that the USSR was several years ahead of the United States in

ABM development. This dramatic confrontation ended, however, with a resounding defeat of the Thurmond amendment by the Senate in a 16-58 vote.[36]

Joining the majority in this overwhelming endorsement of the administration's plan to work toward an improved ABM system were many powerful figures in the Senate, among them, Richard Russell and Stuart Symington. Russell, chairman of the Armed Services Committee, strongly urged against going into production, because of the unproved effectiveness of the Zeus against strategic missiles. He also contended that it was economically unwarranted, due to the $2.8 billion net loss that would allegedly be incurred by deploying Zeus immediately rather than waiting until the operational effectiveness of Nike-X was established. Symington, former secretary of the air force, simply regarded the earlier members of the Nike family as "worthless" and considered the $7 billion expenditures on the entire Nike series, including Zeus, as money "down the drain." [37]

Despite the sizable majority mustered to reject the Armed Services Committee's bill and the Thurmond amendment, pressure from ABM partisans in Congress and key committees in the annual budgetary investigation was to become a common phenomenon in future congressional-executive feuds over ABM funding.

In August 1963 President Kennedy signed the Limited Nuclear Test Ban Treaty, an act which he described as "an important step—a step toward peace—a step toward reason—a step away from war." In preparation for Senate ratification, the draft treaty was then referred to the Foreign Relations Committee for review. The extensive hearings conducted by the committee were to reflect congressional attitude toward the BMD issue and to provide valuable insight into some of the motivations behind later decisions on ABM taken by the secretary of defense.[38]

While the Foreign Relations Committee for the most part endeavored to evaluate the impact of the Test Ban Treaty on the present and future military balance of power, its questions more and more were directed to three areas which impinged upon problems affecting ABM development: "These are the penetration capability of missiles; anti-ballistic missile development; and the survival capability of sites and systems." Indicative of this profound interest were the frequent queries on the three areas of knowledge needed for anti-ICBM development most intimately related to nuclear testing–the blackout problem (i.e., the effect of nuclear detonations on radar), warhead technology, and warhead lethality.[39]

Conscious of the Senate's long-standing interest in BMD, McNamara in his opening policy statement elaborated the major threads of the central argument on ABM and the cessation of atmospheric testing that would constitute the official policy. Basically, McNamara argued, in designing an ABM system, several major factors have to be taken into account: reaction speed, missile performance, traffic handling capacity, capacity for decoy discrimination, resistance to blackout effects, and warhead technology. Only the last two, he claimed, depend on nuclear testing. With regard to warhead design and development, he argued that even without further testing the United States possessed ABM warheads with the yield range for the Nike-X system. Any upgrading of the nuclear warhead required in response to Soviet actions could, he assured the committee, be developed through underground tests. As for the blackout problem, he argued that prior atmospheric nuclear testing had given the United States sufficient technical data either to resolve a number of the uncertainties associated with blast interference or to design around the remaining ones in the near future.[40]

The design efforts of the Soviet Union and the United States, McNamara went on to assert, based on the standards of magnitude and success, were comparable. In addition, he believed that the Soviets were capable of deploying an ABM system in the next few years which at best was no more effective than the flawed Nike-Zeus system. Finally, he summed up the basic position of his office by saying:

The ABM problem is dominated by factors unrelated to the treaty. . . . A fuller understanding of the blackout phenomenon–which would result from tests prohibited by the treaty–might at most permit some reduction in the number of ABM radars required per ABM site.

Thus, with or without a test ban, we could proceed with the development of an ABM system.[41]

Except for slightly conflicting evaluations of the relative status of U.S. and Soviet efforts in ABM development, other leading administration officials appearing before the Foreign Relations Committee simply reiterated the basic line put forth in McNamara's testimony. Even the evident divergence of opinion among key administration officials on the comparative American and Soviet rates of progress in the ABM field was minor. Whatever the exact estimate of the relative positions, all were in agreement that the test ban would not inhibit advancement toward an effective ABM system, if indeed one could be fabricated.[42]

Among the major witnesses called before the committee, only Edward Teller (former director of the Lawrence Radiation Laboratory) and John Foster (current director) articulated views radically at odds with the Kennedy administration's official stance on the treaty. In brief, their dissent was based on a negative assessment of the likely outcome of banning above-ground nuclear testing for ABM development. Starting from the premises that missile defense is possible and that the USSR was ahead of the United States in this area, Teller argued that a policy of abstention from above-ground testing would have a highly deleterious effect on the progress toward that objective. Questioning McNamara's judgment, he challenged the central argument outlined by the defense secretary. He declared that the treaty would stimulate rather than prevent the arms race, since it was directed not against the arms race but against knowledge. The types of knowledge involved had to do with better understanding of the blackout problem and ways of circumventing it, a greater satisfaction with American ABM warheads, and a surer determination of the operational effectiveness of any future ABM system. Without complex experimentation of various ABM systems components in the atmosphere, without ultimately field-testing the entire system under simulated general war conditions, the United States would be prohibiting itself, he argued, from acquiring the knowledge indispensable to ensure confidence in the effectiveness and reliability of any ABM defense it might presume to deploy.[43]

Foster, agreeing generally with Teller, focused his remarks on technological developments which Kistiakowsky had attempted to close off as technically infeasible. For Foster, atmospheric tests were critical in the development of hardened warheads to penetrate a more sophisticated Soviet ABM or in the design of a more advanced ABM warhead to further reduce blackout.[44]

Despite the minority status of their opinions of the test ban hearings and perhaps in the scientific community, their doubts and fears did have substance. Indeed, one of the basic reasons suggested by the secretary of defense himself a scant eight months earlier for not deploying an ABM system was paucity of information about "the effects of a nuclear detonation from one of our intercepting missiles on other elements of the defensive system." Since no American atmospheric test of the blackout problem could have taken place during that intervening period, no technical grounds could be adduced for McNamara's revised estimate of the issue. Moreover, his radical separation of two factors going into the design of an ABM system (blackout effects and warhead technology) from the others and his claim that these two elements could be tested independently of the rest of the constitutive elements violated the dictates of one of the key components of his technique of analysis–systems analysis. Even Dr. Glenn Seaborg acknowledged that "the vulnerability of warheads and other systems components can be examined for many effects associated with a nuclear explosion. However, complete studies involving blast and fireball as well as radiation effects at major weapons delivery systems would be impossible to carry out. Also the study of effects which are completely dependent on the atmosphere at operational altitudes would be essentially impossible and would thus limit the acquisition of new knowledge bearing on radar and communications." Thus, while individual components studies would not be hampered by the test ban, the possibility of an integrated full-systems test, as McNamara himself conceded, would be proscribed under terms of the treaty.[45]

In defense of his basic judgments, McNamara asserted that knowledge obtained from underground nuclear tests and simulated experiments would be sufficient to warrant a "reasoned conclusion" regarding a deployment decision. What stands out from the defense of the treaty by McNamara and other members of the administration is that the arms control policy spawned during the first years of the Kennedy administration had powerfully influenced the decision to promulgate the treaty. Evidently, a political decision had been made in the top echelons of government to subordinate the development of an ABM to the politically more attractive issue of a limited nuclear test ban treaty. At one time in the hearings the secretary almost acknowledged the political character of the affair when he responded in the affirmative to a question about whether he would still recommend adoption of the treaty if he believed that the ABM could not be developed without aboveground testing. Herbert York in his testimony admitted that the partial test ban treaty under review was a first step to a political solution to national security–a solution that only politics, not science and technology, could achieve.[46]

But as 1963 ended, the technological race between the offense and the defense continued apace. With a greatly improved radar system (MAR and MSR), a mix of missile types (Zeus plus Sprint), and a new means of discriminating enemy ICBM warheads and assorted decoys, defensive weaponry design had achieved a high state of technical advancement. Equally impressive were the improvements in offensive weapons technology. Indicative of these improvements was McNamara's disclosure before the Senate Armed Services Committee that all funds which went into the Nike-Zeus through 1962 plus the $350 million being requested for Nike-X in 1963 were necessitated by the considerable gains in the area of penetration aids and decoys, underwater-launched ballistic missiles, and submarine-carried, surface-launched cruise missiles, and the requirement to develop defenses against them.[47]

The questions that comprised the basic features of Mc-Namara's ABM decision of January 1963 were: Why institute Nike-X development? Why give priority to a civil defense program over any active BMD? In brief, according to the key decision-makers, the demise of Zeus was dictated by a host of factors, including its exorbitant cost, its relative ineffectiveness, its vulnerability to surface blast, and its inability to handle the decoy problem. Similar economic and technical reasons–like its lesser anticipated cost, its greater success in discriminating warheads from decoys, its superior radar system, and its ability to be hardened–influenced the decision to initiate development of the Nike-X. Finally, the greater cost-effectiveness and technical simplicity of fallout shelters were two evident reasons that informed McNamara's decision to subordinate active defenses to passive defenses.

Two other factors figured with increasing potency in the decision on weapons development and strategic policy relating to advance in BMD: the increasing domination of the technological imperative and the subtle insinuation of the strategic hierarchy of deterrence strategy. The analysis of this chapter has provided the means of giving more concrete expression to the technological imperative promoting defense decision on innovations in offensive and defensive weapons systems during the McNamara era. The human foundations of this dynamic impulse can be seen in the peculiar manner in which the organizational processes of military R&D were centralized and coordinated in the OSD and mutually fed upon the technical achievements in the realms of offensive and defensive technologies. Centralized in the executive agency of the Defense Department and guided by the most advanced techniques of administration and analysis, military R&D in strategic weaponry was institutionalized and pursued during the McNamara years in an organizational framework characterized by the mutual interaction of military R&D in offensive and defensive technologies. In this way, a continuing battle of the weapons laboratories was provoked.[48] In a sense, then, the technological imperative took on all the features of an internal arms race pitting American scientists and technicians in offensive R&D against their counterparts in defensive R&D within the same agency.

Skewed only by the strategic bias of the doctrine of nuclear deterrence (i.e., the primacy of the offensive), this mutually sustaining R&D network in offensive and defensive technologies assured the superiority of American offensive might with little or no regard for any real Soviet threat or developing Soviet capability. Recalling in 1970 what was occurring in DR&E and ARPA, Herbert York has stated: "It is important . . . to note these early developments of MIRV and ABM were not primarily the result of any careful operations analysis of the problem of anything which might be described as a provocation of the other side. They were largely the result of a continuously reciprocating process consisting of a technological challenge put out by the designers of our own defense and accepted by the designers of our own offense, then followed by a similar challenge/response sequence in the reverse direction.[49]

As it operated during this decade, this technological planning process increasingly adopted the features of a closed system where interest in the character of the Soviet threat, Soviet perceptions of specific weapons programs, and other "external" data became of secondary importance to the "internal" requirements of the system. Indeed, the technological developments in the areas of offensive and defensive weaponry more and more took on the image of rational systems evolving in complete detachment from human control and intervention–even, and especially, to the defense planners whose assumptions, decisions, and actions fueled and perpetuated the pace and course of technological change.

This antiempirical bias of the process was only exacerbated by other aspects of strategic planning and programming introduced by McNamara, particularly those aspects dealing with long-range technological planning. The procedure whereby five-year projections of enemy forces and weapons were introduced into American planning produced expectations which were highly conjectural and subject to great variation and uncertainty. As McNamara himself admitted, such projection encouraged–indeed, required–anticipating decisions "which our opponents, themselves, *may not yet have made*."[50] In a situation of such uncertainty, enemy threats and capabilities were projected either on the basis of "worst possible case" estimate offered by the defense intelligence establishment or on the basis of our technological plans for future weapons systems by attributing to the Soviet Union the technological capabilities possessed by the United States.

6

INTERLUDE: FROM NIKE-X
TO SENTINEL

In 1964, despite the appearance of evidence indicating Soviet development of an ABM defense, a decision by the United States to deploy an ABM system seemed far off. Any decision to produce and deploy Nike-X (or some other advanced ABM system configuration) appeared to be contingent on satisfactory solution of a number of basic problems and issues: remaining technical problems relating to system development, testing, and evaluation would have to be resolved; economic analysis would have to be made; political issues, such as the passage by Congress of an ancillary civil defense program, would have to be confronted; and the strategic issue of the likely effect of American deployment on Soviet strategic planning would have to be gauged.

Testifying before the House Appropriations Subcommittee on February 20, 1964, Robert McNamara confessed that many key problems had yet to be solved before OSD could decide whether or not to produce and deploy the Nike-X system. Amplifying on this point, he said, "A large number of detailed technical, strategic, and economic problems, however, must still be solved before an effective ballistic missile defense system can be deployed. Components must be developed to withstand very high accelerations and temperatures. Manufacturing techniques must be devised for the production of thousands of efficient, reliable tubes and components. While none of these problems is considered insuperable, they could result in delays and increases in costs." [1] Until 1965, when the results of various test projects at Kwajalein and White Sands were evaluated, a decision would be premature.

McNamara in his testimony also expressed concern about

the cost-effectiveness issue. Having articulated for the first time his notion of damage-limiting strategy as the most practical and effective strategy for the United States in this year's posture statement, he went on to argue that, given the anticipated high cost of the system in its present design (approximately $16 billion), its effectiveness would have to be proved. However, he pointed out, at this juncture, higher priority over ABM development should be given to a very austere fallout shelter program, because the Nike-X alone could not save sufficient lives in an all-out Soviet nuclear assault and because the Soviets could easily penetrate the system at a fraction of the cost of a heavy American Nike-X deployment.[2]

A year earlier, McNamara had remarked on the relationship of ABM and the arms race:

As the arms race continues and the weapons multiply and become more swift and deadly, the possibility of a global catastrophe, either by miscalculation or design, becomes ever more real. More armaments, whether offensive or defensive, cannot solve this dilemma. We are approaching an era when it will become increasingly improbable that either side could destroy a sufficiently large portion of the other's strategic nuclear force, either by surprise or otherwise, to preclude a devastating retaliatory blow. This may result in mutual deterrence, but it is still a grim prospect. It underscores the need for a renewed effort to find some way, if not to eliminate these deadly weapons completely, then at least to slow down or halt their further accumulation, and to create institutional arrangements which would reduce the need for either side to resort to their immediate use in moments of acute international tension.[3]

Its pertinence for decision-making on the ABM in 1964 was verified by Harold Brown's testimony before the House Armed Services Committee, particularly his statement that the technical capability of the Nike-X would not be the sole ground for deciding whether or not to deploy it.[4] More salient strategic factors might forestall deployment.

The army's position on Nike-X was remarkably congenial to McNamara's decision. No basic conflict between the army and OSD emerged during congressional hearings on the budget. General William Dick, chief of army research and development and main spokesman for the army at these budgetary hearings in 1964, disclosed that because test information on the multiphased array radar (MAR) would not be compiled and evaluated completely until the end of 1964, no actual production decision would be feasible until 1965 or 1966.[5]

Meanwhile, the army's efforts to improve the design of Nike-X and to enhance its overall capabilities over the phased-out Nike-Zeus system continued with undiminished vigor. One area of prime concern was the matter of developing means of defeating the "fireball blackout" problem. The army in mid-May announced its plan to reconfigure its radar system by interconnecting MAR and MSR components and by placing MSR a certain distance from MAR. By interconnecting the two radars, the Nike-X system would have multiple-look angles; and, by siting the missile radars far enough away from MAR, these radars could continue to send information on attacking reentry vehicles into the data processing complex, even if the main radars had been blacked out.[6]

The second area of technical progress in the Nike-X concerned the missile components. Intercept tests of the Zeus under way in 1964 were yielding phenomenal results. Some Defense officials could not recall when they had had an intercept miss in the test program. Sprint, on the other hand, had yet to go beyond the initial design stage, and completion of missile design was not expected until the beginning of 1965. Moreover, testing of the Sprint warhead and hardening of the Zeus warhead were still to be scheduled as part of the U.S. underground test program. All these technical activities made postponement of any deployment of the Nike-X system likely for at least two years.[7]

OSD's attempts to keep on top of the ABM issue were highlighted in 1964 by the preparation of the Threat Analysis Study, subsequently dubbed the Betts Report.[8] Ordered by the defense secretary in July 1963, this series of studies of ABM defense, directed by General Austin Betts under the army's chief of research and development, had as its fundamental purpose the accumulation of the broadest possible base of information on which to make a decision on production and deployment of the Nike-X ABM system. The study thus examined every conceivable facet of BMD–including the strategic implications of deployment, the Soviet ICBM threat, and Russian ABM progress. Finally, a number of war game scenarios were conducted in order to postulate the various ways in which nuclear war could occur and to demonstrate the contributions of a BMD system at various levels of deployment, in conjunction with various other "damage-limiting" strategic forces, and with varied levels of civil defense programs.

The study also inquired into whether an ABM system should be deployed by this country, even if an effective one could be developed. In particular, the issue of the possible provocative or destabilizing nature of the Nike-X was reviewed. In addition, the Betts Report tackled the argument that ABM deployment by both major nuclear powers would provide a safeguard against enemy duplicity in any arms control agreement involving the reduction of long-range offensive weapons and might serve as a hedge against the risks of continued nuclear proliferation. One other basic area to which the Threat Analysis Study addressed itself was certain ancillary considerations in deploying an ABM system, including possible introduction of the Nike-X–or some derivative–into NATO in order to provide a means of protecting Europe against the large Soviet force of medium-range ballistic missiles. The value of this study (actually a series of quarterly oral briefings with the secretary of defense and supplementary written reports) was to grow in the next two years.

Two other events that were to have important, but conflicting, effects on the ABM decision occurred during the year: revelation of a Soviet ABM and mounting opposition to deployment within the scientific community. The Soviet Union had begun placing a network of ABMs around Moscow early in 1964. Later in November the Soviets paraded a Galosh ABM during a holiday celebration. No official confirmation of a Soviet ABM deployment, however, was released by the Defense Department at this time or for some time to come.[9]

Beginning in 1964 and continuing in ensuing years, a

number of noted scientists, scientific organizations, and public figures carried on vigorous lobbying efforts to publicize their arguments to prevent deployment of an active ABM defense. Included in this movement to halt ABM deployment were such individuals as Jerome Wiesner, Herbert York, Freeman Dyson, and Roswell Gilpatric, and such groups as the Federation of American Scientists and the editorial board of the *Bulletin of the Atomic Scientists*. The basic argument put forth by the members of this movement comprised the following tenets and propositions. Since the Cuban missile crisis, a period of detente had marked the relations between the United States and the USSR. The strategic arsenals of both nations were characterized by a mutual deterrent capability. Furthermore, no advance in major weapons innovation could improve either nation's security.[10]

The policy implications of this situation are twofold: military technology can no longer enhance national security, and a policy of "mutual example," a term coined by Khrushchev, might be the most appropriate strategic policy if East-West tensions were to continue to ease. This policy of abstinence meant that the United States should not deploy an ABM system because it would destabilize the strategic balance introduced by mutual deterrence and lead to a leveling off at a higher point with no material improvement in the security of either nation. Furthermore, even if the Soviet Union should begin to deploy an ABM system, the United States simply should equip American strategic forces with the means of penetrating them. Congress and the American public must be convinced that Soviet ABM systems posed no deadly threat to American security. While McNamara was apparently still unsure of the place of ABM systems in the overall strategic forces of the United States in 1964, this vision and its accompanying arguments were to have increasing weight in his thinking and calculations in succeeding years.[11]

The activities of various scientists and scientific groups in the BMD dispute stemmed less from either the clash of individual personalities within American science or from the party affiliations of these scientists than from fairly coherent and stable sets of attitudes relating to national security and the arms race advanced by three enduring schools of thought within the scientific community. As Robert Gilpin has demonstrated in his work *American Scientists and Nuclear Weapons Policy*, at least since 1947, American scientists have been divided into three distinctive groups: the infinite containment school, the finite containment school and the control school. Gilpin has traced this permanent splintering among American scientists to the conflicting assessments and reactions within the scientific community to the failure of the Baruch Plan to be passed by the United Nations and therefore to achieve international control of atomic energy. For nearly five years, between 1942 and 1947, leading American scientists had repressed their differing political views to take part in the Manhattan project and then in the common endeavor to create a politically feasible and technically perfect plan to freeze forever military technology at the subnuclear level. In the wake of its defeat in the United Nations, members of the scientific community had to orient themselves to a wholly new and frightening situation fundamentally characterized by a developing arms race between two powerful and hostile rivals–the United States and the Soviet Union.[12]

The scientific community divided over conflicting sets of temporally stable assumptions about the origin of the arms race, the essence of security and its relation to technology, the nature of the enemy, and the prospects for negotiation. According to the members of the infinite containment school, headed for nearly twenty-five years by Edward Teller, the strategic arms race was unavoidable under the conditions of modern science until the deep-seated political disagreements fueling the arms race were settled. The context of modern science was emphasized because these scientists believed that "a completely open world is the only alternative to security through arms." That is, because "modern science and technology create novelties which cannot be anticipated, and there is no guarantee that a control system developed on the basis of an existing body of knowledge will be able to detect covert developments made possible by new knowledge," any effort to control technological advances while the cloak of secrecy veils part of the world would be technically impossible and militarily foolhardy.[13]

Exponents of the infinite containment philosophy were thus grounding their argument for security through armaments on two further presuppositions. First, they were claiming that the character of technological developments was unpredictable and its pace uncontrollable. Under these conditions, technology had largely replaced geography as the prime component of national power. Hence, he who sets the pace of technological development controls the world. This view meant that the lead-time that one nation had over another in the discovery and application of new knowledge might prove decisive in weapons competition or in war. Moreover, a decisive military advantage automatically accrues to the country which is first to construct such weapons; and therefore, under any system to arrest technological progress, there would always exist a temptation to abrogate the system and achieve a technological coup which would shift the balance decidedly to one's advantage.

The major premise of this school concerning the arms race and the essence of security is based, second, upon a particular perception of the USSR as a totalitarian political system. The implications of this characterization of the enemy for prospects for negotiation are no doubt evident. As Gilpin has put it, from this view, the infinite containment school drew the inference that "whereas a democracy by its nature will not violate a control system, a totalitarian state could infringe on the system," i.e., it would likely engage in such infringement.[14] From the assumptions of this school, the safest course for an open democracy like the United States was to foreswear any effort to shackle technological development in the military realm by bilateral or international agreement until the political system of the USSR was radically transformed into an open and democratic society.

The finite containment school, in contrast, was more hopeful regarding the possibility of ending the strategic arms race. This group believed that limitation of the arms race by international accord was both technically feasible and politically desirable at some point prior to the resolution of political conflicts separating the United States and the Soviet Union, while Soviet aggression was simultaneously contained.[15]

In part, this position sprang from a somewhat more benign view of the Soviet Union and its capacity to realize its self-interest in bringing the nuclear arms race under control. But, beyond this differing evaluation of the enemy, these scientists believed that in comparing the risks of an infinite and unconstrained arms race with those of a finite cutoff of that race, the greater probability of catastrophe lay with the former. The dangers of nuclear accident, strategic misperception or miscalculation, and the sheer complexity of each new generation of strategic weapons appeared to the members of this school to pose greater threats to mankind's survival than the risks arising from the margin of trust that might be necessary to reach international agreement on arms control. Finally, the finite containment school has shown at various times during the first quarter century of the arms race a profound concern for the corrosive impact upon democratic institutions and norms of arms development and its attendant environment of secrecy, suspicion, and fear. From the standpoint of public policy, this stance meant that the United States should always be prepared to seek means of arresting the arms spiral in spite of its simultaneous commitment to contain acts of aggression by the Soviet Union in the world.

The third school of thought perceived by Gilpin—the control school—has had negligible influence in weapons debates, except during the mid-1950s when the discovery of the genetic and pathological effects of radioactive fallout from nuclear weapons testing provoked members of this school to trigger an international controversy over these revelations.[16] Perhaps the main reason for its slight political influence lies in its general lack of acquaintance with the character and scope of military technology and the complexity of problems associated with arms control. The membership of this school was drawn from the biological sciences, as well as other sciences which impinge upon issues relating to radiation and human organisms.

Part of the reason for its ability to stimulate such a large public furor in the mid-1950s had to do with its links with other scientists throughout the world and its active involvement in the Pugwash Movement.

The fundamental belief of the control school is that the nuclear arms race originated from and continues in misunderstanding, ignorance, and irrationalism. Moreover, with the advent of mutual deterrence and the dangers of radioactive fallout, nuclear war is no longer a genuine option for reasonable and informed people. From this perspective, these scientists concluded that they must refuse to share in the complicity of nuclear arms development and that, as an international force for peace, science "as an international community and language can provide a means of communication and peaceful accommodation between East and West." [17]

In the years following the inception of the nuclear arms race, members of these three schools of thought within the American scientific community gravitated toward their respective outlooks at crucial junctures in the evolution of America's nuclear weapons policy. The critical points included the decision to construct a hydrogen bomb (1949), discussions over alternatives to strategic nuclear bombing (1951-1952), the reemergence of efforts to attain international control over nuclear weapons (1955-1962), achievement of a partial nuclear test ban treaty (1963), and formulation of a nonproliferation agreement (1968).[18]

As the executive and legislative debates over the defense budget requests began in late January and early February 1965, a favorable decision on Nike-X deployment seemed no closer than the year before. McNamara introduced and interrelated the twin components of American strategic doctrine—assured destruction and damage limitation. The particular way that he connected them in his annual presentation before the congressional Armed Services and Appropriations committees in these two months was to pose a further obstacle to deployment of any active BMD.

By differentiating between assured destruction and damage-limiting capabilities, McNamara took the unprecedented step in strategic policymaking of integrating into a single analytic framework strategic offensive and defensive forces. After a lengthy and involved examination of alternative combinations of weapons systems which would yield the most lives per dollar invested, he concluded that "at each successively higher level of U.S. expenditures, the ratio of our cost for damage limitation to the potential aggressor's cost for assured destruction becomes less and less favorable for us." With the prospect of deploying the Nike-X system in mind, he said: "This argument is not conclusive against our undertaking a major new damage limiting program. The resources available to the Soviet Union are more limited than our own and they may not actually react to our initiatives as we have assumed. But it does underscore the fact that beyond a certain level of defense, the cost advantage lies increasingly with the offense, and this fact must be taken into account in any decision to commit ourselves to large outlays for additional defensive measures."

McNamara estimated that a nationwide fallout shelter program "would provide the greatest return, in terms of lives saved, from any additional funds spent on damage-limiting measures." In comparison to the relatively inexpensive $5 billion five-year systems cost for this program, the estimated $24 billion cost of a five-year Nike-X program was inordinately high. Therefore, while deferring for another year any decision to deploy the Nike-X, he requested $23.4 million in the fiscal 1966 budget for emphasizing four aspects of the civil defense program.[19]

McNamara's annual posture statement during this year was also noteworthy in another respect. While not abandoning the notion of damage limitation, he had clearly committed his office to placing highest priority on the goal of assured destruction. This choice was revealed less through public avowal than by his introduction of the idea of Greater-Than-Expected-Threat into strategic force calculations for the future and by his instructions to his new chief of DR&E regarding priorities in military R&D in strategic weapons technology.

The impetus for Greater-Than-Expected-Threat estimations

lay in McNamara's refinement of his strategic thinking and in his commitment to maintaining a level of military capability sufficient to destroy a certain percentage of the Soviet population and industry even after absorbing a Soviet first-strike blow. As this capability assumed the status of keystone of American national security from 1965 onward, it dictated, as Enthoven and Smith observed, that "requirements calculations be made on the basis of *extremely conservative* assumptions." These estimations were based on all possible technological improvements which were conceivable and within the reach of Soviet technology–a level which was "even more severe . . . than that shown at the high end of the predicted range in the National Intelligence Estimates." [20]

The second clue to McNamara's strategic choice was evidenced in his program priorities in military R&D: "Number one–R&D in Vietnam. Number two–assured penetration. Number three–ABM, *but don't precommit me.*" [21] His concluding proviso, of course, was superfluous because his hierarchy of priorities would inevitably structure the results of military R&D in these fields. But, in so doing, he explicitly enshrined the priorities of deterrence strategy which skewed the interaction of weapons R&D in the strategic offensive and defensive realms that became the concrete organizational expression of the technological imperative as it operated in the United States in the 1960s.

Once again, the army, after a year's hiatus, recommended deployment of the Nike-X system and, once more, the defense secretary refused their request. This time, however, eventual political support from a united Joint Chiefs of Staff on the army's project inched closer. In 1965 the JCS were able to agree unanimously to a recommendation that OSD seek funds for procuring certain long lead-time items to hasten the initial operational capability of a deployed Nike-X ABM system. The dispute between the army and its supporters, on the one hand, and the OSD, on the other, was the cost-effectiveness issue. The OSD was convinced that an ABM was of little worth without a supplementary shelter program. So, it seemed, as long as the relative costs of offense and defense favored the former so heavily and so long as Congress maintained such an inflexible position on shelter funding, the likelihood of deployment of the fully configured Nike-X system would remain very slim.[22]

The adamant resistance of the OSD to a comprehensive ABM system directed against the Soviet military threat did not, however, preclude the possibility that other roles might be found for an ABM system. It appeared that other missions for ABM were being assessed within the OSD. For instance, while ruling out a Soviet-oriented ABM system using the cost-effectiveness rationale, McNamara expressed interest in congressional testimony in deploying a modified Nike-X against a primitive Chinese threat which might emerge in the mid-1970s.[23]

Also, early in the year, it was revealed by Charles Herzfeld, deputy director of ARPA, that the Department of Defense was actively looking into the feasibility of developing a relatively low-cost, less complicated antimissile defense system for urban protection. Rather than providing protection against a calculated and sophisticated ICBM attack, its objective would be to protect city centers from an accidental or nth country assault. Thus, in addition to hard-point defense, a limited city deployment was receiving considerable attention within various agencies of the Defense Department. With usual candor and insight, DR&E director Harold Brown in congressional testimony described the developing orientation of the Nike-X program: "We propose in fiscal year 1966 to concentrate on the 'building block' concept of Nike-X to permit maximum flexibility in deployment options and will continue to examine the effectiveness of these options against various threats, including those less than a massive all-out attack by a sophisticated opponent." [24]

This modular ABM system concept vastly extended the types of ICBM threats to which the Nike-X could be adapted. Simply by adding or taking away various components of the full Nike-X system, at least three ABM systems configurations could be designed: in combination with a nationwide fallout shelter program, the Nike-X (Zeus plus Sprint and radar systems) could challenge a deliberate and sophisticated nuclear assault; Zeus, together with a few Sprints and some multiphased array radars, could be highly effective against a crude ICBM attack; and Zeus plus MAR would comprise a light area defense which would thwart suicidal or accidental ICBM firings.

Increasingly, by midyear, speculation grew concerning possible deployment of an ABM against the emerging Chinese nuclear threat. Although the Defense Department had thus far played down China's nuclear potential, congressional and public interest in developing defense measures against China had heightened after October 1964, when the People's Republic of China detonated its first nuclear device. News reports during May 1965 alleged that any American decision to deploy an ABM system would depend upon the pace and nature of the Chinese strategic threat.[25] These estimates ranged between $8 billion and $10 billion. Despite the limited or minimum character of the components that might be initially deployed, this light defense could grow beyond its initial installations to handle more sophisticated threats.

Fueled by a $400 million funding for further development, the Nike-X technical progress continued to be steady and impressive. Earlier in the year, further improvements in MAR were incorporated into its design during its construction at Kwajalein. Then, on November 15, 1965, a Sprint test missile was launched successfully from its underground silo. Finally, modifications of the long-range Zeus were made to improve payload capacity and to extend its range to 400 miles, and it was designated DM15X2, and eventually Spartan.[26]

At the end of the year, belief was widespread in circles attentive to defense developments that political factors would again postpone any decision on deployment. With the cost of the Vietnam War increasingly impinging upon ABM development and the Soviet-American detente still in effect, coupled with continued apathy in Congress toward a shelter program and mounting pressure from an influential school in the scientific community, the chances of a funding request in the fiscal 1967 budget were rated as minuscule.[27]

The defense budget for fiscal 1967 showed no funds for Nike-X production and deployment. Once again, the administration deferred decision, but promoted increased funding of RDT&E. How long this strategy would be viable in the face of growing political pressure from the military and Congress, as well as increased reservations concerning the efficacy of this policy from within some of the agencies of OSD, would be severely tested in the months ahead.

Speaking before the various budget review and military procurement committees of Congress, McNamara in his sixth annual posture statement comprehensively examined the role of damage limitation in the American arsenal of strategic forces for meeting the general war problem. He reached several basic conclusions relevant to BMD. Against a massive and sophisticated Soviet surprise attack, he showed that no mix of damage-limiting measures could reduce fatalities below 50 million. "Accordingly," he concluded, "we should not now commit ourselves to a particular level of Damage Limitation against the Soviet threat—first, because our deterrent makes general war unlikely, and second, because, attempting to assure with confidence against all reasonably likely levels and types of attack is very costly, and even then the results are uncertain." [28]

Responding to the anticipated Chinese nuclear threat in the mid-1970s with damage-limiting measures, he continued, was a different matter. Possibly hedging against political defeat of his position against ABM deployment, McNamara postulated two kinds of damage-limiting postures in the context of a potential Chinese ICBM capability: one that would deploy the Sprint as a terminal defense for a number of cities; and one that would deploy long-range interceptors (DM15X2), in combination with Sprint, to provide an area defense pattern. While the former could be produced and deployed almost immediately, the latter was linked to the development of VHF radars which were being pressed vigorously by the army R&D team. Moreover, as a consequence of the emergence of the long-range interceptor, the defense secretary's assessment of the latter had "changed significantly" from his evaluation in last year's testimony.[29]

According to McNamara, the possibility of developing a moderately priced ABM system which might prove to be highly effective as an area defense appeared promising. With no basic change in U.S. damage-limiting capabilities into the next decade, it was estimated by OSD that the Chinese could launch a nuclear assault which would inflict from 6 to 12 million fatalities. While the former posture, with an estimated $8 billion cost spread over five years, might cut fatalities to a range of 3 to 6 million, the latter posture, requiring an estimated five-year cost of $10.6 billion, might reduce fatalities to a range of 2 million to zero.[30]

In addition to the damage-limiting benefits, McNamara remarked, a light ABM system possessed several other virtues. It promised to retain its effectiveness for some time to come, and such a deployment would give some area protection against even a heavy Soviet attack. Despite the benefits that would accrue to the United States from deployment of this ABM defense, McNamara argued: "With regard to Communist China, the time of a U.S. light ABM deployment should be linked to the pace at which the threat actually evolves. Since we do not believe the Chinese Communists could deploy any significant ICBM force before the mid-1970's, no production decision on that account is needed at this time."[31]

Although McNamara's attention seemed to turn toward eventual production of a Chinese-oriented ABM system, the focus of army, JCS, and congressional concern remained steadfastly fixed on the deployment of a BMD against Soviet offensive might. As General Austin Betts revealed, the army had asked for $188 million for preproduction of long lead-time items, but was turned down by OSD. Then, in a significant departure from past actions, the air force chief of staff lined up with the other Joint Chiefs to form a unanimous recommendation favoring development and production of the Nike-X up to a cost of about $20 billion, which would extend over several years. Thus, the policy of postponement was no longer supported by the Joint Chiefs.[32]

More and more, key sectors of Congress allied themselves with the JCS against the civilian secretary on key political issues relating to military technology and Soviet aid to North Vietnam. And, despite its unflinching opposition to the funding of a comprehensive fallout shelter program, Congress made a strong political effort to trigger deployment of a heavy Soviet-oriented ABM system. During a hearing in April, the Senate Armed Services Committee stimulated another round of ABM debate when it recommended that Congress appropriate $167.9 million to prompt the Defense Department to hasten development and deployment of the Nike-X. The additional funding was to go to the army's missile procurement budget for preproduction items and to the service's R&D budget to finance preproduction engineering on the Nike-X system. These appropriations, the committee argued, would save a year's development time if a decision to deploy were made.[33]

In overriding the Joint Chiefs of Staff on their recommendation which the Senate committee wanted to finance, McNamara now either had to stand alone in opposing a faster pace or acquiesce to Congress and spend the extra authorization. In early May, the House Armed Services Committee added pressure by giving unanimous support to the Senate Armed Services Committee's appropriation recommendation. McNamara's response to these developments was to try to drive a wedge between this emerging political coalition by pointing out Congress's unwavering resistance to legislating favorably a meaningful civil defense program. In addition, he restated the other factors, including the cost-effectiveness element, the uncertainty of Soviet reaction, and the undeveloped nature of the Chinese threat, which made deployment unwarranted.[34]

By midyear, in tandem with rising political support for prompt deployment of a heavy ABM system came signs of a coincidence of Defense Department interest in a Chinese-oriented ABM system with the army's growing capability to assemble and service necessary components for such a config-

uration. Besides developing the DM15X2 long-range interceptor, the army was working on VHF-type radars, which were
designed to extend the acquisition range of Nike-X radars
against small targets of low observability.[35] While lacking the
discrimination capability required for defense against a sophisticated attack, these radars were perfectly designed to meet a
Chinese attack which would involve relatively few enemy
reentry vehicles lacking advanced penetration aids.

These two technical advances triggered speculation that
OSD might be opting for a thin area defense over the entire
United States against the Chinese threat at a relatively low
cost. In mid-June, John S. Foster, new director of DR&E,
stated, "The concept that we now have under engineering
development could provide a thin area defense, that is, a defense that would take . . . missiles or objects coming in
scattered over various targets, for as little as $3-4 billion. That,
of course, is a new concept from anything talked about before
this committee in prior years." As envisioned at this early stage
of development, this system would consist of a dozen long-
range Zeus missile batteries, associated MSRs, and a smaller
number of new VHF radars. Moreover, rather than springing
from the modular concept, its design was being tailored to fit
the specific needs of the projected Chinese strategic threat of
the 1970s.[36]

Sure to intensify further the widening debate over ABM
deployment was the first official public acknowledgment of
Soviet deployment of a ring of ABM installations around
Moscow. This event occurred on November 10, 1966, when
McNamara announced that "there [is] now considerable
evidence that they [the Soviets] are deploying an anti-ballistic
missile system." The Soviet Galosh ABM system–as it was
code-named by NATO–was believed to be composed of a network of radars and a two- or three-stage, solid-fueled interceptor missile designed for long-range, exoatmospheric
interception of incoming ICBMs. Similar in concept to the old
Nike-Zeus, the Soviet ABM apparently did not incorporate any
terminal defense component into its design.[37]

In December 1966 reports of administration efforts to

forestall a deployment decision indicated that the president, urged on by the secretary of defense, was considering inviting the Soviet Union to join them in formal talks to seek a moratorium on ABM deployment–and, thus, prevent a costly upward spiral of the arms race. Public announcement early in 1967 might successfully check congressional moves to spur ABM deployment, thereby delaying an ABM decision for at least another year. On December 21, 1966, Secretary of State Dean Rusk at a news conference expressed hope that the two superpowers could reach agreement to halt the arms race. He argued that deployment of ABM systems by both major powers would stimulate wholly new major levels of expenditures on armaments without contributing to the national security of either side.[38]

Thus, as the year ended, the administration seemed to be falling back on the political gambit of strategic talks as a means of preventing political decisions on ABM deployment which it had thus far resisted.

7

THE DECISION TO DEPLOY

ON September 18, 1967, Robert McNamara delivered one of the most momentous speeches in the history of ABM before the editors of United Press International in San Francisco.[1] In the course of that speech, the following basic tenets of his vision were enunciated and defended: 1) that an assured destruction capability, not a counterforce doctrine or a combination of assured destruction and damage-limiting capabilities, was "the very essence of the whole deterrence concept"; 2) that the United States and the Soviet Union could deter each other and that this condition of mutual deterrence provided both countries with the strongest possible motive to avoid triggering nuclear war; 3) that the number of separate warheads available and capable of being delivered accurately and reliably on individual high-priority enemy targets with sufficient force to destroy them is the most meaningful and realistic standard measuring nuclear capability; 4) that the "intrinsic dynamics of the arms race" can be seen in the way the United States and the USSR have mutually influenced each other's planning of strategic weapons in the past by a process defined by Mc-Namara as the "action-reaction phenomenon"; 5) that as a consequence of the operation of this interaction process, both nations built up their strategic forces to a level that greatly exceeds the requirements of a credible second-strike (or assured destruction) capability; 6) that preferable to an unceasing arms race driven by the "action-reaction phenomenon" is the achievement of an arms limitation–and eventually an arms reduction–accord between the superpowers which would arrest the dynamism of the strategic arms race.

McNamara then discussed the Soviet deployment of an ABM system, suggesting that offensive steps to ensure penetration of this defensive shield had already been taken by the

United States. Therefore, such a development will not pose any threat to the U.S. ability to inflict unacceptable damage on the Soviet Union. To the question of whether the United States should deploy a similar ABM network against the Soviet system, McNamara argued that the overriding problem involved in this decision was not money, but rather the penetrability of the proposed shield. A technically perfect and impenetrable ABM shield is impossible, since the enemy can simply fortify its offensive warhead delivery system and thereby exhaust or overwhelm the deployed ABM systems. This capacity to offset ABM deployment is the "whole crux of the nuclear action-reaction phenomenon." McNamara hoped that a strategic arms limitation agreement between the two superpowers would be reached in the near future. But if it were not forthcoming, the proper response to a Soviet decision to expand its modest ABM deployment into a massive BMD network would be to increase our offensive forces.

Another use for an ABM system would relate to China's emerging nuclear capability. A decision on deployment of a light ABM could not be postponed any longer. In examining the potential Chinese threat, McNamara painted a picture of a country in great internal ferment, fearless in its propaganda of America's power, yet rational and respectful of the awesomeness of nuclear power in its actions. Whatever China's future military designs, he maintained, the United States has the power to assure its effective destruction for the foreseeable future—and that should deter its leaders from reckless military action against the United States. Yet, "there are marginal grounds for concluding that a light deployment of U.S. A.B.M.s against this possibility is prudent."

At least four such marginal grounds were then cited by McNamara:

1) The system would be relatively inexpensive . . . and would have a much higher degree of reliability than the much more massive and complicated system that some have recommended against a possible Soviet attack.
2) Such an A.B.M. deployment designed against a possible Chinese attack would have a number of other advantages. It would provide

an additional indication to Asians that we intend to deter China from nuclear blackmail, and thus contribute toward our goal of discouraging nuclear weapons proliferation among the present non-nuclear countries.

3) Further, the Chinese-oriented A.B.M. deployment would enable us to add . . . a further defense of our Minuteman sites against Soviet attack, which means that at a modest cost we would in fact be adding even greater effectiveness to our offensive missile force and avoiding a much more costly expansion of that force.

4) Finally, such a reasonably reliable A.B.M. system would add protection of our population against the improbable accidental launch of an intercontinental missile by any of the nuclear powers.

After due consideration of the pros and cons of this ABM design, McNamara concluded, "We have decided to go forward with this Chinese-oriented A.B.M. deployment, and we will begin actual production of such a system at the end of this year."

In his closing remarks, McNamara recognized two possible psychological dangers inherent in the decision to go ahead with limited ABM deployment against the Chinese military threat. One concerned the false sense of security that might be engendered in the capitals of independent Asian nations if such deployment were conceived as a substitute for their maintaining their own conventional forces. The second danger would come from the temptation to expand this light ABM system into a heavy Soviet-directed system and the pervasive political pressures that might surface and impel the United States to succumb to its meretricious appeal.

Why, after such a critical description of the "action-reaction phenomenon" and an elaborate brief against deployment of a heavy ABM shield oriented against the existing Soviet military threat, did McNamara decide to deploy a light, Chinese-directed ABM system for a nonexisting threat?

Despite his formal position as chief executive, the president in the past intervened only infrequently in the ABM decision-making process. More typically, he simply affirmed the authority of the secretary of defense to make effective decisions on the multitude of issues relating to this weapons system. For example, in a rare public statement on ABM, President Kennedy in 1963 supported McNamara's resistance to deployment of the Nike-Zeus system. Prior to this incident, President Eisenhower's impatience with interservice feuding over roles and missions in the 1950s spurred McElroy to renovate defense management and, concomitantly, to enforce some tentative resolution of the army-air force squabble over jurisdictional rights to ABM development.[2]

A president, however, cannot remain completely free of the responsibility of choice or the ramifications of decisions made by a delegated authority. Events may compel him to take up the issue and decide–or accept the consequences of a decision that he did not really formulate. As the most visible figure in the United States and politically accountable every four years, he has his own peculiar stakes in the outcomes of different political struggles, as well as his own special perspective on issues and events. For President Johnson in 1967 the stakes that guided his perception of the situation and his actions lay primarily in the domestic arena, and the currency of these domestic stakes tended to be defined in terms of votes, resources for domestic and foreign policy programs, presidential power, and his relations with congressional leaders and his own staff.[3]

Even during the waning months of 1966, President Johnson had begun to play a more active part in determining the fate of the American ABM program.[4] No doubt, unsettled by the heightening furor over ABM in the Congress and concerned about its possible impact on his chances for reelection in 1968, he surely saw important political stakes in the balance on this matter. Moreover, because a basic requirement in presidential administration is that the chief executive annually make budget decisions and defend these decisions publicly in a state of the union address before Congress, Johnson could not evade discussion of this increasingly sensitive political issue. And, given the great congressional and public interest in ABM stimulated by the preceding year's national debate, the announcement of Soviet deployment, and the disclosures of the quickening pace of Chinese nuclear and ballistic developments, his response would be carefully assayed by politicians and the public alike.

In January 1967 the contours of the president's basic strategy on the ABM issue took shape with increasing clarity. Early in the month, President Johnson, in a letter of instruction to the American ambassador to the Soviet Union, asked that Soviet agreement be sought to discuss ABMs. Then, in his 1967 State of the Union Message, he said that, although no decision had been made on the deployment of an ABM system, he was requesting standby funds in the fiscal 1968 budget for its production, awaiting the outcome of his approaches to the Soviet Union to initiate negotiations leading to a strategic arms limitation agreement. Finally, in a public statement, the president announced that no United States ABM deployment would be made until completion of arms control negotiations between the United States and the USSR. Apparently the president had embraced McNamara's option in the closing months of 1966 to delay presidential commitment to BMD by exploring the prospects of arms control talks with the Soviets that might lead to a moratorium on deployment of new offensive and defensive weapons.[5]

The extent of the president's ongoing interest in the ABM issue throughout 1967 was manifested by a meeting that took place at the White House on January 23, 1967.[6] What was exceptional about this gathering was the spectrum of participants assembled before the president to review the question of ABM defense. In addition to the major executive protagonists in the ABM controversy, including the president himself, McNamara, and the Joint Chiefs of Staff, were all past and current special assistants to the president for science and technology (James R. Killian, Jr., George Kistiakowsky, Jerome Wiesner, and Donald Hornig) and all past and current directors of DR&E (Herbert York, Harold Brown, and John S. Foster, Jr.). The president was interested in the participants' evaluations of American ABM technology. The substance of Johnson's inquiries to the scientific community was, "Will it work?" The answer was in the negative.[7] To underscore this point, McNamara related to the president that if the United

States had proceeded in 1953 with the Nike-Zeus system, it would have had to dismantle the system and lose $13-14 billion that had been put into the project.[8] (In later testimony before the Senate Armed Services Committee and in his San Francisco speech announcing the decision to deploy the Sentinel ABM system, McNamara was to use both this argument and the unanimous negative opinion of these presidential scientific advisers to bolster his case against a Soviet-oriented ABM.)

Clearly, from one point of view, the president preferred not to deploy a costly and probably defective ABM system; and he might succeed, he felt, if Moscow would join with Washington in serious and fruitful arms negotiations. On the other hand, his long tenure in the Senate made his friends and former colleagues in that body a major reference group on national security matters. His close friendship with and deep respect for such senators as Richard Russell, Henry Jackson, and John Stennis could not help but influence the way that he perceived his political stakes and his conception of the national interest.[9]

Further complicating his efforts to resolve the issue were clear signs that the Republican party was planning to make Johnson's failure to deploy Nike-X a major issue in the 1968 presidential campaign and to exploit the "ABM gap" in an analogous way to President Kennedy's trumpeting of the "missile gap" in the 1960 election. The first hint of this political design surfaced in February 1967, when the Republican National Committee issued a fifty-five page booklet entitled *The Missile Defense Question: Is LBJ Right?* which argued for immediate deployment of the Nike-X ABM system against the Soviet nuclear threat. This was followed in August with a similarly long *Statement on the Deployment of an Anti-Ballistic Missile System.* Cast in unvarnished political and partisan terms, both documents foreshadowed what would doubtless be a key plank in the 1968 Republican platform.[10]

As a longtime member of the congressional wing of the Democratic party and a close student of Speaker Sam Rayburn, the president was very much inclined to try to strike some compromise that would minimize his costs. Moreover, given his lack of any strong commitments to foreign policy and national security issues, he was predisposed to view the question of ABM deployment almost solely in domestic political terms. Thus, the stakes in this controversy were, for him, predominantly viewed in terms of his relations with his secretary of defense, with the JCS, with the politically influential members of Congress concerned with national defense, and in terms of the ramifications of any decision for the 1968 presidential election.[11]

In the succeeding months of 1967, two questions would weigh heavily in Johnson's calculations with respect to the issue of whether to produce and deploy an ABM system for the United States: would the Soviet Union relieve him of the fundamental choice on the ABM question by initiating serious negotiations on strategic arms limitation? Or, if not, what kind of compromise settlement in the realm of domestic politics could be forged that would distribute dissatisfaction as equally as possible and thereby cut his political costs to a minimum?

McNamara had to marshal all his political resources and use all his political skills to influence President Johnson's perception of the domestic and political consequences of any deployment and to ease the political pressures being brought to bear on the president to give approval. Viewing the ABM as the symbol of the arms race, McNamara strove in the closing months of 1966 and in 1967 to perform these tasks. Unfortunately, his former sources of political strength were gradually evaporating and his past political adversaries were growing stronger and more vocal as each month passed. Not least of all, the Soviet Union's cooperation did not seem to be forthcoming.

In his seventh annual posture statement, delivered in February and March 1967, McNamara enumerated the reasons why the United States should not deploy either a heavy Soviet-oriented ABM system or a thin area defense against the developing Chinese strategic threat at this time. Concerning the Soviet military threat, he noted that, as of October 1966, the United States possessed at least a three-to-one superiority

(1,446 to 470) over the Soviet Union in ICBMs and an even greater superiority in terms of overall combat effectiveness.[12] In the area of BMD systems, the Soviets, after several abortive starts, had begun to deploy the Galosh ABM system around Moscow, as well as another type of defensive system (thought to be geared to the American bomber force) elsewhere in the Soviet Union. But, whatever the exact character of these systems and pace of their deployment by the Soviet Union, American defense planners, for the time being, were predicating their strategic forces on the assumption that by the early 1970s the USSR would have deployed a heavy ABM protection around all its major cities.

As a hedge against Soviet deployment, OSD took a number of actions the year before, including the acceleration of Poseidon missile development, approval of production and deployment of Minuteman III forces, and development of penetration aids for Minuteman ICBMs. For fiscal 1968 McNamara proposed to take some additional steps to enhance the future capabilities of U.S. assured destruction forces: 1) produce and deploy Poseidon missile; 2) produce and deploy improved missile penetration aids; 3) increase the proportion of Minuteman III in the planned force and provide it with an improved third stage; and 4) initiate the development of new reentry vehicles, specifically designed for use against targets heavily defended with ABMs. McNamara stressed that this action to increase the size and penetration effectiveness of U.S. offensive forces *was* the American response to the deployment of a series of ABM complexes around Moscow. From his perspective, "the question of whether we should or should not deploy an ABM is not really directly related to their deployment." [13]

In an attempt to make his case against U.S. deployment of a Soviet-oriented ABM system, McNamara argued that, because of the crucial importance of assured destruction capacity to national security, the United States must be prepared to cope with Soviet strategic threats which are greater than those projected by latest intelligence estimates. From this standpoint, the most severe threat which the Soviet Union could pose in the foreseeable future would be the deployment of an extensive, effective ABM system, in conjunction with a deployment of a substantial ICBM force with a hard-target kill capability. Such a combination of offensive and defensive weapons would put in jeopardy a substantial proportion of the Minuteman missile force and seriously undercut our second-strike capability. To hedge against this imaginary and extremely unlikely eventuality, the Defense Department had authorized the development and production of the Poseidon missiles (with MIRV warheads) and their retrofitting on thirty-one of the forty-one submarines in the Polaris fleet.[14]

Turning to the politically sensitive area of BMD, McNamara tried to convince his audience that the Nike-X system should be categorized in damage-limiting capabilities and that therefore Soviet efforts to undermine America's assured-destructive capabilities by deployment of an ABM system need not entail equivalent response. Rather, since the cost of offsetting defensive measures with offensive capabilities was low, the proper U.S. response continues to be enhancing its offensive striking power and penetration capability. In addition, the Soviets could effectively negate any damage-limiting advantages accruing to the United States from deployment of an ABM system by spending about a quarter of the American investment in defensive capabilities on their offensive forces. This would be the case, he continued, whether the United States deployed a damage-limiting force that was comprised of a light U.S. defense against Soviet missile attack on our cities and costing $12.2 billion or a damage-limiting force that was composed of a heavier defense against a Soviet attack with an area coverage of twice as many cities and costing perhaps $21.7 billion.[15]

McNamara further contended that the USSR possessed the requisite technical and economic capacity to expand its offensive capability and that it would be compelled to react to a threat against its assured destructive capabilities by increasing its offensive nuclear force. But the result of this action-reaction process, he pointed out, would be that "the risk of a Soviet nuclear attack on the United States would not be further decreased" and that "the damage to the United States from a Soviet nuclear attack, in the event deterrence failed, would not be reduced in any meaningful sense." Given the $4 billion spent on BMD research and the $1.2 billion on the development of penetration aids, he maintained, the United States has the technology to counter any offensive or defensive force alterations the Soviets might undertake in the foreseeable future.[16]

Concluding his case against a Soviet-oriented ABM system, McNamara stated: "We can predict with certainty that there will be substantial additional costs for updating any system" due to "technological developments in offensive forces over the next 7 years that may make obsolete or drastically degrade the Nike-X system as presently envisioned"; "deployment of a Nike-X system would also require some improvement in our defense against manned bomber attack" and "we would want to expand and accelerate the fallout shelter program" in order to balance our defensive forces–at an increased cost of perhaps $4 billion; and there would undoubtedly be tremendous pressures exerted to expand the ABM systems network to cover more and more major cities with point defense until an expenditure on the order of $40 billion would be reached over a ten-year period.[17]

As Phil Goulding, former assistant secretary of defense for public affairs, recounts in his book *Confirm or Deny,* the language in the annual posture statement for fiscal 1968 on the possibility of a Chinese-oriented ABM system had been written with great care in November and December of 1966 by McNamara and Deputy Secretary Cyrus Vance.[18] If political pressures subsided or favorable international events arose during the year, perhaps the ABM would not have to be deployed. Otherwise, the secretary could fall back on the less expensive and less provocative anti-Chinese system.

McNamara agreed that an austere ABM defense, requiring a total investment of approximately $3.5 billion, would likely offer a high degree of protection against a possible Chinese attack at least through the 1970s. With this modest investment, U.S. fatalities, in the event of a Chinese first strike, could be reduced to near zero. Indeed, he claimed, with only slight additions and improvements funded by relatively modest outlays, the Chinese damage potential would be maintained at very low levels well beyond 1985. However, the lead-time for deployment of a significant Chinese ICBM force is longer than that required for United States ABM deployment; therefore, he concluded, the decision for the latter need not be made at this time.[19]

In addition to postponing decision on deployment of a thin area defense against the emerging Chinese strategic force, the secretary proposed three actions in the realm of BMD:

1. To pursue with undiminished vigor the development and evaluation of the Nike-X system (for which purpose a total of about $440 million has been included in the fiscal year 1968 budget), but to take no action now to deploy the system.
2. To initiate negotiations with the Soviet Union designed, through formal or informal agreement, to limit the deployment of antiballistic missile systems.
3. To reconsider the deployment decision in the event these discussions prove unsuccessful; approximately $375 million has been included in the fiscal year 1968 budget to provide for such actions as may be required at that time–for example, the production of Nike-X for the defense of our offensive weapons systems.[20]

As this series of decisions discloses, funds for deployment–some $375 million–were being requested for the first time by the secretary of defense (acquiescing to the wishes of the president), to be used in case the American offer to convene arms control talks went unanswered by the Soviet Union.

Although McNamara was constantly pressed in committee hearings to amplify on the possible reasons for Soviet deployment of an ABM complex around Moscow and to justify why the United States should postpone a decision on deploying its own advanced ABM system, members of Congress seemed in a less combative mood on the ABM issue than in previous years.[21] Perhaps they felt that the decision on deployment no longer resided in the OSD. Perhaps they believed it was only a matter of time before executive decision on deployment would be forthcoming, given the course of international events and the continuing success in mobilizing political support for deployment of a heavy ABM system within the legislative and executive branches, as well as from the military.

A cause for even greater concern for McNamara was the increasing disintegration of political support from his traditional bases within his own office for his position of unqualified opposition to any deployment. Within the OSD, all the civilian secretaries (the air force's Harold Brown, the navy's Paul Nitze, and the army's Stanley Resor), the director of DR&E (John Foster), and the director of ARPA (Charles Herzfeld) in congressional testimony on the fiscal 1968 budget expressed favor for deployment of a light, area defense version of the Nike-X system, which would include protection of Minuteman ICBM silos, on the condition that negotiations with the Soviet Union on limiting ABM deployment failed to produce mutual accord. Besides its mission, these officials had reached consensus on the technical feasibility and the operational readiness of this configuration of the Nike-X system. Options of the secretary in the ABM controversy were to diminish to a point where, in Phil Goulding's words, "our choice in the Pentagon in the late summer and fall of 1967 was not a small ABM versus none at all, but rather a small ABM versus a big one." [22]

Within the Department of Defense bureaucracy, the army had long fought for a role in the highest status activity of this organization–the strategic offensive mission. Having been rebuffed in its attempt to gain operational control of ICBMs in the Thor-Jupiter controversy, it turned its attention–with the advent of the missile age–to the BMD field. In the late 1950s and early 1960s, the army continued to mobilize political support among the other service departments and within Congress to gain a favorable decision on production and deployment of the Nike-Zeus and Nike-X ABM systems.

Ironically, coincidental with rising political support for deployment of its anti-ICBM system, there appeared in the middle 1960s waning military interest in the army for this strategic mission. In the past, the army had tried hard to put forth a strong case to Congress for the signal importance of

BMD for the nation; and the offices within the Department of the Army which had overseen the ABM advancement had themselves developed strong organizational stakes in a deployment decision and had, as a consequence, been vigorous spokesmen in congressional hearings for Nike-X. Part of the reason for the army's flagging interest in BMD, no doubt, related to its obvious preoccupation with the land war in Vietnam during these years. But the cause of this reordering of normative interest in the ABM role stemmed from the shift in strategic doctrine in the early 1960s to a strategy of multiple options. From 1961 to 1967 the army's military concerns and operations had become more diverse and more heavily funded as some of its more traditional missions gained a new lease on life and were joined by new roles and missions distinctive to a more insurgent and revolutionary epoch.

This decline in relative priority of the army's role of operational control of the ABM was reflected in the deeper concern for its limited war mission in Vietnam and in the relative equanimity with which some of its top spokesmen anticipated the type of ABM decision toward which McNamara was moving. While General Harold K. Johnson (army chief of staff) voiced support for a more advanced program for Nike-X deployment, both Secretary of the Army Stanley Resor and General Austin Betts (army chief of R&D) seemed quite disposed to accept the milder version of the Nike-X system. Thus, despite the army's official budgetary request for approval to release funds from money already appropriated the preceding year for preproduction of Nike-X items and its expectation that 1967 was the right year for deployment to begin, it seemed quite prepared to accept deployment of a very light defense.[23]

The analysis conducted by the army's R&D office was designed to determine the cost of a very thin ABM system developed out of Nike-X components that would protect against a likely level of a Chinese attack in the 1970s, provide terminal defense for some of the Minuteman force, and eliminate the danger of an accidental ICBM launch. The office reached a judgment, according to General Betts, that "for something a little over $4 billion, we could provide that level of defense." But, he reiterated, "the $377 million [deployment] program recommended is adequate to go ahead with either of the deployment levels that have been discussed in the Secretary's posture statement, or in our recommendations to him." Thus, despite the army's apparent awareness of McNamara's effort to co-opt them should political pressure force a deployment decision, the service took few steps to counter that threat.[24]

During the 1950s when interservice rivalry dominated defense politics, the voice of the Joint Chiefs of Staff tended to be dissonant. "Each Service tended to support its own deployment," as Morton Halperin observed, "and except where specific deals were made, to oppose controversial deployments for other Services, particularly expensive ones, which might upset the existing arrangement allocating shares of the defense budget." [25] With no strong secretary of defense, the JCS saw no threat to their autonomy and preferred to deal separately with the secretary or president on specific issues. As a consequence, splits on recommendations and divergence of opinion within the JCS during budgetary debate became the norm.

This pattern changed dramatically with the entrance of Robert McNamara to the OSD. With his defense management ideology and alternate basis of expertise, as well as his perception of his role in policy leadership terms, he was able to undercut the influence of the Joint Chiefs in congressional debate on the defense budget and to use their division to reject weapons programs supported by less than a majority of the services. In succeeding years, dispute within the Defense Department began more and more to cleave along civil-military lines, as the JCS sought to counteract the civilian secretary's influence. By compromising their positions on controversial issues, the Joint Chiefs of Staff were able to present a united front on many salient defense issues in their periodic budgetary confrontations with the secretary of defense.

Increasingly, then, a united JCS began to line up against McNamara to the detriment of the secretary's influence in

Congress. In 1965 the Joint Chiefs in unison recommended funds for preproduction of Nike-X component parts. In 1966, for the first time, they unanimously recommended production and deployment of the Nike-X according to the first posture design described in the secretary's statement. During this same year, they also dissented from McNamara's position about the impact of Soviet military aid to North Vietnam in its war effort. A united Joint Chiefs of Staff became a strong political force in legislative dealings on defense spending from 1965 onward.

In 1967 the JCS and the secretary of defense diverged sharply on two politically crucial issues: deployment of the Nike-X ABM system and the effectiveness of the bombing campaign in North Vietnam. For the first time, the JCS presented a unanimous recommendation in favor of immediate production and deployment of the Nike-X. Significantly, the Joint Chiefs had to modify their stance under pressure from Air Force Chief John McConnell, to include as a first immediate step the deployment of a light ABM system, which incorporated a measure of protection of the United States land-based ICBM force.[26]

General Earle Wheeler suggested some of the basic motives behind the recent and continuing Soviet buildup of strategic offensive and defensive forces which the JCS imputed to these moves. Among these aims, he included:

First, to reduce the United States assured destruction capability –that is, our ability to destroy their industry and people.
Second, to complicate the targeting problem which we have in directing our strategic forces against the Soviet Union.
Third, to reduce U.S. confidence in our ability to penetrate Soviet defense, thereby reducing the possibility that the United States would undertake a preemptive first strike against the Soviet Union, even under extreme provocation.
Fourth, to achieve an exploitable capability, permitting them freedom to pursue their national aims at conflict levels less than general nuclear war.

He then questioned the defense secretary's assumption that the Soviets would inevitably have to respond to an American

ABM deployment by increasing their existing offensive nuclear force. Given their historical defense-mindedness, the Soviets might simply add more defenses to compound the American targeting problem. And, because of the high competition for relatively scarce resources in the USSR, Soviet leaders might not be willing to increase their defense to offset any American countermove.[27]

An equally important point of contention between the secretary and JCS centered on their varying conceptions of the essence of security. While McNamara saw the keystone of national security lying in a real assured-destruction capability, the Joint Chiefs felt that deterrence was "a combination of forces in being, and state of mind." Amplifying on this point, Wheeler argued:

Should the Soviets come to believe that their ballistic missile defense, coupled with a nuclear attack on the United States, would limit damage to the Soviet Union to a level acceptable to them . . . , our forces would no longer deter. The first principle of our security would be gone.

I should say here that while I certainly agree–and so do the Joint Chiefs–that the basis of deterrence is the ability to destroy an attacker as a viable nation, as a part of this, there is also the ability of the nation to survive as a nation–in other words, the converse of the first point.

The JCS was really more concerned, in contrast to the defense secretary, with extending the damage-limiting capacity of the country's strategic arsenal. In addition, the Joint Chiefs expressed fear that American failure to deploy an ABM would create a strategic imbalance both within American forces and between U.S. and Soviet forces. Finally, Wheeler said, "It could lead to Soviet and allied belief that we are interested only in the offensive–or that our technology is deficient, or that we will not pay to maintain strategic superiority." [28]

As for the possible benefits of deployment of such an ABM system, Wheeler said that it would:

First, provide a damage limitation capability by attrition of a Soviet attack.
Second, introduce uncertainties that would inhibit Soviet lead-

ers from concluding that the United States could not survive a Soviet first strike or that the United States would not preempt under any circumstances.

Third, stabilize the nuclear balance.

Fourth, demonstrate to the Soviets and our allies that the United States is not first-strikeminded; in other words, that we don't put all our eggs in the offensive basket.

Fifth, continue to deny to the Soviet an exploitable capability.[29]

While McNamara tried carefully to refute each of these aspects of the JCS recommendation in his posture statement and in congressional testimony, the fact that this was the second consecutive year that he had rejected a unanimous ruling of the Joint Chiefs was sure to bring more legislators into the movement for deployment of a heavy ABM. McNamara's only solace from the recommendation of the JCS was its willingness to accept a light area defense as a stepping-stone to eventual heavier ABMs.

The second major confrontation between McNamara and the JCS was over the importance of the bombing of North Vietnam. Speaking before the Preparedness Investigating Subcommittee of the Senate Armed Services Committee in August 1967, McNamara articulated some basic realities about the bombing campaign against North Vietnam and about its capabilities. Essentially, he argued, "the primary objective of the air compaign in the North is to reduce the flow of men and supplies from North Vietnam into South Vietnam," not to serve as a substitute for the land and air war in the South. Furthermore, since the volume of supplies needed by the enemy to support the war in the South was significantly under 100 tons per day, this minimum flow "cannot be stopped by air bombardment"–short of virtual annihilation of North Vietnam and its people by indiscriminate bombing. Any effort to cut off war-supporting imports into North Vietnam from Russia and China would be equally futile and risky. Nor, he asserted, is there any reason to believe that Hanoi "can be bombed to the negotiation table." [30]

As sound as these arguments might have appeared, Mc-

Namara was striking at the heart of some of the most strongly held beliefs shared by the military and its allies in Congress. For these people, the bombing of North Vietnam had become the very symbol of air power—and its most supreme test. Whatever McNamara's motives in advancing these arguments, the immediate impact was to widen the civil-military gap and to intensify the conflict between the executive and legislative branches on key defense issues. At this point, one can only speculate what weight this incident and its ramifications carried in President Johnson's calculations on the ABM deployment issue; but, certainly, it could not have been small.

Each year, since the beginning of serious controversy over ABM, efforts were made to trigger a production and deployment decision from the executive branch. During the late 1950s, Congress raced ahead of the administration and OSD by including funds for production of long lead-time items for the Zeus. Then, in the 1960s, this hardware addition became almost a regular routine—with the same result: executive noncompliance. For a time, the dazzle and polish of the civilian secretary's performances (as well as those of his civilian advisers in DR&E and ARPA) overwhelmed ABM proponents and mollified would-be supporters. But the long-term executive appropriation of perceived constitutional prerogatives brought mounting frustration and rebellion in Congress and cries for retribution. As the major symbol of misplaced power and perhaps the foremost perpetrator of executive imperialism, the Pentagon—and, in particular, the OSD—became the chief object of criticism in Congress. Moreover, for some legislators, the policy of postponement promoted by OSD in the case of ABM was to become the specific focal point of efforts in 1966 and 1967 to redress the historical imbalance between the executive and legislative branches of government. An interesting point in this respect is the ambiguity of this grievance. This battle cry has been the banner employed by two coalitions in Congress—to promote ABM in 1967 and to halt deployment in 1969 and 1970. There has been only one constant—antipathy toward the Pentagon.

In part, the inclusion of funds in the fiscal 1968 budget for deployment if arms negotiations failed was a political ploy by the president and defense secretary to mollify congressional criticism and check political pressures to spark a decision for immediate deployment of a heavy Soviet-oriented ABM system. In so doing, it prevented the Nike-X proponents from campaigning to add funds to the defense budget for this purpose in 1967. Unfortunately, during the year, congressional disenchantment with this policy increased, rather than subsided. Indeed, during the summer months of 1967 a number of congressional committees went on record favoring immediate deployment of an American ABM system. In August, for instance, the Joint Congressional Atomic Energy Committee released a comprehensive report on the "serious threat" of China's rapid progress in thermonuclear weapons and their delivery, followed by a declaration by Senator John Pastore in September to fight for an ABM from his position as chairman of this committee. The Senate Committee on Appropriations followed suit. Finally, the furor caused by McNamara's assault on the sacrosanct issue of the bombing of North Vietnam was sure to promote heightened political efforts to halt the trend toward the accrual of power in the executive. Given the prominence of the ABM debate, this area was a likely place for a fight against the executive to be mounted during legislative debates over the following fiscal year's budget.[31]

In early August McNamara was briefed on a study performed by the Nike-X Systems Office concerning the probable reaction and capability of China to respond to an American deployment of a light anti-ICBM system. At the end of August word was released by *Aerospace Technology* that a draft presidential memorandum from the secretary to the president recommending a thin anti-Chinese ABM system had been prepared by the Systems Analysis Group and was currently circulating in the offices of the Defense Department. On September 8, 1967, Dean Rusk launched an apparent last-ditch effort to elicit Soviet response to a U.S. offer to initiate arms-reduction talks before the United States would be compelled to deploy its long-postponed Nike-X system. In the wake of the failure of this request, McNamara announced on September 18, 1967, the decision of the United States to deploy a thin Chinese-oriented ABM defense.[32]

The decision that emerged was the result of a bargaining process composed of individuals with different perceptions of the situation, pursuing a variety of goals defined in divergent currencies (strategic, organizational, interpersonal, personal). It was political, moreover, because it was the outcome of a mix of rationales, all of which were taken into account by the authoritative decision-maker. So despite the powerful influence of the technological imperative upon decision-making in the realm of strategic weapons development, it must be acknowledged that with the displacement of the locus of decision from the Pentagon to American domestic (and presidential) politics, a whole range of forces came to bear upon a decision whose stakes had made it a fundamental responsibility of the executive.

Still, while Lyndon Johnson decided in late 1966 to deploy an ABM, he allowed his defense secretary to determine the size and character of the system. From this perspective, three questions can be raised: Why deploy an ABM system at all? Why deploy a thin Chinese-oriented ABM system rather than a heavy Soviet-oriented one? Why make a positive decision now and not earlier?

An ABM system was deployed because McNamara's options had simply run out. Partly as a stopgap, partly as an expression of his view of the prime stimulus of the arms race and his hope of halting it, McNamara had urged Johnson in the formulation of the fiscal 1968 budget to seek out Soviet participation in arms control talks to limit the size of the overstocked strategic arsenals of both countries and to negotiate a moratorium on deploying ABMs. His strategy in forestalling any deployment rested on international events beyond his control and on domestic political and military pressures the intensity of which would depend in part on his own diminishing influence and political skill in mollifying the fears underlying these pressures. McNamara's discussion of the U.S. response to Soviet deployment of an ABM in congressional testimony was part of his campaign to accomplish the latter. When his efforts failed to convince his critics, and when some of his other actions actually exacerbated the civil-military and executive-congressional antagonisms, McNamara had to rely on the slender hope of timely assistance from the Soviet Union. Moscow's eventual willingness to enter into strategic arms limitation talks came too late for McNamara. For, in late summer and early fall of 1967, with the time for meetings on the fiscal 1968 budget approaching, the president either had to decide soon or report in his next state of the union message that he would maintain the policy of postponement. McNamara found that his options had simply been exhausted and thus he was forced to announce a favorable decision on ABM which he had resisted for nearly seven years.

Why was a thin, Chinese-oriented ABM system chosen over a heavy, Soviet-oriented ABM system? McNamara had long hedged against the possibility of political defeat of his ABM policy of deferring production while funding development. The groundwork for this fall-back system was laid at least as far back as 1965. If an ABM system was forced upon him, the "marginal" reasons for its deployment might even spring from a measure of prudence.

In addition, the thin area defense system, incorporating some defense for the Minuteman force, was also the least common political denominator among the types of ABM systems that most of the constituents of the opposing coalition of forces would accept. While some advocates of ABM would be satisfied with nothing less than the Soviet-oriented system, certainly the civilian secretaries, the director of DR&E, and the director of ARPA within the Defense Department would applaud it. And even the JCS and some senators and congressmen would be satisfied if it appeared that its potential for growth into a large system had not been stymied.

Above all, McNamara's objective remained to prevent the deployment of a large-scale ABM defense that could be regarded as provocative to Soviet leaders and defense planners. Properly advanced and sharply differentiated from its Soviet counterpart, a Chinese-oriented ABM could be more easily limited than a small ABM system designed to blunt and complicate a Soviet ICBM attack.

To further these objectives, McNamara prepared an ABM information campaign on the eve of delivering the speech, with the major thrust being, as its coordinator notes, "to review the public record . . . so that they could keep his speech in proper perspective." He also rechristened the thin ABM configuration as the Sentinel and ordered that its development, production, and deployment be an entirely different project from the Nike-X development program. Furthermore, he assigned the Sentinel program to the Sentinel System Command under the direction of Lieutenant General Alfred Starbird, while retaining the old Nike-X program as a separate organization with Betts as its director.[33]

An affirmative decision was made at that time because by late 1966 McNamara could no longer define the context of decision, although his previous actions had helped shape the milieu. With effective decision in the hands of the president, his role was reduced to that of one major participant in the political contest of influencing the decision of the chief executive. In the past, the decision not to deploy was underpinned by many motivations. But if the perspective of 1967 permits any warrant for generalization, it may be suggested that two basic factors can be isolated to explain why a deployment decision was not formulated until September 1967: cost-effectiveness analysis and the technological imperative.

Cost-effectiveness analysis, as it became ever more deeply integrated into the policymaking process, served to clarify the economics of weapons decision-making and to sharpen the relationship between assured-destruction and damage-limiting capabilities, as well as the relative costs and contributions of offensive and defensive weapons systems. In the specific case of ABM, it acted to rationalize perpetuation of ABM development and the postponement of production and deployment on the basis of the greater contribution (and less expense) of offensive forces, in comparison to defensive forces, to both components of the United States strategic arsenal.

The technological imperative had the effect of pitting American offensive and defensive R&D efforts in an unceasing struggle for supremacy, while allowing the assumption that the offensive had to win to insinuate itself into "rationalization" for nondeployment of an ABM system. If penetration-aids technology of the United States can defeat any American ABM design, however advanced, then it must be assumed that advancing Soviet offensive capability will be able to negate any ABM system that the United States might deploy.

In the end, despite the powerful force of these two factors, McNamara was compelled to yield to the political necessities of election-year politics. Thus he deferred to his political executive and deployed what was more aptly described as a "Republican-oriented" ABM system.

8

SAFEGUARD, SALT, AND THE
McNAMARA HERITAGE

THE year 1968 was marked by continued efforts within the
Johnson administration to stimulate agreement with the Soviet government upon negotiations over strategic arms reductions in offensive and defensive weapons systems.[1] It was also
a period characterized by the administration's attempts to
avoid strong pressures to move beyond the limited Sentinel
program to a full-scale Soviet-oriented ABM system, as well as
to block an incipient movement inside Congress (primarily the
Senate) working for a legislative cut in funding for ABM. A
presidential election year, 1968 was a period where an in-
cumbent president withdrew, the Democratic party's nominee
strove to assume a position of independence without antag-
onizing party regulars, and his opponent sought to capitalize
upon discord and dissent.

With the victory of the Republican nominee, Richard M.
Nixon, the stage was set in early 1969 for a thorough review
of the Kennedy-Johnson policies on foreign affairs and a complete reconsideration of the Robert McNamara-Clark Clifford
programs in the realm of national defense. Many individuals,
including a number of Democratic senators, looked upon Nixon's election as providing a new opportunity to squelch
BMD before production and deployment, when chances of its
overturning would be virtually nil. Anti-ABM critics were
buoyed by the announcement from the Soviet Union (coin-
ciding with the inauguration of the new president) of its
desire to participate in strategic arms limitation talks. In addition, the bipartisan congressional forces found immediate
satisfaction in the growth of public opposition in those areas
of the country where land had been purchased for Sentinel

missile sites. Encouragement was only reinforced by the discovery that leadership in the grassroots was being taken up in many cases by anti-ABM scientists and then by liberal public officials on state and national levels.

When, on February 6, 1969, Secretary of Defense Melvin Laird ordered a halt to the army's entire Sentinel program (including all land acquisition, site surveys, and construction) pending the results of a month-long review, it was widely believed that the president might opt for a permanent cessation of ABM deployment in order to establish good relations with the Democratic leadership in Congress and to make a friendly gesture to the Soviets in response to their initial message to him.[2]

Between February 6 and March 14, as the Nixon administration deliberated, a flurry of intense lobbying took place at all levels of national government among political, corporate, labor, scientific, religious, and academic groups. In Congress, the influential Joint Committee on Atomic Energy began circulating a paper entitled "What's Wrong with Sentinel?"–one that questioned the Chinese orientation and area defense concept of the Sentinel system. Then, later in February, the Senate Foreign Relations Committee announced that its Subcommittee on Disarmament under Albert Gore's chairmanship would begin holding educational hearings into the strategic and foreign policy implications of ABM systems. With the subcommittee chairman and many of its members skeptical of Sentinel's value, its hearings would surely serve as a public forum for airing doubts over any BMD system.[3]

In tandem with the congressional actions were developments in the scientific community to put pressure on the president at least to postpone decision on any ABM deployment until the SALT negotiations had run their course. The president, as well as many senators and congressmen, were inundated with letters and telegrams from scientists opposing any deployment decision. Part of this avalanche of mail could be traced to a national strike to protest against the misuse of science and technology on March 3 and 4, 1969, radiating from the Massachusetts Institute of Technology and extending to other college and university campuses throughout the nation. The anti-ABM movement among scientists was then channeled into the political sphere through actions such as the Gore subcommittee's invitations to top scientists opposed to ABM who had served as advisers to past presidents to testify and Senator Edward Kennedy's hiring of a private panel of scientific experts headed by Jerome Wiesner and Abram Chayes to report on the BMD issue.[4]

While lobbying activities continued, President Nixon pondered a decision which would greatly influence executive-congressional relations on defense and foreign policy matters, but which would reveal a great deal in addition about his image of the presidential style, his view toward arms control negotiations between the superpowers, and his attitudes toward the role of the scientific-technical elite in defense decision-making.

On March 14 President Nixon announced the fate of Sentinel.[5] Speaking before a gathering of reporters, he indicated that three policy alternatives had been rejected. A defense against a heavy Soviet attack was not as yet feasible; the Sentinel program would not be able to respond to the growing Soviet threat to American deterrence forces; and R&D would not provide answers to practical problems in a way that actual production and deployment would.

Hence, the existing Sentinel program needed to be modified and its purposes be reoriented. Dubbed the Safeguard, this new program would be designed to protect American land-based ICBMs against a direct assault from the Soviet Union; to defend the American people against the kind of nuclear threat which China might pose in the coming decade; and to protect against the danger of accidental attacks from any source. The overriding objective of the Safeguard was to provide protection of U.S. deterrent forces.

The proposed Safeguard ABM system exhibited additional features. Because of its change in basic purpose from a population defense to a missile defense, the system would not require installations near major metropolitan areas. Moreover, since its deployment would be a phased one (beginning with protection of ICBM sites) and its value would be periodically reviewed and related to the actual developing Soviet threat, the decision to initiate deployment would not be a once-for-all deployment and its implementation would not impinge upon the success of future arms talks with the Soviet Union.

Despite the importance in the democratic process of an educated citizenry for the quality of American public policy, recent studies have indicated that public opinion has had little impact on policymaking.[6] This was particularly true in foreign policy and national security affairs–realms where presidential prerogative has traditionally been less constrained. And, although more recent studies have found that long-term secular trends in public opinion on international issues do have a cumulative effect, the capacity of a president to mold, deflect, and manipulate public attitudes in these realms continues to be impressive. At best, then, social scientists have concluded, the role of public opinion can be interpreted as setting broad parameters within which a president or chief policymaker may move with great freedom of action and initiative.

Throughout the 1950s and 1960s, the extent of public knowledge and interest in BMD was virtually nil. In fact, a poll taken in 1965 showed that fully two-thirds of the American people believed that the United States was already protected by an ABM system. Nevertheless, while public opinion is often vague, ill-informed, and subject to drastic change, there is perhaps 5 to 10 percent of the American public which does influence the character of public policy. In fact, in the case of the Nixon decision to deploy Safeguard, the decision was in large measure triggered by grassroots opposition which developed in urban areas out of irritation and then anger at the army's program of site location, land acquisition, and construction.[7]

Despite earlier plans to locate Sentinel sites away from population centers in order to provide adequate area defense for the entire United States, the army began instituting land acquisition procedures in or near some of America's largest cities.[8] Among the first cries of public outrage were those of Seattle residents who in late summer 1969 objected to the army's plans to construct a site within a mile of the downtown area. In short order, this public outcry was translated into political pressure from Seattle's Congressman Thomas Pelly upon the army to begin hearings on the matter. This movement of mounting public concern shortly found allies in the Chicago area in November when the army started test drilling at five sites. Protest by area residents was organized and then headed by five scientists who formed the "West Suburban Concerned Scientists Group" to repulse Sentinel construction in Chicago and its suburbs. This group asked the army to cease acquiring land for further drilling and to hold hearings so that concerned citizens could air their objections to proposed sites. In addition, these scientists raised questions concerning the dangers inherent in erecting sites within residential areas–particularly the specter of accidental detonation at the missile site or at an altitude too low above the city, thereby obliterating the city it was supposed to protect.

In Boston, grassroots opposition was perhaps the most formidable and well organized. Headed by Abram Chayes, a former legal adviser to the State Department, the organized opposition of local citizens, area scientists, and well-known government advisers coalesced into the "New England Citizens Committee on ABM." [9] Supported by wide technical knowledge, adequate money, articulate spokesmen, and a sizable membership, the committee provoked intense educational and lobbying campaigns in Massachusetts, as well as in those cities where deployment sites were projected. The effect was catalytic. An ever-widening circle of senators and congressmen was bombarded with letters and telegrams expressing vigorous opposition to the Sentinel deployment program in the fall and winter of 1969. While the wider public quietly supported or remained indifferent to the administration's policy on ABM deployment, a small but increasingly vocal segment of the public began to press its views on this issue into the political arena.

A shift in the climate of opinion surrounding defense decision-making began to take shape. Aided by continued frustration over the Vietnam War, mounting reports of waste and collusion in the Pentagon, and increasing public attention to the military-industrial complex in American society, a new and more skeptical mood toward military budgets was generated. How this erosion of support among the attentive public for foreign and defense policies in the cold war would affect the substance of the new administration's programs and decisions in these areas was problematic. But on January 20, 1969, when Nixon took his oath of office as the thirty-seventh president of the United States, one thing was certain: a new political force in opposition to ABM would have to be reckoned with.

The genesis of congressional restiveness over ABM goes back to the early 1960s and the growing sense of anger and frustration provoked by constant rebuffs by the Defense Department to congressional initiatives in defense spending and military strategy. Repeatedly, congressional appropriations earmarked specifically for programs like ABM, the RS-70 advanced bomber, and other weapons projects in final defense appropriations bills were left unspent at the end of the fiscal year.

Compounding this felt grievance within Congress was an evolving attitude among legislative members outside the charmed circle of powerful and largely conservative committee chairmen or chairmen-in-waiting that the deliberative and watchdog functions of Congress–especially with regard to defense expenditures–had been undercut by the dominance of the cold war environment and the erosion of the traditional powers and prerogatives of the Congress as stated in the American Constitution. Circumstance and the skillful organizational and political strategies of past presidents had conspired to give the executive branch an upper hand especially in foreign affairs and defense policy.[10]

In past decisions on ABM, political pressure from Congress to executive action was directed almost solely to furthering policy options far in excess of what the dominant view in the administration was prepared to accept. By late 1968 and early 1969, however, the increasingly skeptical mood of the public had begun to filter into the deepest recesses of Congress. In the case of the army's Sentinel ABM program, the set of political, social, and technical factors which had congealed in late 1967 to make its production and deployment the most feasible compromise for all the contending forces centered around the BMD issue had begun to disintegrate. While Robert S. McNamara could not be the beneficiary of this shift in public mood and congressional sentiment, the legacy of his strategic thought and analytic techniques were to play a major role in the first concerted congressional effort to overturn a presidential decision on a major strategic weapons program.

The factor that prompted the beginning of a long and protracted battle over ABM was the willingness of Senator John Sherman Cooper to challenge on technical and political grounds the wisdom of this limited ABM deployment.[11] Apparently prompted to review his own support of Sentinel funding by a one-page memorandum from his legislative aide (William C. Miller) which questioned the system's technical readiness, the widely respected Kentucky senator in April 1968 launched a legislative attack on Sentinel and then Safeguard funding bills which came within a single vote of blocking funds for production and deployment of President Nixon's Safeguard ABM system in August 1969.

The fight triggered by Cooper's decision to oppose Sentinel deployment began uncertainly with the coalition of senators who rallied behind his cause, operating from a number of distinct disadvantages. For one thing, their doubts tended to spring not from a pervasive knowledge of the niceties of military strategy or the intricacies of weapons systems, but instead from a concern to give priority to domestic and social welfare needs over swelling and seemingly insatiable defense demands. The political clout of this small group appeared feeble and lacking in any likely reservoir from which to draw strength. Worse still, if they were to be successful in halting ABM deployment in the United States, they would have to challenge the vast might and authority both of the Defense Department and of the most powerful committees in the Senate–the Armed Services and Appropriations committees. With only the position and forum of the prestigious, but hardly influential, Foreign Relations Committee around which to marshal allies and direct attacks, the likelihood of even the most energetic assaults gaining the fruit of victory seemed small.

Yet scarcely ten months after Cooper hurled the first challenge against the Sentinel program in Congress, these meager forces had managed to put together such a powerful coalition of liberal Democrats and moderate Republicans that in early February Laird was forced to call a temporary halt in installing the ABM system, at least in part because of the fear that the Senate would reject requests for further deployment money. The salient elements of the tactics employed by the anti-ABM forces in an effort to defeat BMD deployment in the United States can best be examined through a survey of the three periods during which these elements unfolded: April 18, 1968-February 4, 1969; February 5-August 6, 1969; and August 7, 1969-August 12, 1970.

The first phase was born on April 18, 1968, when Cooper offered an amendment to the weapons procurement authorization bill, proposing that Sentinel not be deployed until McNamara had certified that the system was practicable and its cost was accurately determined.[12] Due to the surprising closeness of the vote (28-31), Cooper was sufficiently encouraged to carry on a battle that two previous senators (Albert Gore and Joseph Clark) had taken up before him only to fail. Cooper then devoted his energies to a study of the political and technical issues relating to BMD and to the organization of a broad base of bipartisan support in the Senate.

Among his first recruits was Senator Philip Hart, who was respected by liberals and conservatives on both sides of the aisle. Then, in short order, through private briefings and memoranda distributed to his colleagues, Cooper was able to pick up a group of hard-core supporters, including Senate majority leader Mike Mansfield and Senators Robert F. Kennedy, Frank Church, Stuart Symington, George McGovern, J. William Fulbright, and Charles Percy. As this coalition grew in confidence, numbers, and knowledge, it began to devise a strategy for blocking Senate passage of Sentinel funding and to delegate authority and responsibility for specific tasks. In terms of overall organization, the anti-ABM group assigned Cooper, a Republican, as floor leader of the battle, with Hart as his assistant on the Democratic side, and the job of behind-the-scenes lobbyist going to Percy.

In their recruitment and coalition-building activities in the Senate, the anti-ABM forces was assisted by several events that facilitated their lobbying efforts. First of all, in order for the Johnson administration to obtain legislative approval of a 10 percent surcharge tax as a device to curb spiraling inflation in 1968, it had to compromise with fiscal conservatives in Congress by agreeing to cut spending in the fiscal 1969 budget by $6 billion.[13] Because domestic programs had been pared for years to finance the Vietnam War, the natural choice—albeit a reluctant one—for budget cuts was the swollen military budget. And if cuts could not come from funds earmarked for Vietnam, military programs like the Sentinel ABM deployment seemed prime candidates for possible budget chopping.

A more detailed review of Sentinel by Congress appeared even more appropriate in the light of developments in the international realm. In the first place, McNamara revealed in his parting annual posture statement that the Chinese ICBM threat was a year behind the progress anticipated in 1968 by American intelligence estimates. For the Senate foes of ABM, this revelation implied that the urgency of Sentinel deployment had diminished. Second, on June 27, 1968, the USSR formally expressed its willingness to enter into discussions with the United States on mutual limitation of strategic offensive and defensive weapons. This announcement was followed by President Johnson's declaration at signing ceremonies for the Non-Proliferation Treaty on July 1, 1968, that the United States and the Soviet Union had agreed to initiate SALT negotiations in the near future. The signing of the treaty also took on specific symbolic importance to Senate opponents of ABM because one of its articles took the form of a pledge by the superpowers to work to end the arms race and reduce strategic weapons stockpiles.[14]

A third source of encouragement for the anti-ABM coalition sprang from the rising tide of public opposition to the army's construction work on Sentinel bases in or around America's largest cities. The decision to deploy ten of the fifteen continental ABM sites in or near the major metropolitan areas had been an integral part of the anti-Chinese or area defense orientation of the Sentinel system. Significantly, the political backlash to the army's deployment efforts was felt even by Sentinel's staunchest advocates. For example, Senator Everett Dirksen, shaken by the deluge of constituent protests against building a Sentinel base in suburban Libertyville, twenty-six miles northwest of downtown Chicago, conceded that "the time has come to take a cooler and more deliberate look at this proposal." [15] Public dissent also reached into the Senate Armed Services Committee, when Daniel Inouye of Hawaii and Henry Jackson of Washington ran into political dissension from constituents. Jackson's success in persuading the army to switch the Seattle site from the downtown area to Bainbridge Island, across the Puget Sound, only served to arouse Congressman Thomas Pelly, who owned a home on the island. While these incidents brought no converts into the anti-ABM fold, they did serve notice on Sentinel stalwarts that public restiveness on this issue was rampant.

Though relative amateurs in this unprecedented confrontation with the Defense Department and its traditional seats of vested interest in the Congress, the Cooper-led forces devised a multifaceted strategy to contest this controversial issue. In this battle, they drew first upon the technical expertise of eminent scientists who had been intimately involved in ABM decision-making in the early 1960s–people like Jerome Wiesner, Herbert York, and George Rathjens–in order to question the technical judgment of Pentagon spokesmen in committee hearings. In addition, the senatorial combatants used their increasing command of the technical issues and problems surrounding BMD to put on the defensive members of the old guard in the Armed Services Committee, who tended to rely too much on the official word of Pentagon witnesses and too little on their own understanding of the complex problems of military strategy and national defense.[16]

The Sentinel opponents then turned to articulating a general rationale for checking the army's production and deployment program, as well as working on the specific language of amendment to military authorization, procurement, and appropriations bills that would become the focus of legislative action in June, August, and October 1968. The criticisms raised by the Senate opposition to Sentinel spanned the full spectrum of strategic, economic, political, and technical issues. The questions included: How valid is Sentinel's anti-Chinese rationale? What is its likely impact on international affairs and United States-Soviet relations? What is its effect on arms control? What implications did its production and deployment hold for domestic programs? Does it enhance national security or jeopardize it? Is the system really technically feasible and fully proved? Increasingly, however, the issues fueling legislative opposition were reduced to the political judgments of concern over its effect upon the strategic arms race and doubts about its value in comparison to the higher urgency of the domestic needs of the nation.

Given these concerns and doubts, Senator Cooper and his allies framed the Cooper-Hart amendment which sought to delete funds for BMD deployment. Its limited and moderate character is revealed by the fact that its objective was simply to delay Sentinel deployment for one year, while allowing the R&D component of the program to continue. The rationale for this postponement was grounded initially in the one-year delay in Chinese ICBM progress, later combined with the belief that restraint in weapons development was required in view of the movement toward the SALT negotiations.

The first real political test of the anti-ABM coalition occurred on June 13, 1968, when Cooper offered his amendment to the military procurement appropriations bill. After more than a week of Senate debate, the Cooper-Hart amendment was defeated 34-52. On the same day, Stephen Young introduced an amendment to strike the $277.3 million allocated for constructing Sentinel facilities. Young's amendment was defeated by a 12-71 margin. These setbacks were followed by a second test of strength in early October. In this last congressional attempt to block Sentinel ABM deployment, the Cooper-Hart amendment was once again offered, this time as an amendment to delete $387.4 million from the Defense Appropriations bill.[17]

The signal event of the nearly two-week Senate deliberation over defense appropriations and the ABM issue was the agreement of the Senate on October 14 to go into closed session–at Cooper's request–to discuss Sentinel. This session not only drew a majority of senators to hear, perhaps for the first time, the main arguments on the ABM conflict but also allowed a degree of candor seldom found in Senate debate. Anti-Sentinel forces were able to win political points in the candid and freewheeling session. Under sharp and probing questioning, J. William Fulbright succeeded in getting Richard Russell to admit that the Senate Armed Services Committee had heard only Defense Department witnesses on the Sentinel issue during committee hearings on the defense budget. Russell then promised that the committee would hear independent scientists suggested by Sentinel foes.[18]

When the Senate returned to open session, the Cooper-Hart amendment was defeated 25-45 and the Defense Appropriations bill passed by a wide margin.[19] Even in defeat, however, the Sentinel program foes could count many political gains from the first round of political dispute over the army's ABM program. With deployment funds authorized by Congress, the army now began in earnest to work on land acquisition and site construction for the Sentinel. These operations only stirred up further community opposition, thus bringing additional political dividends to the anti-ABM movement. As the year ended and a new administration prepared to take over the reins of government, the anti-ABM forces under Cooper's leadership began elaborating new plans to muster a Senate majority.

The combination of mounting grassroots turmoil over the metropolitan location of Sentinel sites and rising congressional resistance to BMD undoubtedly caused Melvin Laird to call a halt to the Sentinel deployment program and to begin a one-month review of the ABM issue on February 6, 1969. Less publicized, but equally significant to the Senate drive to delay ABM deployment was Congressman L. Mendel Rivers's action of using a legislative device to block further land acquisition and construction of Sentinel missile sites on February 5, 1969, pending administration clarification of its overall position on the ABM system.[20] According to legal statute, each branch of the armed services is required to inform both Armed Services committees of the date and military purpose of their acquisition of land. If the committees raise no objections within a month, the military service may proceed with its project. By calling hearings on further acquisitions for the Sentinel system, Rivers in effect brought deployment to a temporary halt. Evidently, chairman Rivers was feeling the political heat.

In the early months of 1969, the developing strategy of the anti-ABM forces became increasingly clear. Perhaps the most adventuresome aspect of its overarching political strategy was the employment of Albert Gore's Disarmament Subcommittee of the Committee on Foreign Relations to challenge openly the authority of the Senate Armed Services Committee over its traditional jurisdiction over military matters, including the oversight of strategic weapons development.[21] Beginning in mid-March, the subcommittee began encroaching upon traditional military interests of the prestigious and powerful Senate Armed Services Committee by holding educational hearings into the foreign policy and strategic implications of military decisions, such as the ABM deployment. In retaliation, the Senate Armed Services Committee convened hearings into the military implications of the treaty to halt the spread of nuclear weapons. The basic intent of the former subcommittee's maneuverings was to capitalize upon the latter's neglect to review seriously the ABM issue, thus providing a procedural rationale to justify its intrusion into this jealously coveted province. With the Nixon decision rendered, the subcommittee now had a precise target to attack in succeeding months. Through these months, the investigations of the Gore subcommittee became the fulcrum of Senate efforts to overturn the Nixon Safeguard decision.

A second central feature of the Senate coalition's strategy

was its promotion of growing alliances with anti-ABM scientists. Gore and Fulbright lined up noted foes of BMD in the scientific establishment like Herbert York, George Kistiakowsky, Jerome Wiesner, and George Rathjens to appear before the Senate Armed Services Committee, as well as before the Gore Disarmament Subcommittee. No longer were the decisions and recommendations of the old conservative guard uncontested. Moreover, given their belief in the sufficiency of the strategic offensive weapons, their ability to suggest practical alternatives to the hard-point defense, and their grasp of the technical problems involved in BMD, these scientists provided impressive support for the case against Safeguard.

Because the political climate in 1969 was suffused by an even deeper mood of skepticism toward the military, concern over the power of the military-industrial complex, and interest in reordering national priorities, the anti-BMD movement was broadened in the Senate and to a degree in the House, and the issue was translated, at least in part, into the currency of domestic politics. Some legislators, like William Proxmire, sought to shift the substance of discussion from the realm of foreign affairs and defense policy, where the executive had long possessed unique prerogatives, to the realm of national economy, where Congress had traditionally been most influential. This tactic was evidenced by the launching of subcommittee hearings on defense and the economy by Senator Proxmire's Joint Committee on the Economy and by his almost single-minded pursuit of waste and collusion in the military-industrial complex in weapons programs during 1969 and 1970.[22]

The anti-Safeguard forces also sought out scientists as policy advisers and as participants in private seminars and conference deliberations. A Conference on the Military Budget and National Priorities was convened on Capitol Hill March 28 and 29, attended by some fifty-two congressmen, many scientists, a number of renowned social scientists, such as Kenneth Boulding and Hans Morganthau, and over a dozen ex-government officials who had served under one of the three administrations. Ranging from the proposed Safeguard ABM system and the burgeoning military budget to strategies to end the Vietnam War and restore a better balance between the executive and the Congress in foreign and defense policies, the participants of this two-day conference prepared the way for the founding of the Members of Congress for Peace through Law and the formulation of the first comprehensive set of alternative budget recommendations on military programs and foreign policy to emerge from Congress.[23]

A final noteworthy element of the Cooper force's strategy in the second round of the ABM controversy during these years was the appropriation of McNamara's strategic outlook toward deterrence and BMD and the skillful application of his analytic techniques to defend their opposition to Safeguard on the Senate floor and in committee debates. Partly schooled in that vision and those methods by McNamara in his years of staunch opposition to the Nike-Zeus and the Nike-X deployment, partly educated in its assumptions and techniques in 1968 and 1969 by those scientists predisposed to McNamara's policy, these senators brought persuasive arguments and detailed charts to Senate chambers and committee rooms which put administration and congressional proponents on the defensive and won new allies to their cause.

Starting with the "Battle of Charts" beginning in Gore's hearings on the ABM on March 26, 1969, and ending with the introduction on the eve of the final Senate vote on the Cooper-Hart amendment of three secret Defense Department studies in an effort to demonstrate that the Safeguard system was ill designed for hard-point defense, the Senate opposition hammered away at the technical shortcomings, political flaws, and strategic errors of the Safeguard program with a confidence that had no precedent in the Senate–except, perhaps, for McNamara's broad and copious cases against earlier efforts at ABM deployment.[24]

By mid-July, the anti-ABM movement had gained such strength and momentum that it counted support from forty-seven or forty-eight senators, with three or four uncommitted senators holding the balance of power. As the Senate showdown on Safeguard edged closer, the outcome seemed to hinge on the decisions of perhaps no more than one or two senators. On August 5, 1969, Margaret Chase Smith declared her opposition to the Safeguard system and indicated that she would offer an amendment to the military authorization bill for fiscal 1970 to prohibit use of military funds for any facet of Safeguard ABM development and construction. On the following day, the Senate began voting on three amendments attached to the military authorization bill. Smith's first amendment, which would have barred all spending on the Safeguard missile defense system (including R&D) was defeated 11-89. The second Smith amendment, which was apparently worked out as a compromise with the Cooper-Hart forces, was then introduced. Intended to ban the Safeguard system but permit other BMD research, this amendment was voted on and defeated by the tie-breaking vote of Vice President Spiro Agnew, 50-51. Then the Cooper-Hart amendment was rejected 49-51, with Smith voting against it. In casting her vote, Smith was expressing her opposition to the continued authorization of any research funds for the controversial Safeguard defense project.[25]

Both sides in the battle saw this narrowest of possible victories for the Nixon Safeguard program as a cause for celebration–the victors for having eked out a winning margin, the losers for having put the administration and its Senate supporters through the most searching congressional review of a weapons program in the entire postwar period. In retrospect, this vote proved to be the high watermark of Senate opposition to the Safeguard. Finally, in December, when the $69.9 billion Defense Appropriations bill came up for final Senate approval, it was passed overwhelmingly after Smith's amendment to delete all funds for the Safeguard program was rejected 36-49.[26]

Renewed Senate debate over Safeguard was triggered by reports in mid-January and presidential confirmation on January 30, 1970, that President Nixon had decided to proceed to phase two of the Safeguard expansion. The president revealed that he had authorized a one-month review to determine the exact nature and scope of the modified Safeguard system. But even prior to full disclosure of the kind and size of the Safeguard expansion, Mike Mansfield and other ABM foes fired shots in the opening of a new protracted congressional debate.[27]

On February 24, 1970, details of the expanded program were outlined by Laird to a joint session of the Senate Armed Services and Defense Appropriations subcommittees. The secretary of defense stated that the administration would request funds for a third Safeguard site that would protect the Whiteman Air Force Base Minuteman complex and for land acquisition and preparation at four other sites, including the nation's capital. Four of the sites were to serve as the start of a thin, anti-Chinese area defense; the fifth was to defend the cluster of Minuteman ICBMs around Warren Air Force Base, Wyoming.[28]

In many ways, the 1970 contest looked like a replay of the 1969 debate, except for the administration's shift in its main rationale for deployment and the program's increased vulnerability. Concerned by the growing Soviet strategic threat emerging from its continued deployment of ICBMs, the president in his Foreign Policy Message to the Congress in February 1970 expressed the view that ABM deployment was necessary to protect American land-based strategic forces. In succeeding months, however, a modified Safeguard deployment program was looked upon as a strong "bargaining chip" at the SALT negotiations.[29]

The anti-ABM movement in the Senate clashed with the president's modified program and its varying rationales at every point. In contrast to the administration's conviction that Senate passage of the revised Safeguard package would serve as an incentive to the Soviets to negotiate, the Cooper-led Senate opposition was convinced that the expanded Safeguard would give the Russians the impression that the United States was moving vigorously on all fronts of the arms race. Moreover, Safeguard opponents also charged that the envisaged system would not be able to protect Minuteman bases effectively against the kind of sophisticated Soviet attack that the USSR could launch by the time the Safeguard hard-point defense had been fully deployed. The final criticism which the opposition lodged against the administration's proposal concerned the area-defense element of the modified program. Here, Cooper and his allies adopted arguments similar to those put forth by Henry Jackson and John Pastore, claiming also that the Russians might interpret an area defense as a step toward a heavy city or damage-limiting defense directed toward blunting a Soviet attack.[30]

Before the Senate opposition's final effort to block expansion of the Safeguard system was mounted and voted on in August, these forces were given an assist by the Senate Armed Services Committee when, in a move lauded by the chairman, John Stennis, it eliminated funds to start preliminary construction on the four sites designed to provide a thin area defense against the Chinese threat.[31] By an 11-6 vote, this committee on June 17 deleted those funds from the Military Authorization bill while approving the administration's request for $1.3 billion to expand the hard-point defense elements of the phase two program. This move testified to the lack of pervasive support in any quarter for the original Sentinel area-defense concept.

Finally, on August 12, 1970, the most protracted and hotly contested Senate debate on ABM was effectively ended with the defeat of the new Cooper-Hart amendment (47-52), which would have permitted continued construction at two Montana and North Dakota Minuteman ICBM sites but withheld authorization for the third site in Montana and preliminary work on the fourth site in Wyoming. The administration victory, however, was not assured until a telegram from U.S. chief negotiator Gerard Smith was circulated, stressing the need for Safeguard for successful negotiations. The political nature of this ploy was clear from the fact that earlier in the year at congressional hearings Smith was more sanguine about the role of Safeguard expansion for productive talks.[32]

As the public furor over the placing of ABM sites in metropolitan regions of the country spilled over into the political realm and was linked to rising congressional opposition to ABM in late 1969 and early 1970, the lobbying and consulting activities of renowned American scientists concomitantly increased. Indeed, evidence indicated that the initiative in provoking active public controversy had clearly been taken prior to the full-fledged public imbroglio by those scientists associated with the finite containment school. Individual scientists set about the task of building a broad, powerful coalition of political forces at all levels of government to repulse what they believed would be one more escalating step in the arms spiral. In so doing, they forced a less-organized and more reluctant circle of scientists, sympathetic to the major beliefs of the infinite containment school, to defend the imperative need for the United States to respond to Soviet ABM deployment with an equally energetic production and deployment program.

Opposition within the finite containment school to the deployment of ABM systems in the United States went back at least to late November 1960. At that time, Jerome Wiesner presented a paper entitled "Comprehensive Arms Limitations Systems" before a gathering of East-West scientists at the Sixth Pugwash Conference in Moscow.[33] In it, he offered a number of detailed proposals aimed at bringing about a condition of mutual deterrence between the United States and the USSR and maintaining a state of strategic parity. From his perspective, the strategic equilibrium that would obtain from mutual deterrence and strategic parity would not be strengthened by the introduction of a highly effective ABM system, but would in fact be thrown out of balance by such a development. If it should become technically feasible to fabricate such systems, he argued, then agreements should be sought to prohibit their development and deployment.

Between 1960 and 1969 the assumptions, beliefs, and arguments underpinning Wiesner's proposals took on increasing clarity and coherence. But crucial to the finite containment view of BMD was the assumption that the United States and the Soviet Union needed to acquire and retain an invulnerable second-strike posture. The resonance between this viewpoint and McNamara's strategic vision of assured destruction is hardly coincidental. During the early 1960s the key leaders and spokesmen of the finite containment school were in favorable positions of influence within the executive. Between 1959 and 1963 Wiesner was a top scientific adviser in the Kennedy administration, York was the first DR&E director, Kistiakowsky was a member of the president's Scientific Advisory Committee, and Rathjens was chief scientist of ARPA. Even after their departure from government service, these men continued to influence the direction of American public policy in the areas of science and technology. They informed fellow scientists in respected scientific journals (*Bulletin of the Atomic Scientists, Scientific American,* and *Science*) of the growing threat of technological advances in active defense to the strategic balance, and they organized scientists sympathetic to the perspective of the finite containment school.[34]

Despite McNamara's unwillingness to acknowledge a direct role by these scientists on his reformulations of his view on deterrence strategy and on his evolving ABM policy from 1961 to 1968, their indirect influence was significant. The affinities of the outlook on strategic doctrine and BMD advances by McNamara and the leading proponents of the finite containment school are too great, and the proximity of these scientists to McNamara during these years was too close, for these views to have emerged independently and in isolation from one another.

By 1968 the focus of the lobbying efforts of these scientists lay in Congress and among the activated public. Whether appearing before a congressional subcommittee, speaking before a town meeting of outraged citizens, or condemning ABM before an audience of striking students, the themes and arguments expressed by these key American scientists were essentially the same. From the thousands of pages of congressional testimony and the countless speeches offered by these scientists in their campaign to halt ABM deployment, eight basic propositions stand out.[35] Taken together and integrated, they constitute the overriding argument advanced by the finite containment school against deploying an ABM system in the United States and in favor of an international agreement prohibiting or at least limiting deployment of such systems.

1. The keystone of security in a world populated by powers possessing vast nuclear and conventional weapons is a condition of mutual assured destruction–a condition that must not be jeopardized by the development of ABM systems. Such defensive measures, which seek to develop a significant damage-limiting capacity and which therefore threaten to undermine the other side's assured-destructive capability, only threaten to unbalance the strategic equilibrium and thrust the arms race into a new realm.[36]

2. In the historical and strategic competition between offensive means of destruction and defensive measures of countering them, an intrinsic advantage lies with the offense. Historically, the offense has always managed to best the defense because its job is less complicated than the task of defense. Furthermore, with the advent of atomic weapons, the task has been made even easier, since only one or a few nuclear weapons need (and will) get through.[37]

3. Development of strategic offensive weapons is sufficient to assure the maintenance of a nation's security. It is argued that serious efforts in technological development and deployment of defensive systems only threaten to raise arms competition to a new level and, as a consequence, imperil genuine efforts to limit the strategic arms race.[38]

4. A technological plateau appears to have been reached in the development of strategic offensive weapons. No genuinely new concepts capable of producing a dramatic technological breakthrough within strategic offensive weaponry appear to be on the horizon. Therefore, the period from 1965 onward was propitious for promoting a policy of restraint in an effort to enlist the Soviet Union in tacit or overt negotiations to limit strategic arms–particularly in the area of ABM systems.[39]

5. The likelihood of technological breakthroughs shifting the strategic balance quickly enough to give the other side a

decisive advantage is negligible. In other words, the lead-time possessed by one nation over another in a certain weapons area is no longer decisive.[40] This conviction is based in part on satisfaction with the tremendous advancements made by the United States in surveillance and detection techniques (spy satellites, radar, listening devices) since 1960. It is also grounded in belief in the length of time required for the Soviet Union (or any other nation) to move a new weapons concept through development, testing, evaluation, production, and deployment stages. Given the sensitivity of existing American surveillance techniques, such a potential breakthrough would be discovered sufficiently early for the United States to respond. In the context of the ABM controversy, this meant that the United States could afford to wait and see if the SALT negotiations would succeed before investing sizable funds into ABM deployment.

6. The prime impetus of the nuclear arms race is the operation of the action-reaction phenomenon, wherein strategic advancements in the arsenal of one superpower compel the other superpower to respond with equivalent innovations in its strategic arsenal.[41] In the context of the ABM controversy, these scientists drew the inference that the United States should restrain technological innovation in BMD lest the Soviet Union be provoked to react to the deployment with its own ABM system. Even if the USSR deployed its own ABM system (as it did), these scientists argued that the United States should still abstain from response in the area of defense measures, but instead should fortify its strategic offensive forces to neutralize the slight impact of the Soviet's missile defenses upon our assured-destructive capability.

7. Additional increments in economic and technical resources for weapons development and production no longer bring increments in national security.[42] With the arrival of mutual deterrence, these scientists argued that it is foolish to pour money into weapons—whether offensive or defensive—which simply put another turn on the arms spiral without adding to the nation's security.

8. The dynamism of offensive technology in strategic weapons development cannot and must not be impeded. For reasons stated above (especially 2, 3, and 4), members of the finite containment school pinned their hopes on maintaining an assured-destruction capability through continued exploitation of offensive technological development. Unimpeded R&D in offensive weapons also served as a partial hedge against significant progress or a true breakthrough achieved in Soviet ABM development. More evanescent, but also equally operative, was the conviction voiced by Herbert York, particularly in offensive weapons development, that the "technological side of the arms race has a life of its own, almost independent of policy and politics." [43] Thus, like the proponents of the infinite containment school, York and other key figures in this school were extremely pessimistic about the possibilities of harnessing military technology under conditions of modern science and technology.

Within the framework of these assumptions, the conclusion that deployment of an ABM system must be limited or prohibited followed with iron-clad logic. But the tendency on the part of this school to reify military technology and to portray its impetus as stemming from some technological imperative only masked the real stimulus of military technology and the strategic arms race in the 1960s, which lay in the systematic interconnection of R&D programs in offensive technology with R&D programs in defensive technology–skewed only by the doctrinal bias of the reigning strategy of deterrence. This shortcoming was shared commonly by McNamara and the finite containment scientists, and this tendency to obscure rather than clarify the basic drives of the arms race did much to confuse the real issues of the ABM, namely, the search for ways to shackle the dynamism of American technological development in the offensive realm. In the end, there was some grudging acceptance of the importance of this issue, as some American scientists and senators came to realize the far more dangerous destabilizing impact of MIRV–a technological breakthrough whose basic concept was spawned, nurtured, and developed along with ABM development by these scientists without the faintest understanding of its revolutionary character. Unfortunately, almost before the radical import of its development was recognized, it was too late. With little or no fanfare, it was deployed.[44]

The second influential segment of the scientific community–the infinite containment school–active in political debate over ABM deployment between 1969 and 1970 began its campaign in support of Sentinel and Safeguard at a distinct disadvantage compared to the finite containment school. While outspoken on the need for technological development in BMD as early as 1963 in congressional hearings on the nuclear test ban treaty, their efforts lacked the organization, governmental positions of authority and influence, and numbers enjoyed by their finite containment counterparts–though they did possess some sources of political influence. At least since the late 1940s, key spokesmen of the infinite containment school were well known and greatly respected in Congress and the military. Edward Teller's technical genius, especially his instrumental role in the development of the hydrogen bomb, as well as his political views, were highly regarded by congressmen; and his technical knowledge and political assessments of the effects of new weapons systems and proposed arms control measures on American national security were frequently called upon.

Leading scientists of this school seemed far more comfortable raising technical and political arguments within the science and engineering agencies of OSD and exerting their influence through the R&D programs of the military services. Yet, until 1965, no key exponent of the infinite containment school held an office of comparable stature in the military-scientific bureaucracy of the Defense Department as had Herbert York and George Rathjens. Only with the elevation of John S. Foster to the top administrative post of DR&E in that year was this imbalance somewhat altered. Moreover, coming at a time when widespread interest in ABM deployment had been aroused, his position as chief of DR&E assured proponents of this school a strong voice for technological superiority in strategic weapons development and for the maximum exploitation of technological developments in strategic offensive and defensive realms.

In the three rounds of the political imbroglio over ABM deployment, members of the infinite containment school reacted only with the greatest reluctance to the efforts of their colleagues in the finite containment school to stymie the administration's deployment program. Once activated, however, their energies were channeled into two fronts–both ultimately centering on the congressional debates. From their position outside of the government bureaucracy, some of the leading members of this school were brought in during 1969 by Senate ABM proponents as independent scientists who could offer technical interpretations of the Safeguard system, specifically to contradict the technical judgments of anti-ABM scientists from the finite containment school. The spectacle of Herbert York confronting William McMillan before a packed gallery in hearings held by the Senate Armed Services Committee was but one example of a skillful chairman's attempts to neutralize the persuasive arguments put forth by a key spokesman of the finite containment school.[45]

Foster used his official authority as DR&E chief to release selected portions of scientific studies and intelligence data at critical moments in the congressional debate in an effort to sway wavering senators. An example of this was the timing of his public disclosure of a questionable intelligence report in August 1969 on Soviet testing of MIRVs capable of attacking three Minuteman missiles, only one day prior to the crucial vote in the Senate on President Nixon's original system. Additionally, in the debate itself, he took every opportunity to advance the central tenets of the infinite containment school. Finally, in the wake of legislative approval of both phases of Safeguard deployment, he began publicizing the presence of a "technology gap"–wherein the United States had supposedly fallen behind the Soviet Union in expenditures on weapons research and development.[46]

The four general propositions comprising the general outline of the infinite containment school's case for ABM deployment were:[47]

1. The essence of security lies in the maintenance of the quantitative and qualitative superiority of one's strategic arsenal and through the continued and unhindered exploitation of weapons technology.[48] Owing to the conditions of modern science and the totalitarian nature of the Soviet system, America's security depends upon its ceaseless pursuit of technological and strategic superiority.

2. Because the novelties that modern science and technology may create can never be anticipated, the decisiveness of lead-time in technological advances in military technology remains valid. Despite the discovery of new means of surveillance and detection and the necessity of standardizing and institutionalizing RDT&E (research, development, test, and evaluation) procedures for fabricating new weapons, the possibility of technological surprise in the strategic realm is ever-present. Consequently, restraint in nuclear weapons policy simply undermines the real source of a nation's security.[49] In the context of the ABM controversy, this assertion implied that the technical feasibility of a highly effective ABM system required its immediate production and deployment.

3. Failure to exploit the full spectrum of weapons possibilities offered by modern science risks the danger of a technological coup being achieved by one's rival.[50] Constant innovation of all weapons developments is therefore dictated.

4. Because no one can forecast under the conditions of modern science and technology from what domain fruitful ideas in military technology may spring, ceaseless and unrestrained technological development in offensive and defensive weaponry is necessary.[51] Also implicit in this assertion is the assumption that technical feasibility is sufficient warrant for production and deployment. Thus, efforts to develop more discriminating concepts, like assured destruction and damage limitation, are superfluous, since weapons technology in this view develops in accordance with its own logic.

Despite the surface differences between proponents and opponents of ABM on the status of technology, the technical feasibility and strategic importance of BMD, and the type of policy in the strategic realm that the United States should adopt over against the Soviet Union, these individuals shared a fundamental attitude: an unquestioning belief in the efficacy of funding ABM development and a basic conviction in the value of continuing unhindered R&D in military technology. What is strange and perhaps inconsistent in the views of the ABM opponents within the finite containment school is how they could sustain a belief in a "technological plateau" while participating in an institutional milieu that was exploring the most exotic of weapons ideas (laser beams, plasmas, X-rays) and paving the way for development and deployment of MIRVs.

In comparison, then, the proponents of the infinite containment school mystify all military technology (whether offensive or defensive) and treat its uncontrollable logic as a solution to national security, whereas advocates of the finite containment school reify only half of military technology (believing the defensive side to be capable of control) and treat its uncontrollable imperative as a perhaps insoluble problem. In either case, the arms race continues unabated in its incredible destructive potential–both its material and ideational roots still obscured by the men whose ideas and institutional processes fuel its operation.[52]

Among the first major issues that President Nixon had to face shortly after his inauguration was the BMD question. Public furor in the metropolitan areas and active lobbying within the Senate over this issue in preceding months were clearly generating a political controversy of sufficient magnitude to command his immediate attention. How the new president would react to this development and the defense issues fueling it, however, was uncertain. On the basis of his past public record and the individuals whom he chose to fill key posts in the Defense Department, the chances were not favorable to the anti-ABM coalition. An ardent advocate of a strong and unrivaled military establishment, Nixon in the 1968 campaign had tried to make the existence of a "national security gap" created by McNamara a key campaign issue and had pledged "clear-cut military superiority" over the Soviet Union if he were elected.[53] Congressman Melvin Laird, a longtime vigorous exponent of military interests in Congress, was appointed as secretary of defense and David Packard, hitherto director of General Dynamics, was appointed as deputy secretary of defense.

McNamara's decision to deploy Sentinel in September 1967 had effectively defused the issue of an "ABM gap" as a potential issue in the 1968 presidential campaign. Thus Nixon came to the office of the presidency with no prior commitment on this controversial issue. Moreover, the conciliatory tone of his inaugural address and its expressed wish that the United States move from an "era of confrontation" to an "era of negotiation" with America's chief rival offered encouragement to Sentinel's foes that he might take the initiative in restraining possible developments in the strategic arms race.[54]

The decision-making process leading to the Safeguard decision was highly internalized, mainly operating through the machinery of the National Security Council. In relying upon the private channels of this small staff of administration officials, the ultimate decision appeared to spring generally from the currency of presidential politics—from the president's consideration of the effects of his action upon the various audiences associated with his multiple roles as the nation's chief executive, the political leader of the Republican party, and the commander-in-chief. Of equal importance to the substance of the Nixon decision on Safeguard was the weight of the McNamara legacy.

Soon after his inauguration, President Nixon charged Laird and Packard with the tasks of preparing two major studies: an overall military budget review and a general assessment of the nation's strategic posture.[55] Charged with major responsibility of directing the latter review, Packard grappled with the question of the ABM system. Having inherited the $1.8 billion Sentinel system from the Johnson administration, the new administration needed to decide whether to proceed with its deployment, to seek out some other approach, or to scrap the system altogether.

On February 20 Packard presented a preliminary report outlining the major policy alternatives available to the president. These options were a heavy ABM system designed as a population defense for the twenty-five largest American cities; the thin Sentinel system providing a lighter area shield for approximately fifteen urban areas; a modified Sentinel system, known at the Pentagon as Plan I-69, which would use essentially the same hardware as the original Sentinel configuration but which would be moved away from cities and placed around Minuteman bases and other parts of the nation's second-strike retaliatory force; and no system at all. Packard made no recommendations. Reacting to this report, President Nixon requested Packard to prepare further studies on each of the four options and to seek counsel from the State Department on the likely diplomatic consequences of each alternative.

At this juncture, the membership of this policy review on ABM had expanded to include Henry Kissinger, the president's assistant for national security affairs, and Lawrence Lynn, a staff member of the National Security Council. Since the review process by this time was operating largely within the framework of the National Security Council, Kissinger's role increased, as he moved to organize and stabilize the decisional process. Among his first actions as de facto co-chairman of the policy review was to assign Lynn to assist Packard. In addition, he charged Lynn with the task of writing papers devising the strongest possible case against each of the four policy options and, in particular, the I-69 option. Meanwhile, Kissinger began consulting with fellow civilian strategists and scientists in the Boston-Cambridge region in order to gain advice on the technical feasibility of BMD as well as to ascertain their feelings toward ABM.

While still far from reaching a policy decision on the resolution of the ABM question, the president was reported to be leaning toward deployment as a means of restoring balance to the system of mutual deterrence. In recent months, he had grown concerned with the combined accelerated buildup by the Soviet Union of its strategic offensive capability and its deployment of more than sixty ABM sites around Moscow. The I-69 system particularly attracted him, because its purpose of protecting America's second-strike capability stood the best chance of being construed by the USSR as being a defensive, stabilizing, and nonprovocative gesture.

On March 5 the National Security Council was convened. Packard strongly recommended the I-69 option. Such a modified system of deployment, he argued, would protect the American deterrent against the Soviet Union's increasing offensive capability and would, moreover, dampen the political furor building up in major cities, without being sufficiently provocative to stimulate a new round of the arms race or to deter future arms control agreement. Laird and Gerard Smith, director of Arms Control and Disarmament Agency also endorsed a redesigned Sentinel system.

On March 7 Kissinger completed a lengthy briefing book on the ABM issue which the president would consult in his review of this policy question. After being briefed by three prominent senators (Javits, Percy, and Cooper) on their staunch opposition to ABM deployment, Kissinger added a summary of their remarks into the briefing book. Included also were a concise summary of the main argument advanced thus far, a review of the major alternatives originally presented by Packard, and Lynn's paper opposing I-69.

Sometime over the weekend of March 8-9, President Nixon reached an initial overall decision on ABM. He decided first to move ahead with a revised Sentinel program, concentrating on protecting the nation's capacity to respond after a nuclear attack. The second decision, largely tactical, involved a determination of the pace of the modified Sentinel system's deployment. Between March 11 and 13 a series of meetings was held under Kissinger's leadership to resolve the tactical issue. Joining Foster, Packard, and Elliot Richardson, then undersecretary of state, Kissinger carefully surveyed the range of options open to deploy the ABM system. The available alternatives were quickly reduced to four: 1) the Sentinel system could be packaged and shifted from the cities to the ICBM bases at a cost of $1.8 billion in 1970; 2) the Johnson system could be deployed at bases starting the following spring (early 1970), reducing the fiscal 1970 outlay to $1.1 billion; 3) the Sentinel program could continue at the level of research and development; and 4) the ABM system could be deployed in phases, thus requiring only $800-900 million in fiscal 1970 to begin work at two of the twelve sites and to continue R&D, while subjecting the efficacy of deploying the other ten sites on phased schedules to annual review.

On March 12 the president and his advisers met in a National Security Council session to make a decision. It soon became clear that the first two options were untenable: both choices necessitated simultaneous starts on twelve of the fifteen sites, thereby committing the administration to a rather large initial expenditure of funds. Both options would also diminish the administration's flexibility to expand or reduce the scope of the system, depending on such developments as an increase in the Soviet offensive threat or the achievement of genuine progress at arms control negotiations with the Soviet Union. The third option, on the other hand, seemed to be the most politically attractive option, and, in fact, it had been urged upon the president and Kissinger by many within the scientific community and in Congress. But, echoing an attitude held by many in the key research and engineering agencies in OSD, the president and his advisers concluded that they had come to the end of the R&D road. Moreover, the group was persuaded that a year's delay would effectively postpone actual deployment by more than two years, since the existing technical team would be lost to other jobs in government and industry.

So consensus coalesced around option four–a phased system of deployment–and the president opted for it. The decision was announced on March 14, and the system became known as Safeguard. Apparently, up to the very day of public disclosure, the modified Sentinel was known only as I-69; the only alternative, "Deterrent," sounded too bland. At a meeting with congressional leaders prior to his public disclosure of the Sentinel deployment, the president had difficulty in differentiating his modified program from the original Sentinel plan. Coming to his rescue, Congressman Craig Hosmer suggested that he christen the system "Safeguard." [56]

By spring 1969 the politics of ABM had decisively shifted from the realm of administrative decision-making and presidential politics to the realm of domestic politics. President Nixon, mindful of this expansion of the political arena, acted to secure legislative approval of Safeguard funding by using his vast official powers and his renowned political ingenuity to orchestrate a political strategy within his office and among key Cabinet officers and legislative aides. The precise character of this strategy disclosed much about the president's thinking concerning attitudes toward his role and prerogatives in foreign and defense policymaking, his relationship toward Congress, his conception of the proper bargaining posture in negotiations with the Soviet Union, his understanding of the strategic requirements of national security, and his image of the proper place of scientists in governmental decision-making. As the events and actions of the legislative contest over the Safeguard system unfolded in 1969 and 1970, Nixon's feelings on these issues became quite transparent.

Global strategy was the first component of President Nixon's overall game plan to win congressional approval. For nearly twenty-five years, the strategy of nuclear deterrence in one form or another had guided executive policy in the sphere of national defense. The belief in the necessity of a sufficient military force capable of deterring any rational adversary from attacking North America had been regarded as the keystone of American defense policy from the middle of the Truman administration to the end of the Johnson years. Its import for BMD had grown clearer and more precisely articulated during the McNamara era as the notion of strategic deterrence became identified almost solely with the possession of an assured-destruction capacity, that is, a sufficiently large, credible, and invulnerable second-strike capability to destroy one's potential adversaries–singly or in combination–as viable societies. In a situation where both the Soviet Union and the United States possessed such capability, deployment of ABMs was potentially destabilizing, since such systems possessed and deployed by one country threatened to undermine the assured-destruction capacity of the other.

At his first presidential news conference on January 27, 1969, Nixon retreated from his earlier campaign demand for clear-cut U.S. military superiority over the USSR, saying that sufficiency rather than either superiority or parity should characterize the nation's strategic needs. In his first foreign policy report to Congress, President Nixon described "sufficiency" as the capacity "to deny other countries the ability to impose their will on the United States and its allies under the weight of strategic military superiority." It was a strategic posture which was both "political and defensive," providing for both "adequacy and flexibility." The following year, in a similar report to the Congress, clear and concrete definition of strategic sufficiency still seemed to elude the president.[57]

Perhaps the best way of conceiving the Nixon strategy of sufficiency is to see it as lying somewhere between decisive military superiority and assured destruction. In this sense, it represents a political compromise between the conflicting pressures and perspectives operating within and upon the executive. On the one hand, the weight of some of the assumptions of the infinite containment school (possibly advanced in policy debate by Foster and others) was felt, especially in the administration's unwillingness to permit the USSR to gain a superior position in any strategic area, even BMD. The drive to maintain technical superiority could also be traced to the outlook of this school. In terms of the ABM decision, these impulses of the strategy of sufficiency led to the conviction that the United States must match the Soviet deployment of such a system in order to prevent the possibility of a Russian breakthrough.

On the other hand, this strategic doctrine also incorporated ideas antagonistic to the strategic vision of this segment of the scientific community. The continued references to the "strategic balance" and the need to maintain its "stability" in definitions of this new strategy provide one indication of this clash.[58] The administration's readiness to enter into strategic arms negotiations with the Soviet Union under conditions of mutual interest was intimately linked to this new strategic posture. The principle of negotiation with an adversary whose political system is closed is anathema to the infinite containment school. Finally, a heavy Soviet-oriented ABM system was never seriously considered by the administration either at this stage of policy formulation and decision-making or in later stages. President Nixon clearly pinned his hopes on the success of the SALT negotiations and, to a degree, rationalized this hope in his policy of strategic sufficiency.

Two sources of counterpressures on the president were the bipartisan coalition of liberal Democrats and moderate Republicans in the Senate and the broad public campaign led by anti-ABM scientists. From our perspective, however, the main wellspring of these movements stemmed from the strategic concepts and guiding vision of Robert McNamara. In shaping the context of strategic policymaking and defense decision-making, the McNamara heritage succeeded in checking serious interest in heavy ABM deployment and in blunting the impact of the infinite containment school's outlook on nuclear weapons policy upon a president who, in a different context, might have been receptive to these ideas.

Between the months of April and June, the second element of President Nixon's political plan to secure congressional passage of his Safeguard proposal was disclosed. This tactic was a soft-sell treatment in sharp contrast to Johnson's hard-driving, oftentimes arm-twisting, political salesmanship during his bouts with Congress. During these months, the president appeared to stand aloof from the controversy, allowing Laird, Packard, and Foster to defend before Congress the necessity of Safeguard deployment. Moreover, neither his two chief aides in charge of congressional relations, Bryce Harlow and Kenneth BeLiew, nor his coordinator of communications, Herbert Klein, were called upon to go beyond the low-keyed nature of the official strategy and apply strong-arm tactics to bring undecided or errant Republican senators into the fold.[59]

Nixon's only departure from his image of one standing above the battle occurred as an act of personal pique, namely, his rejection of F. A. Long's nomination to the post of director of the National Science Foundation because of his opposition to the Safeguard antimissile system. For two months, the president sought to portray himself as a principled national leader bent on gaining victory for Safeguard on the merits of the administration's case.

With the ABM issue firmly entrenched in the arena of domestic politics and with his public image and prestige as a political leader, as well as his conception of the nation's security, on the line, the president's aloofness from the political fray could not remain an enduring element of his overall game plan. On June 5, at a commencement address before the graduating class at the United States Air Force Academy, the president launched a blistering attack against critics of the administration's defense policies and the military establishment.[60] Without directly referring to the congressional debate over Safeguard funding, he argued for a strong military and a defense establishment which was neither a "sacred cow" nor a "scapegoat." Scoring his critics as apostles of "unilateral disarmament" and advocates of a "new isolationism," the president was evidently seeking less to put direct pressure upon anti-ABM senators than to respond to the broad-ranging assault in Congress upon executive prerogative in defense and foreign policy areas. In reasserting the worth of the traditional values of loyalty to country, deference to executive decision in strategic and diplomatic policies, and respect for the military, President Nixon was striving to influence the general climate of opinion permeating the congressional activities on defense policies and the military budget.

In this strongly worded criticism of legislative attacks, President Nixon also illuminated his view of the place of the scientific community in defense policymaking. Recognizing the prominent role that scientists were playing in fomenting public and congressional opposition to the Safeguard ABM system, he had concluded that these specialists were exceeding their legitimate function in the weapons policy debate. He reminded his audience of President Eisenhower's Farewell Address in which he had warned the American people of a danger beyond the military-industrial complex: "the equal and opposite danger that public policy could itself become the captive of a scientific-technological elite." [61]

The scientific community has long been an active participant in policy debate over nuclear weapons development and arms control policy. Indeed, whether the responsibilities of the detached scientist and the duties of responsible citizenship are at all compatible is problematic. Scientists themselves have sometimes obscured this issue by interpreting political problems as technical issues, thus mixing unreflectively technical and nontechnical assumptions. In any case, as David C. Phillips has observed, beginning with the president's commencement address, "the Safeguard issue seemed to be a test case of the new Administration's capability to achieve its policy objectives with the assistance of–but not a sole reliance upon–narrowly specialized groups of experts." [62]

Although rattled by continuing assaults upon presidential prerogative and criticism of the defense budget by a growing coalition of senators aided by critics in the scientific community, Nixon moved to mollify this dissenting group while holding to a no-compromise stance with respect to Safeguard funding. In mid-June the White House, in a move laid to rising congressional pressure, ordered cancellation of the air force's manned orbital laboratory program–estimated at $3 billion–as a major step toward reducing military budgets. In July a blue-ribbon panel headed by Gilbert W. Fitzhugh was formed to undertake a one-year comprehensive study of Defense Department management, research, procurement, and decision-making with a view toward recommending organizational reforms. [63]

In the midst of carrying out his efforts to win Senate approval for his Safeguard ABM proposal, the president sought to secure for Gerard Smith and his fellow negotiators a bargaining chip at the arms control talks which would strengthen the United States' position at the negotiation table. [64]

President Nixon in his first two months in office reached two key conclusions having a bearing on the ABM issue: because little more could be derived from further R&D in ballistic missile defense, ABM was to that extent technically feasible and could therefore be deployed and expanded; and a political and defensive strategic posture larger than assured destruction but less than clear-cut military superiority was necessary for the nation's defense. From these two conclusions, he came to see ABM deployment as neither a necessary asset nor a sure liability. Its fate would largely depend upon Soviet actions either in the realm of strategic weapons development and deployment or in the realm of diplomatic negotiation. In confronting the former, he would link the pace and scope of American deployment of ABM systems to increases in the Soviet offensive threat; with respect to the latter, he would be prepared to respond with any quid pro quo settlement that maintained the strength and integrity of the American offensive retaliatory force.

Throughout diplomatic negotiations, the president viewed the position of negotiation from strength as the essence of our bargaining stance with the Russians. In part, he was no doubt influenced by scientists of the infinite containment school. The genesis of his views on bargaining with the Soviets, however, lies in the long diplomatic tradition of negotiating through strength which, as Coral Bell has convincingly shown, was born around 1950 in the United States and has variously informed U.S.-Soviet relations in foreign policy and defense dealings for over two decades.[65] If this view is accepted, then the interpretation of ABM deployment as a critical bargaining chip must be accepted not as a mere political ploy designed to induce Senate ratification of administration policy, but as a sincerely held conviction of the president concerning the most appropriate bargaining posture with the Soviet Union. This interpretation is reinforced by other actions taken by Nixon relating to the American negotiating position. Throughout most of the Safeguard debate during 1969 and 1970, a vocal segment of the anti-ABM coalition tried to prevail upon the president to declare a moratorium on the air force's MIRV testing and deployment program. Nixon's resistance to such recommendations of unilateral restraint in this case was defended with the same reason: that such action would undercut the American team's ability to negotiate from strength. Drawing upon this longtime tradition of diplomacy, the president seemed to be claiming that success could only be assured through this approach—and it would have done so, if genuine belief in the existence of mutual interests in strategic arms limitation had brought the United States and the Soviet Union to the negotiating table.

The diplomatic rationale for Nixon's no-compromise policy on Safeguard may, of course, have had political roots as well. After congressional passage was assured in early August by defeat of the Smith amendment to the military authorization bill, at least one political analyst tried to fit elements of President Nixon's game plan into his southern strategy which had brought him victory the preceding November.[66] But in terms of his prerogatives for defense programs and future diplomatic negotiations, the president's victory in the Senate in August 1969 and the following year on the issues of Safeguard expansion gave him a mandate—however slim in both cases—in the Strategic Arms Limitation Talks to "negotiate through strength."

In many ways the period from August 1970 to May 1972 marked the closing chapter in the history of American strategic doctrine and BMD. Between the final Senate endorsement of Nixon's modified Safeguard plan and the early summer of 1972, the United States and the Soviet Union entered into the SALT negotiations, wrangled over the nature of the negotiable issues and the scope of mutual agreement, and finally reached a permanent settlement on offensive weapons systems. It may take decades before the ramifications of these arms control negotiations upon American and Soviet strategies, the arms race, and prospects for general disarmament will become apparent.[67] From the vantage point of the close of SALT I, however, some tentative conclusions can be drawn on its meaning and the future of BMD.

To understand the significance of the bilateral accords signed by President Nixon in May 1972 and ratified by the Senate in October 1972, one must have some knowledge of the background to these negotiations—particularly, their origins in the Johnson-McNamara efforts from 1964 to 1968 to place the BMD issue in an arms control context. During these years, the strategic views of the finite containment school of scientists became increasingly influential in administration policymaking circles in discussions concerning arms control and disarmament. In fact, even prior to President Johnson's elevation to office, official thinking within the Arms Control and Disarmament Agency (ACDA) tended to reflect a basic interest in blocking the defense realm from arms competition. For example, during congressional debate over the Test Ban Treaty, William Foster, then director of ACDA, stressed that one positive benefit of the treaty would be its likely curtailment of ABM development on both sides. Later on, after the Test Ban Treaty had been signed, he suggested that the technical infeasibility of an adequate defense against a sophisticated ICBM attack required us "to rely on a strategy of deterrence" and to seek to "provide for the security of the free world, in the absence of a classic defense situation." [68]

Increasingly, then, during the Johnson administration, U.S. policy toward arms control and disarmament tended to be dominated by the search for international and bilateral means of maintaining the strategic equilibrium between the United States and the Soviet Union and prohibiting those measures which threatened to destabilize this balance. The earliest formal expression of this concern came on January 21, 1964, when the United States offered a five-point arms control proposal before the Eighteen Nation Disarmament Committee in Geneva. Specifically aimed at preempting the deployment of ABM systems, this proposal called for a verified freeze on the "number and characteristics of strategic nuclear offensive and defensive vehicles." [69] Although it was rejected by the Russian negotiators because, among other things, it would have frozen the preponderant American advantage in ICBMs without offering any compensation to the Soviet's strategically inferior force, it represented the first time that an arms control proposal attempted to isolate strategic delivery systems from the larger framework of arms control and disarmament.

By the beginning of 1967, the Johnson administration was hard at work on the diplomatic front to initiate talks between the two superpowers to prevent another surge up the arms spiral. Dean Rusk's news conference in December 1966 and President Johnson's statements in his State of the Union Address in January 1967 both sought to stimulate Soviet interests in such talks. These calls for strategic arms limitation talks received their first favorable response from the Soviet Union on March 2, 1967, when Soviet Premier Aleksi Kosygin agreed to begin procedural discussions in Moscow regarding U.S.-Soviet negotiations on curbing strategic offensive and defensive missiles. Hopes of bringing about an early beginning to the formal negotiations, however, were dimmed in June 1967 following the Soviet Union's reluctance to set a date for formal talks.[70]

During 1967 the Johnson-McNamara campaign to initiate the SALT negotiations and thus check the mounting domestic political and institutional pressures for ABM deployment were stymied by at least two factors. Both Soviet strategic doctrine and the strategic views of prominent leaders in the Kremlin at this time were favorably disposed toward BMD. Most Soviet military strategists and key leaders, owing in part to the prominence of a strong defense tradition in Soviet strategy, had refused to interpret ABM missile deployment from the strategic viewpoint advanced by the United States. As early as 1964, the Soviet defense bias in strategic doctrine and its relation to BMD was given coherent articulation in a paper by the late Soviet strategist General Nicolai Talensky. In the course of his discussion of ABM systems and general disarmament, he observed: "The creation of an effective anti-missile system enables the state to make its defenses dependent chiefly on its own possibilities, and not on mutual deterrence, that is on the good will of the other side." Three years later, in February and again in June 1967, Premier Kosygin gave public endorsement to this view, arguing, for example, after a summit meeting with President Johnson at Glassboro, "We believe that the discussions should center not on merely the problem of anti-missile defense systems. Because, after all, the anti-missile system is not a weapon of aggression, of attack; it is a defensive system." Far from fearing ABM systems as potential destabilizing elements, the Soviets appeared to have been guided by a strategy emphasizing both deterrence and defense. Not adhering to the logic of American strategy and therefore not feeling the sense of urgency concerning domestic and organizational pressures to force American ABM deployment, the Russians met Americans' pleas for arms talks more with puzzlement than with avid interest.[71]

It was not until July 1, 1968, that the Johnson administration could announce superpower agreement to move from preliminary procedural talks to substantive arms discussions. It appeared that the four-year diplomatic campaign by Johnson and McNamara was on the verge of achieving its goal, albeit too late to affect American deployment of an ABM system that neither had wanted. Unfortunately, on virtually the same day that the president was to announce the imminent opening of the arms limitation talks at the summit level, Soviet-led Warsaw Pact forces marched into Czechoslovakia with the immediate impact of bringing these diplomatic interactions to a temporary and uneasy halt.

On January 20, 1969, Richard M. Nixon delivered an inaugural address in which he sought to promote an atmosphere of negotiation between the new administration and the Soviet Union. The Soviets sent a message to the new president acknowledging their readiness to initiate bilateral talks on strategic arms limitations. President Nixon decided not to seize immediately upon this overture and, instead, turned to constructing an American strategic position from which the United States could negotiate from strength. Between January and October 1969, the president worked with the newly formulated Verification Panel, which was instituted to examine verification aspects and strategic implications of curbs on individual (and then combinations of) weapons, in the context of the National Security Council. In the wake of the Senate's passage of Safeguard funding and the defeat of Senator Edward Brooke's bill to halt U.S. testing of MIRV, the president extended an invitation to Premier Kosygin and Chairman

Leonid Brezhnev to begin formal arms limitation talks. Nixon's invitation was then accepted by the Soviet leaders on October 25, 1969, and the first exploratory round of the SALT negotiations commenced in Helsinki on November 17, 1969.[72]

In his first report to the Congress on U.S. foreign policy for the 1970s, President Nixon characterized the first six rounds of the SALT negotiations as "the most important arms control negotiations this country has entered"; Premier Kosygin was only slightly less enthusiastic about their commencement. After a slow start marked by mutual explorations of the other side's bargaining position, the discussion moved to intense negotiations on specific proposals. During the spring and summer of 1970, the talks apparently reached a difficult stage of negotiation as the key areas of disagreement surfaced–one concerning the desirability of a separate agreement on an ABM curb, the other centering on the definition of the term strategic. The United States allegedly took the position that any accord limiting strategic weapons should be comprehensive, covering both offensive and defensive systems. Reportedly, the Soviets favored separate treatment of the systems, with priority given to the offensive. Concerning the definition problem, the Russian view held that the term strategic covered all offensive strategic weapons targeted on the Soviet Union (including American strategic and tactical nuclear forces in Western Europe under the auspices of NATO); and the United States, on the other hand, interpreted the term to encompass only those weapons with an intercontinental range. These differences, which emerged in the second round of talks, then hardened, and, through the third round, the negotiations reached an impasse.

This deadlock was broken the following year when both sides compromised. The United States agreed to work for a treaty on the limited deployment of ABM systems and agreed in the interim to curb some facets of offensive weapons. The Soviet Union softened its stance by allowing the question of the strategic nuclear forces in NATO to be handled through the beginning of negotiations between NATO and the Warsaw Pact on mutual force reduction in Europe. Progress continued during the fifth and sixth rounds, according to news sources and leaks, although some shifts in outlook and temporary reversals of agreement occurred. Meanwhile, both sides vigorously expanded and improved their nuclear arsenals and delivery systems with a complete lack of restraint. Both sides made their greatest strides in the sphere of offensive destructive potential: the United States, testing and deploying MIRVs; the Soviet Union, increasing its land-based strategic offensive force to over 1,600 ICBMs.[73]

On May 26, 1972, SALT I negotiations ended in Moscow with the signing of the first set of agreements by President Nixon and Secretary Brezhnev.[74] The product of nearly two-and-a-half years of bilateral discussions, these agreements were comprised of a treaty limiting ABM systems and an interim agreement (and protocol) limiting strategic offensive arms. The treaty curbing ABM systems was specific and comprehensive, having the following features: an explicit prohibition against either a nationwide or regional ballistic defense; the limitation of ABM deployment to two sites–one for defense of the national command area and the other for the defense of ICBMs–to total no more than 100 ABM launchers and interceptor missiles at each of the two launch sites; a strict control on the qualitative and quantitative aspects of the radars deployed around the two sites; a proscription against the development, testing, and deployment of ABM systems or ABM components that would be sea-based, air-based, space-based or mobile land-based; and a term of compliance of unlimited duration.

The intent of this treaty was to freeze permanently the existing level of ABM technology in the United States and the Soviet Union and to limit forever permissible deployments of ABM systems to two restricted ABM sites. Strategically, the signing of this treaty by both parties symbolized the interment of BMD and the enshrinement of the strategy on nuclear deterrence–or, in the words of Donald Brennan, "the policy of mutual assured destruction."[75] Politically, this event could be regarded as a victory of the greatest magnitude–the closing off of the defensive realm–for McNamara and the finite containment school of the scientific community. Both the energetic pursuit by the defense establishments of both countries of qualitative and quantitative improvements in their respective strategic nuclear arsenals and the character of the interim agreements on curbing strategic offensive weapons, however, make it difficult to resist drawing the conclusion, as Colin Gray has done, that, to both superpowers, SALT has appeared both "as an exercise secondary to their serious strategic preparations for the conduct of the arms race in the 1970's" and "as an exercise that may be manipulable for political advantage, both external and domestic." And if this does prove to be the ultimate outcome of SALT, then the policy of mutual assured destruction will indeed have earned its initials–MAD.[76]

9

SHIELD OF DREAMS:
THE PERSISTENCE OF
BALLISTIC MISSILE DEFENSE

With the negotiation and ratification of the ABM Treaty by the United States and the Soviet Union in 1972, ballistic missile defense as national policy all but faded from the political scene. Working within the provisions of the SALT accords, the Soviet Union and then the United States each deployed an individual ABM site—one around Leningrad and the other near Grand Forks, North Dakota. But the idea of a defense against intercontinental ballistic missiles, the dream of security from the threat of nuclear attack, did not die. Like a temporarily neutralized virus or a repressed desire, it lay seemingly dormant for nearly two decades, lurking in the margins of mainstream politics and inhabiting the inner sanctums of national laboratories. Then, in a powerful and electrifying speech almost wholly unanticipated, it burst back into the headlines as the bold vision of a sitting president intent on transforming the nation's reigning strategic doctrine and rendering would-be enemy ICBMs "impotent and obsolete."[1]

In retrospect, it is baffling that so powerful a legacy as the one Robert S. McNamara and his political and scientific allies had bequeathed to succeeding generations of Americans would be challenged in the context of the cold war's most decisive years. Who would have predicted that so formidable an array of principles and assumptions inherited from the McNamara years would carry with them the seeds of their own potential undoing? Who would have predicted, in changed and changing political, military, and international conditions favoring the final interment of ballistic missile defense, that it would be reintroduced as an alternative— or a complement—to the strategic goal of nuclear deterrence, the mainstay of American military strategy and force planning since the onset of the cold war?

Before trying to puzzle out the answers to these questions, it might be illuminating to recall the key elements of the McNamara legacy in nuclear strategy, the strategic arms race, R&D policy, and strategies of arms control. That heritage can be conveniently distilled into four critical components. The first is the former defense secretary's embrace of *the strategic bias toward deterrence*. Over the course of his efforts to sort out and refine his understanding of the requirements of national nuclear strategy, Robert McNamara slowly abandoned the temptations of war-fighting and war-winning as the foundations of national security in the Nuclear Age and accepted nuclear deterrence as its overriding goal. In so doing, he concluded that mutual assured destruction (MAD) is not mad, but the bulwark of superpower national security. A second cardinal feature of his legacy is *a principled support for continued and unfettered military R&D*. Although the guiding objective of deterrence was in his view the hallmark of any reasonable and enduring nuclear strategy for the United States (and the Soviet Union), he could justify the exploration of ideas across the technological spectrum—including design concepts that ran counter to deterrence—on the premise that it would challenge offensive weapons technologists to find ways of countering such potential innovations and thereby sustain U.S. deterrent capability. Thus, the third component of the McNamara heritage is *the maintenance of unflagging technological bias favoring offense over defense*. That is, given the strategic necessity of protecting our deterrent capability at all costs, military R&D must assure that the offense always gets through and that some minimum level of deterrent capability is never compromised.

Finally, McNamara bequeathed to later policymakers a fourth imperative: *the necessity of pursuing vigilantly, but with due regard for the highest national interests, arms control means to abate, redirect, and check the impulses of the strategic arms race*. Having reached the conclusion that the strategic arms competition was the greatest source of tension between the United States and the Soviet Union and that its perpetuation risked the outbreak of nuclear war through accident, miscalculation, or foolhardy design, McNamara chose many forums at the end of his stint as defense secretary (and later as head of the World Bank and beyond that office) to plead the case for national policies designed to ameliorate the course of the strategic arms race and dramatically lower the size of nuclear weapons stockpiles and the magnitude of overkill capabilities in the hands of both superpowers.

The apparent telos of post–McNamara era development regarding strategy, technology, and arms control raises these key questions: given the persistence of the dream of ballistic missile defense, what accounts for its endurance in an international climate marked by the collapse of the USSR and Soviet hegemony and the rise of the United States to supremacy as the only military superpower? In pursuing the dream of national missile defense, what is the goal or end that certain political forces—especially on the right and within the Republican party—have courted? What explains the shifting rationales and missions and changing technological arrays and configurations of a missile defense system that will not go away but never seems quite ready to meet the challenge of an ever-improving offense (and seemingly endless cheaper countermeasures)? In short, why has the mythos of a shield of dreams gained such a grip upon the political imagination of key elements of the Republican party and the American right, remaining rooted in a field of historical and political possibility?

Although the dream of a defensive shield to protect the United States from the threat posed by ballistic missiles hibernated for nearly eleven years, the technological, political, and even mythic grounds for its revival were quietly, but assiduously, being prepared in this interregnum by a number of agencies. For one thing, as a part of the McNamara legacy, research and development of ballistic missile defense ideas proceeded, albeit with less budgetary support, at several leading public and private laboratories—most notably at the Lawrence Livermore National Laboratory under the directorship of Edward Teller, erstwhile leader of the infinite containment school within the scientific community. Also instrumental, the political right associated with the extreme wing of the Republican party retained its demonic image of the USSR and the Soviet hegemony over Eastern Europe and elsewhere, as well as its dedication to the pursuit of security for the United States against any perceived military threat, a blanket defense premised on military preparedness and technological innovation in virtually all spheres of possible military action. Likewise, careerist national security experts of a strongly conservative bent provided intellectual legitimacy and political backing for the Republican right's black-and-white portrait of the post–World War II international environment. They offered support by generating a strategic framework and technical vocabulary to justify the right's bipolar views of the world and to lend credence to its technological optimism regarding even the most exotic proposals for weapons development.

These powerful background forces shaping the renewal of interest in ballistic missile defense would never have been as influential or formidable without the election of so iconic a figure for president as Ronald Reagan. Nor would these plans have gained such popular appeal and political capital without his catalytic role and salesmanship abilities in persuading American citizens and politicians of the ABM system's credible place within a strategic vision that, he alleged, transcended the limits and inadequacies of McNamara's doctrine of mutual assured destruction. As Frances FitzGerald has so copiously detailed, the beginnings of Ronald Reagan's interest in ballistic missile defense and its underlying strategy of assured survival are shrouded in a "myth of origins" involving conflicting stories composed of truth, myth, and self-serving deceptions by Reagan and his political and scientific associates.[2]

What is uncontested in the historical record is the decisive role played by President Reagan's address of March 23, 1983, in altering the national political climate and resuscitating the idea of ballistic missile defense. In an otherwise standard rendition of the president's stump speech about the nature of the Soviet threat (used so effectively in his 1980 presidential bid), his call for an impregnable defense shield had an extraordinary and galvanic effect precisely because of its mythic-heroic quality. That is, its rhetorical strategy invoked powerful images of a coming era in which a strong and peace-loving nation would rebound from a supposed position of military inferiority vis-à-vis the Soviet Union; by using defensive technology to take command of its own destiny, the United

States would achieve a status of invincibility in the context of a world still haunted by the specter of nuclear weapons.[3]

Early in the speech, the president hinted at his policy's novelty and audaciousness by appealing to the themes of "a new hope for our children" and "for the future" amidst a time of policy drift and national peril presented by a massive Soviet military buildup. Simultaneously, while dismissing the arms control alternative offered by the increasingly popular and powerful nuclear freeze movement, he called for redoubled efforts to challenge the USSR to negotiate with the United States toward significantly reducing the arsenals of the two superpowers. Then, turning to the section of the speech that would establish its historical significance, President Reagan indicated his intention to follow the lead of his military and civilian advisers by charting out a course that "breaks out of a future that relies solely on offensive retaliation for our security" by embarking "on a program to counter the awesome Soviet missile threat with measures that are defensive."[4] With high-mindedness and unvarnished hope, he asked: "What if free people could live secure in the knowledge that their security did not rest upon the threat of instant U.S. retaliation to deter a Soviet attack, that we could intercept and destroy strategic ballistic missiles before they reached our own soil or that of our allies?"[5] Acknowledging that this task might take years—even decades—of sustained military R&D to achieve, he called upon American nuclear scientists and weapons engineers to follow this vision and provide the American people with "the means of rendering these nuclear weapons impotent and obsolete."[6]

In a nationally televised speech lasting less than an hour, the issue of ballistic missile defense was once again thrust onto the center of public debate and restored to the highest level of the nation's policy agenda. Detractors in Congress and within the peace and social justice community quickly labeled the president's vision "Star Wars" in order to pejoratively associate the potential defensive shield with George Lucas's science fiction films. Republican party stalwarts and cold war hardliners within the national security establishment heralded it as a dramatic departure from the old shibboleths and stale nostrums peddled by past liberal Democratic administrations. Within days of its enunciation, the administration's new defense approach was formalized in National Security Decision Directive 85, and shortly thereafter two executive committees were set up: the Fletcher panel would evaluate the state of ABM technology and recommend programs to advance the goal; and the Hoffman panel would assess strategic and policy implications of such a defense effort.[7]

Before its reincarnation as the Strategic Defense Initiative on May 30, 1985, in a document issued as National Security Decision Directive 172,[8] Reagan's ballistic missile program moved forward peripatetically amid executive-legislative skirmishing, international administrative jockeying, uncertain organizational direction, and heavily promoted and often misguided scientific development. In October 1983, the Hoffman report was released and offered two major findings: that development and deployment of missile defenses could significantly enhance deterrence; and that advancement of tactical missile defenses could contribute to the ambitions of developing a national missile defense system.[9] The Fletcher panel subsequently issued its report recommending a $20.9 billion five-year budget to support an aggressive research program, working from the presumption that any anti-missile system would be a multi-tiered defense capable of attacking a ballistic missile at each stage in its trajectory, from the boost phase to the mid-course phase to the terminal phase.[10]

The disclosure of the tentative outline of the multi-layered Reagan "Star Wars" plan by the Fletcher team prompted interested parties to scrutinize closely its technical feasibility and political implications. Congress invited one of its research arms, the Office of Technology Assessment (OTA), to investigate the status and promise of high-energy weapons and missile defense programs in space; meanwhile, the Union of Concerned Scientists (UCS), an organization closely identified with the finite containment school within the scientific community, undertook its own study of overlapping issues related to strategic defenses. Along with the Fletcher panel report, the OTA study, directed by Ashton Carter, and the UCS study, largely authored by Richard Garwin, fomented intense scientific and technical controversy among scientists as well as numerous congressional hearings and extensive media coverage on these disputes. The resumption of heated conflict among prominent and influential spokespeople of different schools of scientific thought signaled the start of yet another chapter in the history of defense strategy and weapons innovation politics within the scientific community.[11]

Both the Carter report from the more nonpartisan OTA and the Garwin report from the openly engaged Union of Concerned Scientists reached similar conclusions—specifically, that none of the technological proposals for missile defense could achieve the level of technical perfection necessary to secure a "leakproof" defense umbrella for the United States (and its allies) against a sophisticated ballistic missile assault, and that none offered any reasonable technological foundation for a major shift in American strategic doctrine.[12] While the debates carried out in congressional committee halls, scientific journals, and weekly television news programs often became entangled in arcane technical issues, the anti-SDI scientists did much to convey a general sense within the Congress and among the public that the pro-SDI scientists' assumption that all elements of the system could work flawlessly as a whole was unreasonable, given the many components of the complex system and the potential for small technical slip-ups and malfunctions to produce large margins of error and major snafus.[13]

No less troubling—and in some respects more assuming—were the battlefield management problems presented in the effort to mount a robust defense against an incoming missile strike. The critical stage of any thick, multi-layered anti-missile system, as Robert McNamara recognized in the 1960s, involves the boost phase of an enemy missile assault. With only a three-to-five-minute window of opportunity to destroy ballistic missiles being lofted into the exo-atmosphere before multiple independently-targetable reentry vehicles (MIRVs) and decoys (chaff, fake warheads, etc.) are released, the tasks of detecting, tracking, discriminating, guiding, and intercepting an enemy missile proved a daunting, if not technically intractable, problem. For a determined adversary, McNamara hypothesized, the offense could always overwhelm even the most sophisticated defense with comparatively cheaper counter-measures—including penetration aids.[14] In the case of space-based high-energy defense weapons (whether X-ray laser or kinetic energy), that the offense would be able to destroy space-based battle stations more easily and at less cost than the defensive battle stations could target and destroy attacking ballistic missiles with computer and radar assistance remained one of the strongest and most persuasive arguments against deploying an expensive and inevitably porous ABM system.[15]

As if these formidable technological impediments and cost considerations were not enough, scientists and defense experts skeptical of the Reagan strategic defense initiative pointed out how the necessity of a "hair-trigger" launch in the face of any real or apparent Soviet missile strike would pose a crisis of constitutional authority. Simply put, the imperative to shoot down Soviet missiles in the boost phase of their trajectory within a few minutes of detection would most likely entail that presidential authorization be replaced by decision by computer.[16]

These complicating factors were explored and acknowledged in the otherwise favorable report by the Fletcher panel in its seventh volume. The panel concluded that indeed "Soviet countermeasures could seriously complicate the capability of the X-ray laser to function as an effective mechanism for antimissile defense."[17] As journalist William Broad[18] and navy science adviser Theodore Postol[19] observed, the damaging character of this finding prompted the Fletcher commission to suppress that critical volume from its overall evaluation, since it found no way to confront and overcome a problem that appeared insoluble with existing or foreseeable means.

For a time, the Reagan administration was able to sustain support and momentum for SDI through a variety of political and rhetorical means. As Gary Guertner pointed out, that formula involved a combination of "incremental funding, technological optimism, ambiguous standards of proof"[20] and, I would add, the idea that a technological solution to the problem of national security exists and simply must be found. Reagan's most passionate boosters of this core assumption were the scientific establishment's infinite containment school, led by Edward Teller, head of the Lawrence Livermore National Laboratory. Largely credited along with fellow scientist Lowell Wood for kindling President Reagan's interest in and enthusiasm for the Star Wars concept in 1981 and 1982, Teller proved to be an unflagging supporter of complex and often arcane missile defenses like laser weapons and boost-phase defenses.[21] In congressional testimony and private executive meetings, he tended to boost such projects "as if these weapons were about to jump off the assembly line."[22] Heavy funding of these ideas and preliminary field testing demonstrated otherwise.

The series of Homing Overlay Experiments taking place in 1984 and the Goldstone experiment conducted in 1985 not only produced results that were especially sobering to supporters of X-ray laser and kinetic energy technologies. These tests also raised serious issues concerning the intrusion of politics into the testing process and the role of bureaucratic pressures in manipulating vehicle design tests to maximize the likelihood of favorable outcomes.[23] While revelation of some of these manipulated results would not come to light until years later, the slow accumulation of evidence of rigged experiments cast greater and greater skepticism on the maturity of the High Frontier technologies being developed and designed under the auspices of the SDI program.[24]

By the mid-eighties, the novelty and luster of the much vaunted SDI program first enunciated by Ronald Reagan in March of 1983 had all but worn off, as the dream of a leakproof ABM system capable of "hitting a bullet with a bullet" had to come to terms with organizational and technological realities as well as increasingly complicated political, diplomatic, and international challenges. Given the insistent intervention of hardcore ABM supporters within the Reagan administration upon the RDT&E process administered by the SDI bureaucracy, the Strategic Defense Initiative Organization (SDIO) found itself caught in the crossfire between the high expectations and political demands of BMD proponents and the profound doubts and close scrutiny of the defense system's critics. As a result, SDIO's bureaucratic structure underwent reshuffling in July 1986 and again in September 1988 in efforts to realign its organizational form with rising political demands and diminishing technological advances.[25]

The internal politics within the White House also impinged upon missile development, as two coalitions strove to shape the president's views on the future of SDI, the direction and prospects for U.S.-Soviet relations, and the promise of strategic arms reductions. One coalition was centered on Defense Secretary Caspar

Weinberger, a staunch advocate of national missile defenses, and the other was organized around Secretary of State George Schultz, something of a skeptic of the value of ballistic missile defense. This fascinating episode in White House politicking over SDI provides insights into the constraining factors militating against a U.S. withdrawal from the ABM Treaty and an administrative decision to deploy at least the first phase of a thick anti-missile system during the eighties.[26]

Two factors had a profound impact upon executive politics: the Soviet political liberalization occurring in the context of the START negotiations seeking sizable reductions in U.S.-Soviet nuclear stockpiles; and the utopian dream of President Reagan of an America—and perhaps a world—free from the fear of nuclear war.[27] In combination, these elements so heavily shaped administration politics that generally conservative, but seasoned, foreign policy actors like Secretary George Schultz and Reagan arms negotiator Paul Nitze were able to keep at bay through guile, experience, and dogged determination militant cold warriors like Defense Secretary Weinberger and Assistant Defense Secretary Richard Perle. As a result, the latter found their efforts to expedite deployment of an anti-missile system, scuttle the START negotiations, and break out of and nullify the 1972 treaty blocked at virtually every turn.[28]

However strenuous was the intra-administrative campaign by SDI proponents to deploy a multi-layered missile defense system, the increasing international and diplomatic pressures brought to bear by the Gorbachev regime in the Soviet Union and the domestic reverberations of the nuclear freeze movement played their crucial parts in obstructing a go-ahead decision. While introducing increasingly radical reforms of the stodgy, overcentralized, and deteriorating Soviet economy, Mikhail Gorbachev seemed equally energetic in throwing the American cold war hardliners off guard by offering dramatic initiatives in strategic arms reduction that appealed to President Reagan's utopian-millenarian inclinations.[29] Whether in Geneva or in Reykjavik, these gestures inspired that side of Reagan's mythic-heroic personality that believed a solution—whether technological or diplomatic—could be found to rid Americans of the risks of nuclear war posed by the deadly and overgrown strategic arsenals of the two superpowers.

But so too did the nuclear freeze movement play its role in constraining elite prerogative in the realm of defensive techno-logical innovation.[30] In many ways a throwback to the movement politics of the sixties, the nuclear freeze campaign had the advan-tage of offering a simple, cogent, and—for many American citi-zens and elected representatives—compelling alternative to incrementalist strategies of achieving arms control and weapons reduction. As the movement gathered political steam and legisla-tive support, the Reagan administration was increasingly compelled to respond to its growing popularity and political clout. Many in the administration rejected the idea of trying seriously to reach agreement with the USSR on significant nuclear arms cuts. In spite of their ability to steal the limelight from the nuclear freeze movement with radical proposals that the Soviets could not ac-cept (given the manner in which such offers would jeopardize So-viet national security), these cold war ideologues discovered that their apparent success in co-opting the nuclear freeze movement only fostered heightened expectations from those strategic arms talks.[31] In so doing, the administration was forced to temper its highest aspirations regarding ballistic missile defense in an effort to counter bold Soviet bargaining positions with dramatic ones of its own during the START negotiations.

The most diehard supporters of the strategic defense initia-tive were never able to disentangle themselves from the skein of interlinked issues ensnaring ballistic missile defense. As the arena of debate and contestation overflowed the boundaries of intra-administrative politics and took the form of executive-legislative wrangling, domestic political jousting, elite prerogative–mass movement mobilization, U.S.-NATO disharmony, and future U.S.-Soviet sparring, wider constituencies and other interests played increasing roles in shaping the technopolitics of ballistic missile defense. Despite the great impatience of key players and insiders like Defense Secretary Caspar Weinberger, SDI-booster Edward Teller, and High Frontier advocate Gen. Daniel Graham to set in motion an early SDI deployment plan, the force of events linked to these other arenas of politics and diplomatic relations, reinforced by the relative immaturity of some of the critical components of the evolving BMD architecture, stymied their best and most strenuous efforts.[32]

In the end, the solitary consolation netted by these cold warriors and technological enthusiasts was the pervasive belief that the dramatic military buildup and massive defense budget increases during the Reagan years drove the Soviet Union to economic bankruptcy and hastened its break-up and the demise of the communist empire worldwide. According to this view, the United States under the Reagan administration was able to draw upon its wider economic base, its more plentiful national and financial resources, and the largest peacetime budget increase in defense expenditures to advance SDI as a "symbolic decoy" or "virtual sword," bringing the USSR to its knees economically and politically.

The "Reagan Victory School," as Gordon Mitchell has labeled it, has many members and spokespeople, not least of whom include former Reagan national security adviser Robert McFarlane, former Carter adviser Zbigniew Brzezinski, and conservative scholar and former Reagan UN ambassador Jeane J. Kirkpatrick.[33] More recent scholarly studies, though, have cast considerable doubt on the assumptions and allegations on which this "vindicationist" history and "peace through strength" theory rest.[34] They point to the facts that Russia's response to the strategic defense initiative took place well before Gorbachev came to power, that no high-level policymaker for Russia has acknowledged any real impact of "Star Wars" on its military force levels or budget plans, and that America's aggressive SDI program more likely had the effect of heightening tensions and slowing the timetable of reaching agreement with the Gorbachev regime, which was prepared at nearly every turn and in every area (except BMD) to move quickly and radically with the United States toward significant strategic arms cuts.

In any event, the collapse of the Soviet Union hegemon and its satellites and the perpetuation of strategic arms talks did little to halt the drive for a defensive weapons system in succeeding administrations. Presidents and the missile defense lobby continued the search for both a mission justifying ABM deployment and a winning political constituency to realize that dream. Indeed, facing the end of the cold war, the further trajectory of the U.S. debate over ballistic missile defense would provide one possible answer to Gorbachev's query to an American delegation before the final summit meeting in Moscow in 1988: "What are you going to do now that you've lost your best enemy?"[35]

The Bush administration's initial efforts to distance itself from the Reagan presidency and its legacy prompted some of its key players—including the president himself—to put ballistic missile defense on the back burner. Key administrative officials, including Defense Secretary Richard Cheney and eventual Joint Chiefs of Staff General Colin Powell, initially showed little interest in the missile defense issue. This pattern of disinterest and ambivalence toward ABM was paralleled in their delay and seeming policy paralysis regarding U.S.-Soviet relations in the first months of the new administration. Once the Bush-led regime did get its bearings, however, the president found himself embracing a tough negotiating position closely akin to his predecessor's.[36] Despite recommendations by the Joint Chiefs of Staff (JCS) that the U.S. negotiation stance drop any insistence on American prerogative to deploy such defense systems in the future and that the national BMD policy revert to an R&D program focused on a distant technological horizon, the George H.W. Bush team coalesced around a new defense concept—the idea of scattering thousands of kinetic energy interceptors in low orbit around the earth using tiny computers and sensors to direct deadly beams to destroy enemy ICBMs in mid-flight.[37] Dubbed Brilliant Pebbles, its core emanated from the technological ideas and weapons architecture spawned at the Lawrence Livermore National Laboratory under Edward Teller and Lowell Wood's administration and direction.

Though at first modestly funded and regarded as a low-end project within the SDIO under Gen. James A. Abrahamson, technological progress and lobbying success by its originators convinced Secretary of Defense Cheney, by the spring of 1989, to give Brilliant Pebbles his imprimatur.[38] As a result, it was elevated in status and funding within the SDIO and showcased in congressional committee meetings and public speeches by President Bush and his national security advisers.

The evolution of the concept, design, and development of

Brilliant Pebbles underwent considerable revision in the mid- to late-eighties. In spite of considerable enthusiasm for Brilliant Pebbles technology among its chief advocates within the Lawrence Livermore National Laboratory, its weapons designers continued to explore a variety of other speculative project ideas, including particle beam weapons, high-power conventional lasers, and orbiting X-ray lasers primed by nuclear detonations.[39] Like so many exotic projects investigated during the McNamara years in the Defense Department, these "blue-skies" schemes proved technologically infeasible though oftentimes enormously attractive to certain political constituencies. When a consensus within the Bush administration coalesced around the less ambitious Brilliant Pebbles program around 1988, this project evoked a sense of déjà vu among defense planners and missile engineers.

Harkening back to the late fifties and early sixties, Brilliant Pebbles bore a number of remarkable affinities to the air force's Ballistic Missile Boost Intercept (BAMBI) project, which also featured "hit-to-kill" interceptors. As noted in earlier chapters, BAMBI had been terminated by McNamara and his weapons designers because of the over-the-horizon character of its technological demands and because of its enormous and uncertain expense, even in optimistic estimates.[40] Brilliant Pebbles distinguished itself from BAMBI in its "distributed network" configuration—it envisaged a network of thousands to tens of thousands of small, independent, and comparatively inexpensive battle stations. Its attractiveness as a design concept diminished, however, as weapons designers were compelled to enlarge these battle stations from pebbles to boulders to take into account complex technological requirements.[41]

With palpable evidence of a thaw in U.S.-Soviet relations largely spurred by the persistent departures from past party lines by Mikhail Gorbachev, efforts designed to break down American resistance to bold initiatives in arms control and foreign relations, new rationales for BMD deployment surfaced in the face of evident progress in the long-standing START negotiations in Geneva. As it became clear that the Soviets were prepared to dismantle more long-range ballistic missiles through a negotiated arms accord than any projected Brilliant Pebbles defensive network could aspire to destroy, the project's escalating funding and promised emplacement in space were given new justifications. The new rationales offered by President Bush and other key aides were that Brilliant Pebbles would serve both as a safeguard against accidental missile firings and as insurance against reckless nuclear strikes by Third World rogue states.[42] This latter role, which would emerge eleven years later as the central mission and defining purpose of the George W. Bush administration's National Missile Defense campaign, was roundly criticized and contradicted in 1990 by JCS chair Colin Powell. The threat from foolhardy and unstable leaders, according to General Powell, was not an imminent one; indeed, he argued, it was less ominous than the greater likelihood of such rogue states launching an atomic offensive through cheaper and less risk-prone means, such as clandestine bomb delivery by suitcase or offshore boat.[43]

Vigorous congressional lobbying and public marketing by the president, the defense secretary, SDIO administrators, and national laboratory scientists could not prevent the tolling of the death knell of Brilliant Pebbles as a serious, viable, and well-funded R&D project by the late eighties. Its interment as a serious military R&D project and possible technological avenue to missile defense was influenced by progress in the START negotiations, by its failure to achieve notable technological advancement, and by sagging congressional support for continued funding of the program. Though not officially terminated as a research project, Brilliant Pebbles was all but assimilated into a somewhat broader, but less ambitious, project by the Bush administration under the aegis of the SDIO. The Global Protection Against Limited Strikes program—shortened to its acronym GPALS in defense policy making, military, and legislative circles—retained as its basic raison d'être the strategic goal of protecting the United States from nuclear assault by Third World countries and from accidental Soviet ICBM launches. With an estimated cost of forty billion dollars or more, GPALS was conceptualized as a two-tier defensive shield comprising a thousand space-based Brilliant Pebbles and five hundred to a thousand ground-based missile interceptors (GBIs).[44]

As subsequent reviews and investigative reports would reveal,[45] the technological viability and defense worthiness of this project were never proved during the Bush years. What saved GPALS—and indeed the entire strategic mission of missile defense—from obscurity at this time was a major international event that erupted in another part of the globe. This event, the Iraqi invasion of Kuwait, provided a significant boost in political and legislative support for BMD development precisely at a time when budgetary funding prospects in Congress and broader public enthusiasm were ebbing. On January 16, 1991, the Gulf War commenced. For some five weeks, a rapt global audience, including a sizable percentage of the American television-viewing public, was treated to a daily diet of a regional military conflict. Spectacular news coverage offered footage of volleys of cruise missiles and smart bombs homing in on their Iraqi targets with unerring accuracy, images reminiscent of a Nintendo battle game.

The other focus of worldwide attention was the fireworks display in the Middle Eastern night sky as Patriot missile batteries targeted the medium-range SCUD missiles Iraq was launching at Israeli and Saudi Arabian cities.[46] With early army reports of Patriot interception and kill ratios of 90 percent or higher, the much-vaunted Patriot became symbolic of the extraordinary precision of these defensive missiles. In addition, it fostered belief on the part of many American citizens that the U.S. military already possessed an effective anti-missile defense or could soon replicate the success of the theater-level Patriot missile in defending allied cities at the national and strategic level.[47]

As Gordon Mitchell recounts, the claims attributed to the Patriot not only proved spectacular; their evidence rested on fallacious data and thus contributed to a campaign of military and administrative deception.[48] Drawing upon the careful scientific studies of MIT physicists Theodore Postol and George Lewis,[49] Mitchell demonstrates how the illusion of Patriot effectiveness encouraged wide support for the Cheney-led Defense Department's Revolution in Military Affairs—a vision of the battlefield of the future grounded in high-tech military projects being politically supported and heavily funded by the Bush administration. He also details the painstaking analyses of actual Patriot performance against Iraqi SCUDs, showing how the pretense of success was often constructed from television footage or videos that failed to take into account the intercept dynamics of the Patriot. His recapitulation of the Patriot accuracy controversy in Congress and within the scientific community also underscores the way that major institutional players like the Pentagon and Raytheon (the Patriot's corporate manufacturer) used the cloak of secrecy and classified information to undercut democratic processes and scientific inquiry into their extravagant claims.[50]

Such charges of "strategic deception" regarding missile performance and field testing would erupt anew over BMD testing during the two terms of the Clinton administration. The Patriot episode in the Gulf War and its aftermath was significant to the unfolding politics of the ABM debate in another respect. The fanfare surrounding the record of near-perfect precision initially attributed to the Patriot fostered the public misconception that the Patriot and SDI missiles being developed and tested were virtually one and the same. Actually, the Patriot was first designed in the sixties and seventies to be an air-defense system and was subsequently upgraded and redesigned in the eighties as a point-defense to protect military troop concentrations or bases against short-range offensive missiles like the SCUD. Accuracy was never the overriding design issue for such weapons, since their objective was to explode within the vicinity of a primitive missile and destroy it, either by debris spread around its incoming trajectory or by forcing it off course with self-detonation. Such a mission was quite removed from the task assigned to ABM interceptors—almost literally, hitting a bullet with a bullet.[51]

On the heels of this public relations victory for missile defense, the political fortunes of the SDI program soared as the Bush administration announced its decision on January 29, 1990, to reorient its BMD program to protect the United States against limited ballistic missile attacks from any and all sources and to request a significant hike in the budget for this mission.[52] Within Congress, mounting legislative pressure for commitment to and early deployment of a phased ABM system was expressed in a bill drafted by senators Sam Nunn and John Warner, the Missile Defense Act of 1991.[53] In addition to calling for a first step in the eventual deployment of an antiballistic missile system within five years, it also pressed the executive branch to initiate talks with the Soviet Union to revise the ABM Treaty to allow such deployment within its amended terms.

Advances in arms negotiations moved apace even as legislative pressure and executive and military bureaucratic endorsement for rapid deployment of ballistic missile defenses gained ascendancy within the domestic political arena. Simultaneously, the United States and the USSR consummated a significant strategic arms treaty through the START process instituted under the Reagan presidency. This achievement was chastened by the unilateral Soviet declaration of intention to withdraw from the treaty in the event the United States abrogated or seriously violated the ABM Treaty.[54] Meanwhile, Republican senators successfully pushed the Nunn-Warner bill through the arms services committee and then the full Senate. Their ability to accomplish this feat would become a pattern in the nineties. This pattern involved the success of conservative forces within an increasingly ideologically solidified Republican party to gain symbolic purchase from an opportunistic event (like the Patriot's alleged achievement in the Gulf War) at a moment when the Democratic party was in disarray and on the defensive.

The political momentum gained by supporters of GPALS during the preceding four years was dealt a serious blow by the failure of President Bush to win reelection in November 1991, a defeat compounded by the breakup of the Soviet Union in December 1991. With the cold war over and the economy still mired in a recession that Bush's Democratic contender, William Clinton, capitalized on during the presidential campaign, the prospects of even a first-phase deployment of a missile defense system were dimmed by independent assessments of the technological status of GPALS and the Brilliant Pebbles R&D projects. A GAO report released in March 1992 disclosed that GPALS still lacked a stable architecture, while the design of Brilliant Pebbles faced many technological hurdles before its value could be determined.[55] Worse still, further legislative investigations and research studies questioned the methodology and findings of the SDIO's testing programs, raising charges of wholesale exaggeration and even willful rigging of some of the technical tests of the missile interceptors.[56]

The changeover in administrations not only meant a new party and a new cabinet lineup; it also prompted a shift in priorities within programs geared to the missile defense mission. The new secretary of defense, Les Aspin, who in Congress had been regarded as something of a critic of past campaigns for sizable defense budget increases and big-ticket items, sought to rein in hopes and expectations for rapid development and near-term deployment of any ballistic missile defense.[57] First, he reorganized the SDIO into the BMDO (Ballistic Missile Defense Organization); then he sought to stabilize and lower expenditures on NMD in present and future years. But more significantly, he revised missile defense policy to change budgetary and developmental priorities within the new BMD organization by reversing the post–Gulf War Bush administration's 4:1 ratio of funding allocated to national missile defense vis-à-vis theater missile defense. This last shift meant that preponderant funding for missile defense development would go to programs to protect American troops and U.S. allies from shorter-range battlefield missiles.[58]

This restructuring of priorities, however, soon led the Clinton White House into a thicket of problems relating to the ABM Treaty and to army-BMDO pressures to achieve notable success in theater missile tests. At the center of both controversies triggered by this change in emphasis was the army's Theater High Altitude Area Defense, known as THAAD for short. Although interservice rivalry fueled competition among the army, navy, and air force for the role of theater defense, the BMDO elected to promote most aggressively the army's upper-tier THAAD program, the navy's Aegis program, and another army program, PAC-3, which grew out of the Patriot missile system.[59] While the THAAD was specifically designed as a theater defense, using faster interceptors and more powerful radars to provide area protection against short- and medium-range enemy missiles, its high-end design raised serious worries among arms control critics that its performance standards would exceed the limitations established by the 1972 ABM accord.[60]

Because the Clinton administration broke with the central tendencies in the Reagan and Bush administrations and foreswore broad interpretation of the ABM Treaty, key administrative spokespeople and representatives in the Aspin Defense Department were increasingly compelled to defend the distinction between the upper-tier theater defense mission of the THAAD system, then undergoing development and testing, and the strategic role of an ABM system targeted against assaults from Russia, China, or any other hostile nuclear power with ICBMs.[61] Yet ambiguities in the language of the U.S.-Soviet agreement to limit BMD systems forced Clinton's defense officials and diplomatic aides to press their Russian counterparts for clarification of the treaty in a manner that would allow THAAD's testing and prospective deployment under a more explicit and generous set of criteria demarcating permissible upper-tier systems from illegal strategic anti-missile systems.

In this context, a new and spirited chapter in the politics of the scientific community was ignited, as reports and congressional testimonies from former finite containment scientists like Richard Garwin, David Wright, and Theodore Postol were challenged by those issued from their counterparts in the past infinite containment school.[62] There, these scientific representatives and other arms control advocates warned that inflating technical criteria for drawing this distinction would amount to a unilateral breakout by the United States of the ABM Treaty limits, while, in a reversal of virtually all past missile deployment campaigns, scientists supporting the army/BMDO Theater High Altitude Area Defense project were charged with "deflating performance evaluations to portray the system as legal under the ABM Treaty."[63] The debate subsided as a political issue only in 1997, when Russia's resistance to accommodating the Clinton position crumbled in the face of its economic tailspin and desperate need for international assistance. As a result, Russian leaders agreed to a settlement of the dispute that excluded THAAD—but no other future (and faster) upper-tier system—from treaty constraints.[64]

As the ballistic missile defense controversy wended its way during the Clinton years in the White House, the often intense divisions at the intersection of physics and politics were also evidenced with the issue of the THAAD testing program.[65] In a pattern that would surface during the first year of the George W. Bush administration over its haste to deploy an anti-missile system, the same cast of anti-ABM scientists and arms control proponents expressed deep misgivings about the BMDO's highly compressed testing timetable evidenced in slipshod testing and questionable reports on THAAD's performance and deployment potential.[66]

The significance of the THAAD testing program for national missile defense lay in the fact that one of the roles assigned it was "to serve as the 'hit to kill' architecture of a Star Wars–style NMD system."[67] In part, the impetus for accelerated testing of the THAAD lay in the heavy pressures brought to bear on the program by the technical milestones and targeted goals set forth in the 1996 Missile Defense Act, as well as the exigencies its political supporters perceived regarding high-end theater defense. These forces coalesced to create a testing and evaluation environment where the BMDO and the THAAD corporate contractor, Lockheed Martin, were prone, as the Welch Commission concluded, to "underestimate the degree of difficulty in achieving HTK [hit-to-kill]" objectives. As testing failures were piled on testing failures, design modification led to hasty design revisions that caused "significant cost, schedule, and technical performance problems."[68] The result was a series of flight test failures that amounted, in the words of the Welch Commission report, to a "rush to failure."

President Clinton's reluctance to commit to deployment of national missile defense, despite formidable political pressures building up within the developing coalition of NMD supporters, was revealed in 1996 when his administration announced its "3-plus-3" policy.[69] Experiencing mounting political heat after the call for a highly effective missile defense at the earliest practical date in the "Contract with America," the rallying manifesto of the Gingrich-led engineers of the Republican congressional sweep ushered in by the November 1994 mid-term elections, President Clinton pursued a political strategy of "triangulation," setting a middle course between foes and skeptics of missile defense and ardent BMD supporters. Citing the uncertainties of the existing and emerging threats that might warrant ABM deployment, as well as the cost factor and impact of such a decision upon standing arms control treaties, the president announced a plan that would involve continuing development of an anti-missile system for three years; the system would then be deployed within three more years if a palpable threat materialized and warranted such an action. Otherwise, military research on NMD development would continue.

As a consequence of the "3-plus-3" policy impetus, the BMDO increasingly refined and diversified its program, and a discernible architecture of the NMD system began to take shape. That system design envisioned a fixed, land-based, non-nuclear missile defense system with an orbiting detection system. Its five key elements follow: ground-based interceptors; a battle management C3 (command, control, and communications) system; X-band, multi-function radar; upgraded early-warning radar; and a sophisticated defense support program of an early-warning satellite network, eventually supplanted by a space-based infrared system.[70]

The Clinton NMD system was designed to evolve over its lifecycle through three capability levels. Its Capability 1 configuration, intended to meet executive-legislative objectives of fielding a capability within three years, sought to satisfy criteria necessary to protect the United States against unsophisticated threats involving a handful of single-warhead missiles and simple penetration aids. Capability 2 was projected to reach performance standards against authorized, unauthorized, or accidental attack by sophisticated payloads (including more exotic penetration aids). The overall and long-term objective of the Capability 3 level of the NMD system was to satisfy performance criteria against a limited, but more diverse, set of sophisticated threats (either 50 ICBMs with 50 individual warheads and simple decoys or 20 ICBMs with 20 warheads and 100 credible decoys). To achieve C1 and C2 performance standards, 20 GBI missiles and 100 GBI missiles, respectively, would be deployed in underground silos in Alaska; the goal of C3 protection would entail the emplacement of 125 GBI missiles in Alaska and the same number at Grand Forks, North Dakota.[71]

This gambit by the Clinton administration to abate increasing political pressures among congressional Republicans to force early and rapid BMD deployment experienced growing strains and difficulties. Over the next two years, notable political events began to erode the counterweight against deployment emanating from within the administration as well as the scientific and arms control communities. In July 1998, a blue-ribbon commission headed by Donald Rumsfeld, former secretary of defense in the Ford administration, raised the specter of "rogue states" like North Korea and Iraq being able to develop and deploy ICBMs with nuclear warheads within a five-year period.[72] Even though a contemporaneous CIA study contradicted this alarming estimate, a surprise North Korean test-firing of a long-range missile over the Pacific the following month blunted this more cautious projection and intensified calls by Republican legislators to speed up testing and deployment of a national missile defense system. In the Senate, threat of a Democratic filibuster blocked efforts led by Thad Cochran (Rep., Miss.) to pass a missile defense bill. But the public disclosure of the Lewinsky episode and the surrounding controversy triggered impeachment proceedings against the president in early 1999, hobbling the Clinton administration's efforts to stave off these mounting political demands for deployment.[73]

Faced with shrinking political space for maneuver and contestation on the BMD issue, Clinton's secretary of defense, William Cohen, announced the administration's commitment of $6.6 billion in additional support over a five-year period dedicated to deploying a missile defense. Acknowledging the palpable nature of the looming threat from "rogue states," Cohen further pledged to press Russia to agree to a modification of the ABM Treaty. In the event the Russian leaders rejected such amendment, the defense secretary indicated that the administration was prepared to set aside the treaty and deploy an ABM system.[74] Oddly, the mounting political campaign to force a deployment decision was occurring against the background of general public indifference.[75]

This concession only strengthened the hand of ballistic missile defense supporters within Congress and among the Republican right. With Democrats under siege, Senator Cochran reintroduced his national missile defense bill, and House Republicans brought forth an even more strongly worded bill endorsing deployment of a national missile defense as a matter of national policy.[76] Despite the president's success in avoiding removal from office in the Senate trial, opposition from the Democratic party and administration dissolved, and the National Missile Defense Act of 1999 was passed in the Senate on March 16, 1999.[77] The next day, Senate passage of the bill was followed by House endorsement of a measure committing the United States to deploy a national missile defense. Subsequent legislation declaring it the policy of the United States to field national missile defenses as soon as technologically feasible came in late May of the same year.[78]

Signing the National Missile Defense Act of 1999 on July 23 provided President Clinton with the occasion to outline the four criteria he would apply in deciding when to deploy such defenses: the character and seriousness of the threat, the cost of any such system, the technological readiness of the NMD, and the status of any such program vis-à-vis a renegotiated ABM Treaty.[79] Strategic arms negotiations between the United States and Russia to determine, among other things, a modification of the ABM began in earnest in mid-August. Meanwhile, conflicting recommendations from high-level bodies cast the future of national missile defense even more completely within the realm of political decision.

In September 1999, the Welch Commission presented its updated recommendations on NMD in light of revised timelines on ballistic missile defense developments and projects. The panel members concluded that the program remained a "high risk" venture and urged the president to consider his forthcoming June 2000 decision as a judgment concerning "feasibility" rather than "readiness to deploy."[80] In the same month, a new National Intelligence Estimate titled, "Foreign Missile Developments and the Ballistic Missile Threat to the United States through 2015," reversed its earlier, more conservative estimate of the emerging danger from missile-capable nuclear powers and predicted that "during the next 15 years the United States most likely will face ICBM threats from Russia, China, and North Korea, probably from Iran, and possibly from Iraq."[81]

With Congress having imposed a deadline of 2005 for deploying a national missile defense, the director of the Defense Department's Office of Operational Test and Evaluation, Philip Coyle, raised concerns in mid-February 2000 about extraordinary and "undue pressure" put upon the NMD testing program.[82] Reports of strategic deception in the testing program during the first two integrated flight tests attempting to intercept a missile using components of the proposed NMD system lent substance and credibility to Coyle's admonition. Claims by the Pentagon that the October 1999 test was a complete success were contradicted by later revelations that the anti-missile actually homed in on the single decoy released by the target missile; defense policymakers declared the January 2000 test, the second, a success despite an intercept failure caused by an infrared sensor malfunction. A third test, which took place in early July 2000, was unsuccessful because the kill vehicle failed to separate from the surrogate booster and the test decoy would not inflate.[83]

In the midst of a close presidential election campaign between Vice President Albert Gore and his Republican rival, George W. Bush, President Clinton chose to postpone any decision on ABM deployment in the closing months of his second term of office. On September 1, 2000, the president announced his decision not to authorize work to initiate the construction of a missile defense, leaving such a determination to the next president. Clinton cited as the reasons for postponing an affirmative decision the immature status of the technology, the continuing opposition of Russia to modifications of the ABM Treaty to permit such deployment, and the reluctance of America's NATO allies to support so radical a shift in nuclear strategy and technological innovation.[84] Thus, as the Clinton-Gore years drew to a close, the fate of ballistic missile defense—and with it the future of the ABM Treaty—appeared to rest on the outcome of the 2000 presidential election. In tandem, so too did the durability of the McNamara legacy.

George W. Bush's election to the office of the presidency in January 2001 foreshadowed a decisive change in nuclear strategy overall and, particularly, the place of ballistic missile defense in such policy. As a candidate, Bush had sent clear and unambiguous signals to Washington politicos and the American people that his administration would move with alacrity to deploy a missile defense system against what he and his campaign advisers regarded as a near-term and material threat from the nuclear weapons and missile programs of nations falling outside the community of responsible powers. Within the first month in office, the seriousness of President Bush regarding NMD was demonstrated in no uncertain terms.

His choices of nominees for all the high-level posts in national defense and the foreign policy establishment as well as the nominees' statements during Senate confirmation hearings made it unmistakably clear that the Bush administration would soon enact policy that would, barring domestic countermobilization or international veto, move toward early deployment of a ballistic missile defense and challenge the continuing relevance and viability of the ABM Treaty.[85] With Condoleeza Rice as chief national security adviser, Donald Rumsfeld as secretary of defense, and Colin Powell as secretary of state, as well as former Ford defense secretary Richard Cheney as vice president, the president appeared to have established a critical mass of presidential advisers who unreservedly embraced technological innovation in the realm of defense.

Formal announcement of such an intention was not long in coming. With his phalanx of cabinet appointments and chief advisers barely in place, George W. Bush chose the setting of National Defense University in Washington, D.C., on May 1 of 2001, to announce his decision to proceed with the early deployment of a national defense system directed against the emerging threat from rogue states and to abrogate, if necessary, the limits imposed by the 1972 anti-missile accord with Russia. Portraying the world at the beginning of the new millennium vastly different from the last half of the preceding century, President Bush called for a "new policy, a broad strategy of active nonproliferation, counter-proliferation and defenses." Arguing for an updated strategic framework to suit the new and unfolding international threat environment, he called for "new concepts of deterrence" that went beyond the biases and purported limitations of the strategy of mutual assured destruction inherited from the McNamara legacy. This new paradigm, he emphasized, would go beyond the constraints of the antiquated ABM Treaty and rely on both offensive and defensive weapons. A major dividend of these steps beyond doctrinal truisms and force structures of the past would include not only protection against the rising dangers posed by rogue states and terrorist groups but also the possibility of maintaining credible deterrence with dramatically less offensive nuclear weapons in the U.S. strategic arsenal. President Bush then acknowledged that the particular shape and substance of national missile defenses required further development and design. But he underlined without equivocation his administration's commitment to move quickly toward designing and implementing a missile defense system to augment America's offensive might.[86]

This formal decision drew considerable applause from President Bush's conservative coalition representatives, while it was sharply criticized by his opponents.[87] International reaction fell along predictable lines, with Russia, China, and North Korea condemning the program's potential focus on countries like China and North Korea. World leaders also voiced the concern that breaching the ABM Treaty would rend asunder the whole fabric of arms control agreements woven since the seventies, including treaties reducing offensive nuclear armaments.[88] In response, Bush and his key aides pointed to the new context of international threat and military preparedness shaped by the dissolution of the Soviet Union and its communist empire, the dangers posed by nuclear proliferation to provocative and terrorist-supporting regimes with developing capacities in nuclear weaponry and ICBMs, and the need for an American presidential administration to mandate a defense system capable of thwarting such inchoate threats.

The least clarified facet of the Bush NMD program was its exact architecture and configuration. From statements by the defense secretary, it was disclosed that the unfolding Bush plan would be a multi-layered system composed of boost-intercept, mid-flight-intercept, and point-defense capabilities.[89] It apparently would also revive the idea of space-based interceptors that originated in the Reagan "Star Wars" plan.[90] This facet particularly worried BMD critics, who saw it as an opening wedge of the enduring campaign among right-wing Republicans to militarize space.[91] Statements by Defense Secretary Donald Rumsfeld about increased budgetary support for military R&D on space-based weapons only exacerbated fears that the high frontier of space would soon become a new realm of military innovation and weapons deployment in the twenty-first-century global battlefield.[92]

The Bush administration's campaign to convince Russian, Chinese, and allied NATO leaders of the limited and nonprovocative nature of its emergent NMD policy was stymied in part by the lack of a precise outline of the ABM system to which it was committing. The president himself admitted that this lack of clarity fueled misunderstanding and dissension among NATO allies.[93] Parallel with its mobilization of the BMDO to launch a program of aggressive development and testing of BMD components, the Bush administration undertook a series of meetings and conferences with Russian officials, including Vladimir Putin, to persuade Russia to join the United States in shelving the Antiballistic Missile Treaty as a prelude to constructing a new relationship between the former adversaries.[94] Yet actions during the first months of the administration left no doubt that a firm political decision had been made to go forward with rapid deployment no matter the extent of allied misgivings or Russian, Chinese, and North Korean antagonism. Rebuffing criticism from noted scientists skeptical of ballistic missile defense, Secretary Rumsfeld argued that continued testing of such a system's components taking place in tandem with phased deployment of the system would allow the weaknesses in the chosen configuration to be improved in situ.[95] Attacks on the administration's readiness to unilaterally go beyond the ABM Treaty boundaries were countered with arguments that the treaty had been overtaken by a new international era and that it constituted, according to National Security Adviser Condoleeza Rice, a "relic of the past."[96]

So intent were the Bush White House and Rumsfeld Pentagon to deploy national missile defenses that, in an environment of prevailing doubt and dissensus domestically and internationally, a first-phase plan was announced in mid-July 2001. Its ostensible purpose was to test more vigorously the components of an overall BMD system; but its underlying impetus seemed to be to put in place NMD hardware and operational components that would violate en passant the existing terms of the ABM Treaty "in a matter of months" and signal to opponents that the controversy was over, a fait accompli.[97] In calling for a $3 billion increase in missile defense funding to $8.3 billion for fiscal year 2002, the administration sketched the rudiments of a testing program that would build upon and go beyond the Clinton-Cohen plans, which involved a program of phased testing and possible implementation centered in Alaska.[98] The Bush plan proposed a "more robust" testing program on highly augmented facilities at Fort Greely and Kodiak Island in Alaska to permit more realistic intercept tests by 2003. In the scenario that national security exigencies required withdrawal from the ABM Treaty, Deputy Defense Secretary Paul Wolfowitz envisaged the possibility of the new Alaskan testing range being used for "emergency deployment" of an ABM system—according to some reports, as early as 2004 or 2005.[99] It remained unclear whether the more vigorous testing schedule outlined in these plans would overcome continuing concerns among arms control advocates and ABM skeptics about consistent evidence of a "rush to failure" in BMDO testing.

In the midst of continued warnings of the flawed nature of BMDO tests in the waning months of the Clinton administration, the first test of the "hit-to-kill" vehicle during the Bush presidency on July 14 raised persisting concerns over the technological status and near-term deployment readiness of the NMD system being developed for the rogue state mission. Although the HTK vehicle did strike its target over the Pacific Ocean, later reports revealed that the vehicle only had to distinguish the actual warhead from a single mylar decoy and that the target itself was equipped with an active electronic beacon aiding the HTK vehicle to home in on it.[100]

For a time, nothing seemed to deter President Bush and his defense team from taking fateful steps toward breaking out of the postwar arms control regime and taking the country and the rest of the world into a new era of international politics and security issues and a new strategic framework for augmented deterrence and arms reductions. Continued politicking over ABM funding and testing by the Democrats, whose political fortunes in the Senate improved with the defection of Senator James J. Jeffords (Ind., Vermont) from the Republican party, did little to diminish the administration's missile defense campaign. Insistent arguments from anti-ABM scientists deflating the imminence of the external threat and the capacity of envisaged hostile nations to neutralize a limited national missile defense system had little impact in weakening the Bush-Rumsfeld resolve to push testing and deployment.

Neither did continued NATO concerns about the impact of the Bush assault on the ABM Treaty, a document viewed by West European allies as the cornerstone of strategic stability over the preceding thirty years. Russian resistance and Chinese intransigence in opposing revision or replacement of that treaty had little more than a delaying effect.

Only the shocking terrorist attacks on the World Trade Center in New York and the Pentagon in Washington, D.C., seemed to slow the missile defense juggernaut within the administration. That event raised anew questions about the value of yesterday's high-tech solutions for tomorrow's dangers. In this new century, "low-tech/high-concept" actions like the plane hijackings of September 11, 2001, presaged a different kind of national security threat—one calling for a patient and protracted twilight struggle against a shadowy adversary and perhaps requiring a new strategy and different weapons of offense and defense. The threat of global terrorism not only provided an answer to Mikhail Gorbachev's question at the close of the Moscow summit in 1988 in a manner that would legitimate a military definition of the United States' international role in a new American century. For the Bush administration, the specter of Al Qaeda and the expanding number of "rogue states" allegedly comprising an "evil axis" added heightened urgency for going beyond the ABM Treaty and McNamara heritage and installing its own "shield of dreams."

CONCLUSION

This work has sought to illuminate one particular aspect of the history and politics of national security policy and arms control negotiations in the United States: the controversy over whether the United States should deploy ballistic missile defenses. The preponderant weight of this analysis has been oriented to examining the trajectory of the first ABM debate, spanning from the mid-1950s through its culmination in the U.S.-Soviet treaty of 1972. The blocking of the defensive realm in strategic weapons innovation and the integration of ABM into an overarching deterrence strategy by the two superpowers were two outstanding achievements of these accords. From the point of view of the arms control ambitions of the Johnson and Nixon administrations, these achievements came as fruits of eight years of military and diplomatic negotiations: over five and a half of those years were spent trying to induce the USSR to join such arms limitation talks; two and a half, trying to reach agreement on the terms of a settlement. The dominant figure in the resolution of the initial phase of the ballistic missile controversy was Robert S. McNamara. He deserves major credit for compelling the leadership in the former Soviet Union to abandon its traditional and doctrinal commitment to defensive means and to recognize that the United States would not permit Soviet deployment of any significant shield against America's strategic weaponry.

Undoubtedly, a focal purpose of this work has been to dissolve the seemingly autonomous and objective character of complex military technology and to disclose its human roots in social action. In the course of analyzing the general background of the politics of defense in the 1950s, the specific political and administrative response of Secretary McElroy in 1958 to this situation was examined. This response took the form of the centralization and coordination of R&D in military technology in the Office of the Secretary of Defense. With this integration of technological development into the executive agency of the Defense Department and allocation of generous funding, significant changes in the form of defense politics were bound to occur in the 1960s—regardless of who was to occupy the OSD in 1961.

The impact of these actions was twofold. In the first place, a new and centralized source of technological dynamism was institutionalized in the Office of the Secretary of Defense. From this state of affairs the organizational framework was laid for harnessing and directing this "technological impulse" in the 1960s. In the second place, the centralization and coordination of R&D at the top of Defense Department administration with ample funding in the defense budget helped to promote further endorsement of the operation of some immanent logic of scientific or technological progress.

In the 1960s, with the assumption of Robert McNamara to the helm of the Defense Department, military technology in the United States was characterized by capital-intensive, systematic, and computerized qualities—which is to say that it was expensive, complex, and esoteric. Moreover, it was subject to rapid obsolescence for a variety of reasons, including the success of technological planners in developing counter-measures that could effectively neutralize its capabilities. But it is precisely the insular character of technological development and obsolescence that requires explanation. Conventional wisdom suggests that the rapid obsolescence of a particular weapons system is caused by the enemy deployment of a weapons system with the capability of countering it. The operation of the technological imperative and the course of the strategic arms race in the 1960s suggest otherwise.

Rather than further mystifying the technological imperative by portraying it as some vague, sinister force dominating the defense policy process, I have sought to express its concrete origins in the peculiar manner in which the organizational processes of U.S. offensive and defensive programs in military R&D were coordinated within the scientific and engineering agencies of the Office of the Secretary of Defense, thereby mutually nourishing technical progress in each sphere. Having examined the genesis and components of the technological imperative in some detail, I would now like to take this analysis one step further by deepening understanding of this imperative and clarifying its role in the 1960s. To achieve these purposes, I wish to consider two more questions: What strategy of technological development underpinned the impulse of American military technology in the 1960s? In what sense was it the controlling factor in stimulating the upward spiral of the strategic arms race during that decade?

The U.S. strategy of technological planning and weapons innovation flowing from the technological imperative may be most aptly termed a technological-breakthrough approach.[1] This approach to military R&D is basically composed of the following features:

• Maximization of uncertainty: Given the tendency of American strategic planners to compete with their own counter-weapons systems designs within their own technological planning process and given their concern for possible strategic threats and breakthroughs by the adversary as much as five years or more into the future, the level of technological uncertainty is only increased by the fact that new performance requirements for new weapons systems tend to exceed the prevailing "state of the art." Under such circumstances, the higher the planning uncertainties, the greater the level of funding that will be required in order to explore as many avenues of feasible technological development as possible.

• Nongeneric prototype design: Because new performance requirements go far beyond the prevailing "state of the art," the design of the new weapons system is likely to be radically different from the design of the existing weapons system that it is to replace.

• Multipurpose design: In order to decrease the cost of each new weapons system, new weapons designs are typically developed with multipurpose requirements in mind. The effort to reduce costs by developing a single new weapons system with multiple missions (rather than several systems with a single mission) is undercut, however, by the tendency of American strategic planners to try to incorporate into the weapons design all possible technological answers to threats to the system's missions. (The plight of the TFX multipurpose plane early in the McNamara era is indicative of the technical and political problems that accompany this approach to weapons innovation.[2]) In order to bring some control to the complexity of the weapon design and to limit costs, cost-effective analysis and other forms of systems analysis are integrated into the planning process.

• Quest for technological superiority: The insular and futuristic nature of the military R&D planning process guided by the breakthrough approach fosters in strategic planners the inherent propensity to seek a position of technological superiority vis-à-vis one's adversary. To underscore the point, this propensity stems less from any real threat or technological adventurism on the part of the opponent than from the strategy and process of one's own weapons planning. Hence, in the cases of ABM and MIRV, the qualitative improvements (and general design and capability superiority) in both offensive and defensive technologies were almost entirely a function of the peculiar way in which their developments were intertwined in the American planning process and mutually nourishing.

• Breakthroughs are constitutive of the strategy: Qualitative change in military technology becomes a constitutive element of this strategy and its administrative forms. The ideal toward which it strives is the leapfrogging of the design and conceivable vulnerabilities of the present generation by a wholly new and more perfect weapons system. Consequently, the search for greater technical perfection in each succeeding generation becomes ceaseless, since the process integrates the parallel search for ways of countering each new generation of weapons into its plans and calculations.

• Problems of stability and control: The difficulties associated with achieving stability and control over weapons technology thus become insurmountable within the institutional framework established. Dynamic change and instability are built-in features of this approach to R&D in military technology. This situation has led some defense policymakers to interpret these intrasystemic problems as systemic problems, that is, to view structural problems peculiar to the institutionalization of technological planning in military weaponry as problems inhering in the strategic interaction between the two superpowers.

• A common technological impetus projected onto one's adversary: If these problems are unmanageable within one's organizational framework and can be mistakenly ascribed to characteristics of the international system, then obviously the driving force of one's military technology can easily be attributed to the military technology and planning process of one's opponent. Thus, the symmetry of technological planning and its attendant problems are assumed to be universal.

• The breakthrough approach is self-referential as to ends: It tends to orient formulations of military strategy to technology itself and even to decouple strategy and strategic power from political objectives. By the implications of the breakthrough approach (and practically in terms of the history of American foreign policy in the postwar period), strategic power does not serve any instrumental function in foreign policy and international diplomacy and thus encourages a politically defensive or reactive foreign policy. At best, this approach promotes the search for solutions to politico-strategic problems through technology, i.e., through the design and deployment of more advanced and sophisticated weapons systems.[3] Finally, it also encourages the misinterpretation that technological stability gained by diplomatic or arms control accords is also expressed in political stability.

The United States based its strategic planning and programming upon a presumed symmetry with the Soviet Union's weapons development. Yet planners showed little concern to factor the actual Soviet strategy of weapons development and innovation into the American weapons R&D planning process. Moreover, nearly all serious analyses of Soviet behavior in developing and deploying strategic weapons systems contradict the assumption of strategic and technological symmetry.

Actually, the Soviet military R&D process seemed to be directed by what has been called a strategy of "technological incrementalism."[4] This approach to technological planning and weapons development includes the following features:

• Minimization of technological uncertainty: This approach is highlighted by a fundamentally conservative orientation toward military R&D at the strategic level. This characteristic is evidenced in the concern to minimize technological uncertainty (i.e., the probability of successful development of a technological concept or design) by keeping the complexity of new strategic weapons innovations low. American scientists often noted the ponderous, unsophisticated nature of most Soviet missiles, as well as their relatively uncomplicated guidance systems.[5]

• Generic prototype design: Another feature of this incrementalist approach is the use of existing weapons systems as generic prototypes on which to add new components or capabilities. The similarity of the Soviet SS-type ICBMs is illustrative of this tendency. In addition, the inherent conservatism of this approach dictates the use of limited deployments of one or more prototypes of a particular weapons system for field testing rather than, as in the United States, immediate deployment of large numbers of a weapons system after RDT&E. An example of Soviet conservatism was the deployment of a limited number of ABMs around Leningrad after 1963, which were subsequently dismantled (apparently because the prototype design was found faulty).[6]

• Single purpose design: Weapons systems according to this approach tend to have a single mission, and only infrequently is the mission of the system altered or multiplied by further technological development; for the most part, any new performance requirements for the next generation weapons system do not go beyond the existing "state of the art."

• Acceptance of technological inferiority: The incremental approach does not necessitate that the USSR compete with the United States or with itself in advancements in military technology. Rather, a degree of technological inferiority is conceded—although technological inferiority does not entail the acceptance of a position of overall strategic inferiority.

• Reliance on numbers and/or megatonnage: To offset any qualitative superiority of an adversary, the former Soviet Union tended to rely on a larger destructive potential in terms of megatonnage, a superior number of strategic weapons, or both. From this perspective, the Soviet development of large-yield warheads (5-25 mt.) in the early 1960s to compensate for the American qualitative and quantitative lead is quite explicable.

• Sources of breakthroughs: Qualitative changes in the Soviet strategic arsenal tended to occur either through successive incremental changes from one generation of weapons to another, which add up to a qualitative transformation, or through the appropriation of the adversary's deployed weapons systems as nongeneric prototypes for its own developments.[7] The case of MIRVs is one instance where the Soviet Union apparently followed the U.S. example. This case may also be one in which a limited and selective "action-reaction" pattern operated.[8]

• Political use of strategic power: Despite a long-term embracement of a strategy of technological incrementalism and inferiority, the USSR did not draw the conclusion that strategic power is politically impotent. That is, they did not assume a politically defensive position diplomatically or in their foreign policies. Instead, as Horelick and Rush have recounted, Soviet strategic power was frequently cashed in for political currency and served as one of the instrumentalities of Soviet foreign policy throughout the 1950s and 1960s.[9] Thus technological conservatism did not breed political inaction, but political assertiveness.

• Deterrence and defense strategy: The Soviets consistently structured their planning for military technology on the basis of a military strategy that combined deterrence and defense components. Owing partly to Russia's historical vulnerability to land incursions from the West, their traditional defense-mindedness is deeply rooted in Russian military establishment and doctrine. This tended to stimulate a basic strategic asymmetry between the United States and the USSR, since the Soviets tended not to interconnect deterrence and defense as American decision-makers and strategic planners have; i.e., increases in defenses (active and passive) by the United States were not associated with any accompanying perception of a decrease in deterrent capabilities by the Soviet Union. Thus, ABM deployment, for instance, was not viewed as destabilizing by the USSR as it was by the United States.[10]

These two highly schematized and idealized portraits of the conflicting and asymmetrical technological planning processes of the Soviet Union and the United States illuminate how their implementation affected the strategic arms race in the 1960s. The major impetus of the arms race was not the action-reaction phenomenon but rather the "technological imperative"—operating within the administrative agencies of the OSD and guided by the technological-breakthrough approach. As Herbert York has admitted from this vantage point, "Over the last thirty years we have repeatedly taken unilateral actions that have unnecessarily accelerated the rate." "Our unilateral decisions," he went on to say, "set the rate and scale for most of the individual steps in the strategic arms race."[11] Even John S. Foster was willing to concede that "in each case [of strategic weapons development], it seems to me that the Soviet Union is following the United States lead and that the United States is not reacting to the Soviet actions."[12]

Through the interaction of this technological imperative flowing from this "continuously reciprocating process" and the consequences of the McNamara twin revolutions in defense policy-making, then, the United States eventually found itself in the worst of all possible technological worlds. It was a world composed of a strategic arsenal many times more powerful than necessary, a modest ABM system strictly ancillary to its strategic offensive forces, and a dynamic arms race fueled overwhelmingly by its own R&D efforts in both offensive and defensive spheres.

If we consider the preceding themes in the context of McNamara's ABM policy, the main outlines of the critique of this policy come to the foreground.

While the category of decision carries with it the image of a decision-maker responding actively to his social situation, two basic criticisms concerning this aspect of McNamara's decisions on ABM have been made. First I argued that the basic motivations of these decisions have been largely unreflected upon in their deeper dimensions; and I tried to demonstrate that the realm of possible action and initiative for pursuing arms restraint by the United States was much broader than McNamara conceived. As a consequence of its pursuit of technological superiority and the Soviet tendency to imitate rather than initiate innovations in the realm of weapons technology, the United States spent most of the cold war as the front-runner in the strategic arms race. Thus, it had much greater latitude than the Soviet Union in showing restraint in new weapons deployments, especially in the offensive realm, as well as in exerting greater initiative in pursuing arms limitations. The "technological imperative," in combination with the normative bias of strategic deterrence, issued in McNamara's refusal to consider seriously the instrumental value of defensive systems for pursuing the political goal of national security.

The rationalizing impulse, too, had a significant impact upon McNamara's decisions on ABM and other weapons programs. The more that cost-effectiveness, systems, and operations analyses suffused the style of decision-making, the more "purposive rational action" was substituted for "symbolic communication."[13] That is, the five-year strategic forces planning program, the systematic interconnection of offensive and defensive weapons planning, and the other techniques for promoting the politics of efficiency in defense management did little to advance the political values and normative assumptions underlying the notion of national security and its pursuit. Indeed, to the degree that the issues of defense decision-making were construed as technical problems requiring information and instrumental strategies produced by scientific experts, they were removed from political debate without being politically resolved. The basic tendency, then, was to obscure genuinely political problems and to enshrine unreflectively the institutional prejudices of the strategic doctrine of the 1950s.

A further criticism I make of McNamara's ABM policy relates to his central hypothesis about the role of the action-reaction phenomenon in fueling the strategic arms race. His contention that U.S. deployment of an ABM system would force the Soviet Union to respond by strengthening its strategic retaliatory forces was highly questionable, if not patently false. Indeed, one of the key flaws of McNamara's outlook on strategic doctrine and ABM was its lack of any empirical concern for the real character of Soviet strategic thought.[14] It is more likely, given the Soviet doctrinal and developmental stress on defense, that the Russians would have reacted by deploying more ABMs or upgrading existing ones. Furthermore, McNamara's own actions in 1961 and 1967 appear to invalidate his central explanatory hypothesis. Both in 1961, when he raised U.S. strategic forces to a four-to-one superiority, and in 1967, when he once again multiplied American offensive might through the introduction of MIRVs into the U.S. strategic arsenal, the level of American response was unnecessary and inordinately high, even if a measure of prudence dictated some reaction.

Perhaps a better and more charitable way to understand McNamara's action-reaction proposition is to see it less as an explanatory hypothesis than as a debating tool in domestic politics and a diplomatic tool in international affairs. To measure the degree McNamara and the scientists of the finite containment school recognized the true functions of their hypothesis is conjectural; but, skilled bureaucratic politicians that they were, it must be assumed that their awareness was not insubstantial. Within internal debate of governmental policy, whatever the forum, the hypothesis that an action-reaction pattern characterized the arms race served as a strong strategic argument against weapons innovation in the defensive realm and, to a lesser extent, for restraint in all technological innovations in America's strategic arsenal.[15] When allied with the other key tenets of McNamara's strategic vision, specifically, adequacy in offensive capabilities and nuclear sufficiency at the assured-destruction level, this hypothesis seemed to possess an irresistible logic. Its persuasiveness is evidenced by the number of important senatorial figures who assimilated it into their cases against ABM deployment and expansion in the 1969–1970 ABM congressional debate.

In the international realm, particularly in U.S.-Soviet relations on strategic and arms control matters, the action-reaction pattern functioned as a partly coercive, partly educational device. Its coercive facet lay in the inferences it tried to force upon the Soviet Union; that is, it seemed to invite Soviet acceptance of the following logic: just as you will have to react to our innovations in an equalizing way, we too will have to respond to your strategic challenges in a compensatory manner. In the case of ABM, the United States first sought to encourage Soviet restraint by a policy of postponement,[16] and then, when the USSR deployed a BMD anyway, the United States multiplied its strategic offensive forces in order to punish the Soviet Union and to show its leaders that innovation in the defensive realm would be futile.

In this latter respect, McNamara was endeavoring to "educate" the Russians in the higher calculus of strategic thought—

American style. During the Kennedy administration, American defense officials undertook the task of schooling the Russians in the requirements of a safe and secure second-strike force. Throughout these years, the Soviets did little to promote the readiness of their ICBM forces, keeping their warheads as much as fifty miles from their missile sites during the Cuban missile crisis. In addition, they lacked even the crudest safety devices and procedures for minimizing the dangers of accidental firing or missile malfunctioning.[17] Likewise, from 1964 onward, the Johnson administration strove to "educate" Soviet strategic planners in the requirements of deterrence strategy.

The urgency of this pedagogical exercise also stemmed from the developing attitude held by McNamara as well as influential politicians and scientists of the Kennedy-Johnson administration that the arms race must be braked and that ABM had become a veritable symbol of the arms race. Consequently, if the Soviet Union did not share America's strategic outlook and doctrinal bias favoring the offense, then it must be taught (or coerced) to abandon its defense strategy and programmatic emphases and embrace ours. These efforts, carried out with such stridency by the Johnson-McNamara defense establishment and with almost equal, but unwitting, determination by Nixon and Laird, reached fruition in the success of the SALT I negotiations. By placing ABM on so high a diplomatic level and interpreting its significance in terms of overall U.S.-Soviet relations in the future, the United States apparently succeeded in bypassing the Soviet defense bureaucracy, with its inherited traditional and doctrinal biases, and in engaging the Soviets at the highest political level, where the issue of ABM was viewed more in the currency of superpower bilateral relations and economic trade.[18]

Implicated in this political strategy of coercive education were the scientists who helped shape McNamara's strategic vision and the politicians who followed his recommendations. The role of the American technological planning process also was profound. From the perspective of the alternative interpretation of the prime stimulus of the strategic arms race offered here, it should be clear that the freezing of ABM deployment and the blocking of innovation in the defensive realm—the two major achievements of the

SALT I agreements—helped resolve an intrasystemic control problem of the weapons technology planning process in the United States.

ABM was born of the hope for an absolute counter-weapon to the guided missile. It met its demise out of a fundamental conviction held by a liberal administration and its scientific aides that some control had to be imposed upon the arms race. Identified as the symbol of the arms race and harbinger of a new round of strategic arms escalation, its deployment was resisted with a sense of determination and single-mindedness seldom exhibited by American leaders in the realm of strategic weapons innovation. Yet forces operating at a subterranean level within the scientific establishment and in domestic politics were conspiring to frustrate these efforts. Compounding these developments were actions within the Defense Department that were making ABM and MIRV so technically and politically attractive that further resistance became futile.

President Johnson and Secretary McNamara failed to reap the rewards of their campaign. But their heritage was felt by the succeeding administration. Indeed, in the strange world of twentieth-century American politics, it appeared at times that President Nixon and his staff were acting as unwitting instruments of a design largely constructed by Johnson, McNamara, and the finite containment school. However crude the tactics used, Nixon appeared to be carrying on the efforts begun by the two previous administrations to "educate" the Russians on the niceties of American strategic doctrine. As SALT I testified, the Russians had learned, and the fruits of that instruction were bestowed upon the Nixon administration.

The McNamara legacy might have been a lasting one but for the circumstances that triggered the second phase of antiballistic missile controversy in the United States. The conditions leading to the resurrection of ballistic missile defense were precipitated by, among other things, the militantly anticommunist cold war attitudes of Ronald Reagan and key scientists and policy advisers in his administration, who entertained utopian dreams of an impregnable shield against an inflated Soviet threat. With the onset of this new debate, which traversed four presidential administrations and nearly twenty years, forces buried deep in the landscape of twentieth-century politics and political culture took shape and eroded the elements comprising the McNamara heritage. These influences have made the deployment of a limited NMD system by the United States by 2004 or 2005 take on the force of a seeming political inevitability.

For ten years, the political and diplomatic solution enshrined in the 1972 ABM accord seemed to hold in check impulses to reconsider innovation in the realm of defense, redirecting American and Soviet military rivalry into protracted arms negotiations and a continuing arms race in the offensive realm. Although the United States did deploy an ABM complex in the early seventies, the weight of the McNamara heritage and the domestic political climate in the United States favored the institutionalization of the ABM control regime. Having closed off innovation in the defensive realm, BMD research and development were relegated to the minor role of assisting in the technological advance of offensive military technology and hedging U.S. bets in the event the Soviets decided to break out of the ABM Treaty.

With the return of a Republican Party standard bearer to the White House, the period from 1983–1992 was marked by the uncertain quest for a strategic alternative to MAD amidst a decisive turning point in U.S.-Soviet relations. It was also characterized by an almost restless and unceasing search by ABM supporters to discover and carve out a mission for defensive technology. In this decade a major American defense buildup in response to perceived Soviet military superiority was punctuated by the implosion of the Soviet Union and the unraveling of its hegemony over client nations within its sphere of influence. Though initially imagined as a utopian scheme to establish a perfect, leakproof shield against enemy ICBMs, the Reagan administration's hope for a system offering assured survival was eventually transformed during Reagan's second term into a mission that would merely complement and reinforce nuclear deterrence through a mix of offensive and defensive weapons. With the end of the cold war, the George H.W. Bush administration converted the mounting political pressures supporting the deployment of some kind of missile defense into a more limited, but expedient, plan to use space-based interceptors to neutralize the threat posed by so-called rogue nations and accidental ICBM launches.

The return of a Democratic administration to the White House in 1993 saw a loosening of the checks on those procedures and norms sedimented into the ABM Treaty regime and the arms agreements that followed. A combination of Democratic Party instrumentalism and accommodationism influenced by the Clinton presidential style and the growing influence of a New Democrat philosophy over the party itself had their effect upon the second ABM debate. Coupled with increasing Republican ideological purism manifested in that party's victory in the 1994 mid-term congressional elections, these attitudes and orientations prompted the Clinton White House to undertake a variety of political feints and dodges that succeeded in keeping a deployment decision at bay while continuing the funding, development, and testing of a modestly scaled defense system. Like Lyndon Johnson and Robert McNamara in the late sixties, President Clinton and Defense Secretary Cohen could find prudential and expedient reasons for a limited NMD system if political exigencies overwhelmed their capacities to resist the campaign demanding deployment.

With no mainstream party opposition at the national political center strong enough to block a deployment decision, the election of George W. Bush to the presidency and the assumption of hardliners and ideological conservatives within the national security establishment to positions of authority and influence tolled the death knell of the old arms control regime. These events also precipitated the beginning of the restructuring of the world system by an America triumphant and the unfolding of a delimited mission for BMD in a new framework dominated by the dialectic of isolationism and unilateralism. In the face of this turn in international and military policymaking, mounting alarm from America's European allies could be discerned as the Bush foreign and military team withdrew from meetings organized around standing problems requiring multinational and even global action. In areas of concern to key European allies, including initiatives on global warming, racism, land-mine disposal, and biological weapons, Bush foreign policy and military officials stood aside, making concerted allied action impossible.[19] In other areas, among them missile defense, the United States forged ahead on an independent path with only token consultation with, and pro forma participation by, NATO allied leaders.

Assessing these developments as part of a larger framework of foreign and military policymaking, especially as it relates to the BMD issues, it appears that the character of the imperative driving BMD decisions has changed. If a technological imperative operates in this second phase of the missile defense controversy, unfolding since Reagan's Star Wars speech, it resides only in the almost relentless drive by rising political forces to compel deployment of an anti-missile system, no matter how shifting or suspect or merely expedient the rationale for such action. In a more fundamental sense, however, the technological imperative propelling ballistic missile defense decisions has become a political imperative, even a cultural imperative embedded deeply in our political culture.

At one level, the political forces arrayed against technological restraint and international multilateralism have ushered in a seeming technological enthusiasm and global unilateralism regarding ballistic missile defense. With the aid of greater distance, objectivity, and documentation, future historians and political analysts will carefully reconstruct the sequence of critical events, meetings, and decisions by presidents and high-level officeholders that contributed to this latest turn in American national policy. From hindsight, such a political history will no doubt illuminate how this technological *cum* political imperative seemed both inevitable and reversible in light of structural realities and contingent actions.

Such future explanations will be incomplete without a profound appreciation of the significant cultural variables influencing and shaping the context and field of political action. I wish to argue that that cultural dimension lies deep in the origins of the American Republic and in the unfolding of a powerful and longstanding tradition of thought in American foreign and military policy. I wish further to argue that this tradition allows us to understand the peculiar interplay of isolationism and unilateralism that has characterized the foreign and military actions of the Bush administration in its first year in office. Drawing upon the subtle treatments by Ernest Tuveson and Frances FitzGerald of the major components of this foreign and military heritage, I seek to enumerate the key elements of this tradition and connect their main lines to the apparent cultural imperative fueling BMD decisions in the George W. Bush (and Ronald Reagan) administration.

In his classic study, *Redeemer Nation*, Ernest Tuveson traces the religious origins of the core idea in American foreign policy that the United States has a redemptive mission in the world.[20] While cognizant of the *real politique* strains in American foreign policymaking, Tuveson underscores the powerful role of America's peculiarly Protestant (especially Calvinist) religious and cultural foundations in molding the contours of this country's view of Europe and the world. He also highlights the special place of America in a narrative of millennial design stemming from a literalist interpretation of apocalyptic prophecies in the Bible. In *Cities on a Hill* and *Way out There in the Blue*, Frances FitzGerald has excavated similar religio-cultural ground to illuminate the powerful hold that this tradition has had upon a segment of the leadership and constituency of the Republican Party based in the American Midwest and mobilized by Senator Robert Taft.[21]

The defining characteristics of this millennial tradition help to clarify the cultural foundations of the Ronald Reagan and George W. Bush decisions in international military policy and in particular the urgency evidenced in both administrations to deploy a missile defense system. Perhaps the most salient elements comprising this foreign and military worldview are these:

• Americans as a chosen people: In the national mythology informing America's founding leaders and running through the colonial and the early Republic's celebrated preachers, poets, and theologians, an emphasis on the parallels between the Hebrew people and Americans, as both chosen by God to fulfill his millennial design for the world, is readily apparent.[22] This idea of being chosen runs like a thread from the Jews to early Christianity to the Protestant reformers to Germany and England. It then settles into American political culture through this national mythological discourse that increasingly takes expression in its view of the world (especially Europe), its role in that international realm, and the principles and actions that infuse this divinely ordained role. As early as 1630, John Winthrop captured this religious notion in his famous sermon, claiming that "we shall be a City upon a Hill, the eyes of all the world . . . upon us."[23]

• America as a redeemer nation: As a chosen people and instrument of God's will, America is called upon to become a redemptive force in the world, an exemplar and a beacon of hope, as well as a crusader wielding the sword of justice and Godly vengeance upon demonic evil in the world. In Tuveson's words, "Providence or history has put a special responsibility on the American people to spread the blessing of liberty, democracy, and equality to others throughout the earth, and to defeat, if necessary by force, the sinister powers of darkness."[24] At the same time, this role is a voluntary responsibility that America may either willfully choose to embrace by shouldering or reject by succumbing to worldliness and the temptations of power, self-interest, and sinfulness. Whether expressed in the language of the good doctor or the righteous preacher, American policy statements about global issues on trade, the environment, and international security have taken on a distinctly religious, almost sermonizing tone. In these pronouncements, Bush spokespeople seek to convince allies and former adversaries alike that the Bush doctrine is right for America and therefore right for the rest of world.

• The domestic imperative of moral and spiritual reformation: To be a true world savior and moral exemplar, America must put its domestic house in order. Righteous action on the international front requires exemplary moral and spiritual action in the domestic arena that transforms the nation into a paragon for emulation by other nations. Sometimes this moral rearmament in the domestic arena takes the form of crusades against evil agencies in our midst[25]; at other times, it is expressed in moral binges against immoral practices[26]; it may also erupt as a form of ideological witch-hunting targeted at supposed internal sources of international setbacks and failures in moralistic foreign policy actions.[27] In whatever guise, these spirited mobilization campaigns often exact high costs on the rights of individuals, particularly on the personal and political freedoms of ethnic minorities and political dissidents. The danger internationally is that this impulse often transforms into moralism in foreign policy and national security policy, licensing violence and punitive military action when high-minded moral preaching fails.

• Europe as a bastion of worldliness, sinfulness, and evil: As the dualism of good and evil played itself out in world history, American elites influenced by this apocalyptic-millennial narrative shortly came to see Europe as a symbol of Old World secularism, worldly pride, and humanist excess juxtaposed against the self-image of America as an emblem of New World innocence, goodness, and righteousness. The ending of the cold war and the collapse of godless communism have prompted a search for new enemies. The political construction of renegade or rogue nations and terrorist groups standing in need of redemption—or obliteration—has been supplemented by the reactivation and expression of older, more traditional perspectives on Europe derived from early American images and narratives.[28]

• Isolationism and unilateralism: Given its divinely ordained mission, American foreign policy oscillates between isolationism and internationalism. But the supposed poles of isolationism and unilateralism really form a hidden harmony. That is, the poles of this international orientation in this interplay are not antithetical or contradictory but complementary, yoked at more subterranean levels in American political culture.[29] As both moral exemplar and world savior, American foreign and military policy must guard against the temptations of compromise with and accommodation of worldly powers to, the dictates of *real politique*. The impulse to retreat from the world and its unwanted political entanglements and the quest to organize the world according to a particular American design or blueprint, thus, are thoroughly compatible. Precisely at a time when the Bush-Powell foreign policy apparatus and the Rumsfeld defense team are pulling back from past multilateral commitments incurred during the Clinton years, a go-it-alone, unilateral bent in foreign relations and military policy—underlined by missile defense—is apparent. Right-wing columnist Charles Krauthammer recently reflected on the dawning era of "unipolarity" in twenty-first century international politics, the global role and responsibilities of the United States in this unique period in history, and the meaning and driving intent of the Bush doctrine and its latest expression in the missile defense controversy. He tersely summed up the purposes of unilateralism in characteristically apocalyptic-millennial verbiage by saying: "we are not just any hegmon . . . [we] run a uniquely benign imperium."[30]

• Imperial isolationism and military action at a distance: Evangelical Protestantism became sedimented in the American Midwest, shaping a world view among this provincial core of heartland Republicans typed by Charles and Mary Beard as "imperial isolationism" or "unilateral imperialism."[31] America's inclination to build a fortress against Old World decadence and nonwestern despotism and inscrutability and its salvic need to intervene in righteous causes gave rise to a strategy of exerting military power at a distance. As a result, midwestern Republicans abjured the buildup and exercise of armed power on land, preferring sea and air power. The latter forms—upgraded and modernized with the advent of missiles and nuclear weaponry—allowed for the projection of American might while Fortress America remained isolated and insulated from distant battlegrounds.[32] Seen in this light, the visions of the electronic battlefield, of futuristic Nintendo wars, the militarization of space glimpsed in the Gulf War, and the computer graphic presentations of Reagan's Star Wars and George W. Bush's ground-based to space-based multi-tiered NMD systems come across as only the latest incarnations of these ideological tendencies emanating from the cultural seedbed of evangelical Republicanism.

•Utopian-millenarian dreams and the neurotic quest for absolute security: Filtered through the lens of political cynicism, the apparent moral uprightness of this international and military orientation strikes one as merely a cloak for imperialistic ambitions driven by crass economic motives and an exceedingly narrow conception of national interest. One need not deny the powerful economic motives shaping corporate-biased national policy in the United States, including the role of defense contractors whose headquarters and assembly plants are strategically positioned to affect the geography and electoral calculus of national—and especially presidential—politics. But one must not overlook the language in which these politics are articulated or the rhetorical battles fought over them.[33]

The political vocabulary of the world vision underpinning Ronald Reagan's SDI program and George W. Bush's NMD system draws heavily from cultural foundations anchored in a uto-pian-millenarian stream of Western religion and theological dis-course. The increasingly powerful influence of the Christian right on the political center and on the ideological substance of the Republican Party reinforces the role played by religion in main-stream U.S. politics and the rhetoric in which its policy initiatives in the domestic and international arena are transacted and negoti-ated.[34] With the war on terrorism declared in the wake of the as-saults on the World Trade Center and the Pentagon, this cultural undertow is likely to become even more powerful rhetorically and materially.

Ironically, if the telos of the utopian-millenarian impulses informing the politics of the latest missile defense controversy were followed and charted, it would appear that its endpoint takes the form of an almost neurotic pursuit of absolute security militarily. For even as Defense Secretary Rumsfeld is scaling back U.S. na-tional strategy to establish force levels adequate to fight only one major war and retooling defense policy to target terrorism glo-bally, the Bush administration is aggressively moving to capitalize on America's solitary superpower status and aspiring to achieve absolute security as a military bulwark. Just as psychiatrists have observed that the quest for absolute safety and a risk-free life is the mark of a particular style of the neurotic personality,[35] so too might it be argued that the pursuit of an analogous goal globally—even by a superpower in a world of stark inequalities of power, wealth, and natural and human resources—constitutes a similar chimera or folly.

No matter how important military technology and other as-sets are to providing some measure of national defense, the route to national security can never be reduced to the achievement of a particular form of military technology or even a mix of technolo-gies. A solution to these problems of national security and inter-national peace can only come from recognizing that the gross inequalities limned above must be overcome by redistributive poli-cies at the global level before the perpetuation of regional and international conflict can be drastically undercut or eliminated at its source. In a world fraught with dangerous, potentially cata-clysmic possibilities from nuclear proliferation, global warming, overpopulation, and ecological scarcity, this daunting task is the central challenge in the new millennium for an enlightened America: to temper its own moralistic-religious excesses and face the community of nations not as obstacles to a *pax America* but as partners in a new multicultural discourse seeking common ground and a collective future free of such global ills.

Certainly, if the genuine intentions and motivations of political leaders and national security advisers backing national missile defenses were aimed at a more pacific and mutually secure world, then BMD could have a major place in diminishing the still huge strategic arsenals of major nuclear powers and supporting further dramatic cutbacks in these instruments of terror and destruction. National missile defense coupled with deep cuts in nuclear weapons could contribute to the foundations of positive peace and international comity.[36] Given its double-edged possibilities, ballistic missile defense has remained, on the one hand, a potential strategic add-on to augment deterrence, a measure of protection for urban populations, and a possible new means to extend American power and hegemony into space. On the other, it has existed as a potential avenue to rechannel the awesome dynamism of the strategic arms race and, ultimately, to rid the world of the hydra-headed nature of the threat posed by nuclear—and thermonuclear—offensive weapons.

The latest politics of missile defense do not provide a strong basis for optimism that the conditions for the realization of this alternate strategy and vision will congeal soon, if ever. But what is self-evident is that a strategic agenda driven by a compulsion to eliminate all potential risks and to extend military reach to the heavens will only exacerbate the problems of international stability. Such an agenda is also likely to set in motion powerful tendencies toward fueling new, more vigorous strategic arms races. Moreover, looking back at the history of arms control since 1972 should give pause to those who advocate isolationist-unilateralist withdrawal from international control regimes. The most likely consequence of dismantling existing frameworks of international control and prohibition will be the erosion of hard-won norms and practices that were slow in being institutionalized and will not easily be restored in an environment where the global hegemon exercises a form of isolationist unilateralism its chief political proponents call "a la carte multinationalism." It is far better to regard these international norms and procedures as valuable prizes not to be cast aside lightly.

Three decades after its institutionalization in the ABM Treaty, the McNamara heritage in ballistic missile defense and arms control may seem little more than a historical curiosity or anachronism. In retrospect, its contradictory elements clearly contributed to its political undoing. Yet the progressive cultural and political forces in the sixties that shaped the political context prompting Secretary McNamara to embrace finite deterrence and an arms control strategy are a reminder of the open-endedness of politics and history. Contrary to the ideologists promoting a grand celebration of the victory of global corporate capitalism and American consumer culture, the End of History has not been reached.[37] If such a simplistic optimism is not appropriate, then neither is political cynicism, fatalism, or terrorism. Instead, sober recognition of how far American politics and culture must be transformed in this post-cold-war era, buoyed by the eruption of new social movements resisting top-down globalization, local/global ecological devastation, and the militarization of space, must be the starting point for any reasonable foundation for critical policy diagnosis, committed political action, and hope in the new millennium.

NOTES

INTRODUCTION

1. Alexis de Tocqueville, *Democracy in America*, ed. Richard Heffner (New York: New American Library, 1991). My colleague Herbert G. Reid first brought this to my attention in several of his scholarly articles on the politics of time.

2. The relevant works here are Dawson and William Lucas, *Organizational Politics in Defense* (Pittsburgh, 1975); Benson Adams, "McNamara's ABM Policy, 1961-1967," *Orbis* 12 (Spring 1968): 200-225; Adams, *Ballistic Missile Defense* (New York, 1971); Herbert York, *Race to Oblivion: A Participant's View of the Arms Race* (New York, 1970); and Anne Hessing Cahn, *Eggheads and Warheads: Scientists and the ABM* (Cambridge, Mass., 1971).

3. Schelling, *Arms and Influence* (New Haven, Conn., 1966), p. 224 and passim; York, *Race to Oblivion*, p. 180; Lapp, *Arms beyond Doubt: The Tyranny of Weapons Technology* (New York, 1970), p. 31.

4. This counterargument has been offered by Alain Enthoven and K. Wayne Smith, *How Much Is Enough? Shaping the Defense Program, 1961-1969* (New York, 1971), pp. 34-35, and Harvey M. Sapolsky, *The Polaris System Development: Bureaucratic and Programmatic Success in Government* (Cambridge, Mass., 1972), pp. 235-36.

5. Gintis, "Alienation and Power," *Review of Radical Political Economics* 4 (Fall 1972): 19.

6. For further discussion of ABM systems functions and components, see William Schneider, Jr., "Missile Defense Systems: Past, Present, and Future," in *Why ABM? Policy Issues in the Missile Defense Controversy*, ed. Johan J. Holst and William Schneider, Jr. (New York, 1969), pp. 3-13.

7. Most of these more exotic ABM concepts were originally explored at the R&D stages by ARPA's Project GLIPAR and quickly abandoned because they were not feasible. It wasn't until the early eighties that these "blue skies" ideas gained new currency and were championed by Edward Teller at the Lawrence Livermore National Laboratory. As chapter 9 reveals, these ideas contributed to Ronald Reagan's Strategic Defense Initiative.

8. Robert Gilpin, *American Scientists and Nuclear Weapons Policy* (Princeton, N.J., 1962), pp. 102-7.

9. See his remarks in *The Essence of Security* (New York, 1968), pp. 65, 116, passim; also exemplary of this position was the substance of one of the conclusions generally accepted by the participants at the Pugwash Symposium held in Copenhagen, Denmark, in 1969 on the implications of ABM systems: "Fears were expressed . . . that Man may not be able to control the rapid advances made in technology, and ABM deployment was cited as a glaring example of the instability of technology itself. Technology makes new weapons available; because they are available political pressures build up within states for their acquisition; political leaders succumb to this pressure and invent policies to justify the acquisition of the weapons. Once the weapons are acquired, strong pressures develop for large-scale deployment, even in the absence of sensible strategic arguments." See C. F. Barnaby and A. Boserup, eds., *Implications of Anti-Ballistic Missile Systems* (New York, 1969), p. 229.

10. See Wiesner's essay, "Hope for GCD?" *Bulletin of the Atomic Scientists* 24 (January 1968): 13. See also Wiesner, "The Case against ABM," *Anti-Ballistic Missile: Yes or No?* (New York, 1968), p. 13.

11. Brennan's statements on the value of active defense measures include: *Post-Deployment Policy Issues in Ballistic Missile Defense: Two Views*, Adelphi Paper no. 43, The Institute for Strategic Studies (London, November l967); "The Case for Missile Defense," *Foreign Affairs* 47 (April l969): 433-48; "The Case for Population Defense," in *Why ABM?*, ed. Holst and Schneider, pp. 91-118; and "Strategic Forum: The SALT Agreements," *Survival* 14 (September/October 1972): 216-19.

12. Seymour Martin Lipset, *The First New Nation: The United States in Historical and Comparative Perspective* (New York: Basic Books, Inc., 1963); Henry Nash Smith, *Virgin Land: The American West as Symbol and Myth* (Boston: Harvard Univ. Press, 1971); David Potter, *People of Plenty: Economic Abundance and American Character* (Chicago: Univ. of Chicago Press, 1958); and Kenneth M. Stampp, *The Peculiar Institution: Slavery in the Ante-Bellum South* (New York: Vintage Books, 1989).

13. Ernest Lee Tuveson, *Redeemer Nation: The Idea of America's Millennial Role* (Chicago: Univ. of Chicago Press, 1968).

14. Charles and Mary Beard, *America at Midpassage—Vol. I* (New York: The Macmillan Company, 1939).

CHAPTER 1

1. *TVA and the Grassroots* (Berkeley, Calif., 1949).

2. This rendering, I feel, fairly mirrors Selznick's interpretation, although some of the concepts are derived from Dawson and Lucas, *Organizational Politics in Defense*.

3. Huntington's *The Common Defense* (New York, 1961) has come closest to performing this historical-analytical task. Also relevant here is Frank Borklund's *The Department of Defense* (New York, 1964).

4. Based upon extensive interviews among key political figures in the Eisenhower administration, Glenn Snyder has conclusively demonstrated that the president's role in shaping the general contours of the New Look policy was paramount. Among the personal characteristics and political convictions that inclined Eisenhower in the direction of the New Look approach were his fiscal conservatism, his sensitivity to the potential hazards to the domestic economy stemming from excessive military spending, and his intense dislike for interservice politicking in all its forms. For an account of the strategic, political, and economic sources giving rise to the New Look, see Snyder, "The 'New Look' of 1953," in *Strategy, Politics, and Defense Budgets*, ed. Warner R. Schilling, Paul Y. Hammond, and Glenn H. Snyder (New York, 1962), passim.

5. Huntington, *The Common Defense*, p. 65.

6. Armacost, *The Politics of Weapons Innovation* (New York, 1969), p. 267.

7. Huntington, *The Common Defense*, p. 378.

8. Armacost, *The Politics of Weapons Innovation*, p. 16.

9. For a detailed case study of the B-36 dispute, see Paul Y. Hammond, "Super-carriers and B-36 Bombers: Appropriations, Strategy, and Politics," in *American Civil-Military Decisions: A Book of Case Studies*, ed. Harold Stein (University City, Ala., 1963), pp. 465-567.

10. Enthoven and Smith, *How Much Is Enough?*, pp. 13-14.

11. Dawson and Lucas, *Organizational Politics of Defense*, pp. 14, 21.

12. York, *Race to Oblivion*, p. 214.

13. Michael Armacost concurs in this judgment (see *The Politics of Weapons Innovation*, pp. 271-72), but any frequent reader of the per-

tinent congressional testimony would quickly reach a similar conclusion.

14. Dawson and Lucas, *Organizational Politics of Defense*, chapt. 4.

15. Armacost; *The Politics of Weapons Innovation*, p. 290.

CHAPTER 2

1. U.S., Congress, House, Committee on Armed Services, *Investigation of National Defense Missiles, Hearings before the Committee on Armed Services*, 85th Cong., 2d sess., 1958, pp. 4197, 4196 (hereafter referred to as *Investigation of National Defense Missiles*).

2. "What We Have Learned from V-2 Firings," *Aviation Week* (November 26, 1951), p. 23; "G.E. Reveals Hermes Missile Milestones," *Aviation Week* (March 8, 1954), pp. 26-32; David Anderton, "Effective ICBM Defense Possible under State of Art," *Aviation Week* (April 9, 1954), p. 44; U.S., Congress, Senate, Subcommittee on Preparedness Investigation of the Committee on Armed Services, *United States Guided Missile Programs*, by Charles Donnelly, 86th Cong., 1st sess., 1959, pp. 1-9.

3. *Anti-Ballistic Missile Defense* (Washington, D.C., 1965), p. 59.

4. On the history of Nike-Zeus, see John G. Zierdt, "Nike-Zeus: Our Developing Missile Killer," *Army Information Digest* (December 1960), pp. 5-6, and "Nike-Zeus: Seventeen Years of Systems Growth," *Flight International* (August 2, 1962), pp. 165-70.

5. Armacost, *The Politics of Weapons Innovation*, pp. 37-42.

6. Ibid., p. 44; James A. Gavin, *War and Peace in the Space Age* (New York, 1958), p. 137.

7. Armacost, *The Politics of Weapons Innovation*, pp. 117-20; U.S., Congress, House, Committee on Government Operations, *Organization and Management of Missile Programs, Hearings before the Committee on Government Operations*, 86th Cong., 1st sess., pp. 746-48.

8. *Organization and Management of Missile Programs*, p. 748.

9. Armacost, *The Politics of Weapons Innovation*, p. 266.

10. Ibid., pp. 121-28, 172-78.

11. U.S., Congress, Senate, Committee on Appropriations, *Department of Defense Appropriations for Fiscal 1958, Hearings before a Subcommittee of the Committee on Appropriations*, 85th Cong., 1st sess., 1957, p. 878 (hereafter referred to as *DOD Appropriations for Fiscal 1958)*; Dawson, "Nuclear Proliferation and the Politics of ABM," p. 5; from Major General Dwight Beach's testimony, U.S., Congress, House, Committee on Science and Astronautics, *Missile Development and the Space Sciences, Hearings before the Committee on Science and Astronautics*, 86th Cong., 1st sess., 1959, pp. 239ff (hereafter referred to as *Missile Development and the Space Sciences)*; Senate, *DOD Appropriations for Fiscal 1958*, p. 890.

12. U.S., Congress, House, Committee on Appropriations, *Department of Defense Appropriations for Fiscal 1960, Hearings before a Subcommittee of the Committee on Appropriations*, 86th Cong., 1st sess., 1959, 1:311 (hereafter referred to as *DOD Appropriations for Fiscal 1960)*; *Investigation of National Defense Missiles*, p. 4216.

13. U.S., Congress, Senate, Committee on Armed Services, *Study of Airpower, Hearings before the Subcommittee on the Air Force of the Committee on Armed Services*, 84th Cong., 2d sess., 1956, p. 711.

14. "First Details of Boeing GAPA Project," *Aviation Week* (February 2, 1953), pp. 32-35; Ernest Schwiebert, *A History of U.S. Air Force Ballistic Missiles* (New York, 1965), esp. pp. 151-53.

15. On the nature, scope, and purpose of Project Wizard, see the

testimony of General Putt, *Investigation of National Defense Missiles,* pp. 4777-91, 4800-4804; ibid., pp. 4799, 4798.

16. Ibid., p. 4802.

17. Stated by Secretary of the Air Force Donald Quarles in U.S., Congress, Senate, Committee on Appropriations, *Department of Defense Appropriations for Fiscal 1959, Hearings before a Subcommittee of the Committee on Appropriations,* 85th Cong., 2d sess., 1958, 1:299.

18. "Wizard Reported Pushed as Top Defense Missile," *Wall Street Journal,* October 22, 1957; testimony by Richard Horner, assistant secretary of the air force, in House, *DOD Appropriations for Fiscal 1960,* 6:165-70.

19. Disclosed and summarized by Jack Raymond, "Air Force Urges Joint Chiefs Ban Army Missile Bid," *New York Times,* November 21, 1957, pp. 1, 8.

20. James Baar, "Talos Turns Triple Navy Threat: Anti-Air, Bombardment, and AICBM," *Missiles and Rockets* (September 21, 1959), p. 24.

21. Cited by Armacost, *The Politics of Weapons Innovation,* p. 38, from Walter Millis, ed., *The Forrestal Diaries* (New York, 1951), p. 392.

22. Maxwell Taylor, *The Uncertain Trumpet* (New York, 1959), p. 168; Huntington, *The Common Defense,* p. 423; Armacost, *The Politics of Weapons Innovation,* pp. 64-71, 107-10; for a lucid and thorough case study of the navy's success in winning approval of the Polaris system, see Harvey M. Sapolsky's work, *The Polaris System Development* (Cambridge, Mass., 1972).

23. The basic source for the background and history of defense reorganization in response to missile technology is *Organization and Management of Missile Programs;* see also Armacost, *The Politics of Weapons Innovation,* pp. 219-49, passim. Unless otherwise noted, it is from the former document that this outline is drawn.

24. *United States Guided Missile Programs,* p. 42; Armacost, *The Politics of Weapons Innovation,* pp. 72, 234.

25. *Organization and Management of Missile Programs,* p. 43.

26. Factors suggested by Armacost, *The Politics of Weapons Innovation,* pp. 226-27.

27. *Organization and Management of Missile Programs,* p. 19.

28. U.S., Congress, House, *Communication from the President on Proposed Additional Authority for the Department of Defense, H. Doc., 298,* 85th Cong., 2d sess., 1958; U.S., Congress, House, Committee on Appropriations, *Department of Defense Appropriations for Fiscal 1961, Hearings before a Subcommittee of the Committee on Appropriations,* 86th Cong., 2d sess., 1960, 6:139 (hereafter referred to as *DOD Appropriations for Fiscal 1961*).

29. *DOD Appropriations for Fiscal 1961,* pp. 139-40.

30. Ibid., p. 147.

CHAPTER 3

1. See William Kaufmann, *The McNamara Strategy* (New York, 1964), and Enthoven and Smith, *How Much Is Enough?,* p. 31 and passim.

2. On these issues, see Armacost, *The Politics of Weapons Innovation,* pp. 222, 224-49, and two pertinent congressional hearings: U.S., Congress, Senate, Committee on Aeronautical and Space Sciences, *Transfer of Von Braun Team to NASA, Hearings before the NASA Authorization Subcommittee of the Committee on Aeronautical and*

Space Sciences, 86th Cong., 2d sess., 1960; and U.S., Congress, House, Committee on Government Operations, *Air Force Ballistic Missile Management, Hearings before the Committee on Government Operations,* 87th Cong., 1st sess., 1961.

3. Discussed by William D. Phelan, "The 'Complex' Society Marches On," *Ripon Forum* 5 (January 1969):9-21, esp. 11-14; and Seymour Melman, *Pentagon Capitalism* (New York, 1970), pp. 11-14.

4. "Defense management" was coined by Dawson and Lucas in *Organizational Politics of Defense.*

5. Arthur Schlesinger, Jr., *A Thousand Days* (New York, 1965), pp. 291, 294. For an insightful account of McNamara's years at Harvard and Ford Motor Company, see Henry L. Trewhitt's *McNamara: His Ordeal in the Pentagon* (New York, 1971), pp. 26-56.

6. W. W. Kaufmann, *The McNamara Strategy,* p. 171.

7. Melman, *Pentagon Capitalism,* p. 13. For a copious analysis and pointed critique of systems analysis as it operated in those various societal spheres, see Ida Hoos, *Systems Analysis in Public Policy: A Critique* (Los Angeles, 1972).

8. See Bernard Brodie, "Strategy Wears a Dollar Sign," *Strategy in the Missile Age* (Princeton, N.J., 1959), pp. 358-89, and Schelling, *The Strategy of Conflict.*

9. Robert Art, *The TFX Controversy: McNamara and the Military* (Boston, 1968), p. 158.

10. For an introduction to PPBS in theory and practice, see Charles J. Hitch and Roland N. McKean, *The Economics of Defense in the Nuclear Age* (Cambridge, Mass., 1963), and U.S., Congress, Senate, National Security and International Operations Subcommittee of the Committee on Government Operations, *Planning-Programming-Budgeting: Defense Analysis: Two Examples,* S. Res. 24, 91st Cong., 1st sess., 1969.

11. Art, *The TFX Controversy,* p. 31.

12. Brodie, *Strategy in the Missile Age,* p. 384.

13. In a sense, this decision is one of the real anomalies of the missile gap controversy and its legacy which no recent analyst on this subject has adequately resolved. David Halberstam has offered one answer in "The Programming of Robert McNamara," *Harper's Magazine* (February 1971), p. 54.

14. The text of this speech appears in the *New York Times,* June 17, 1962, p. 26.

15. On the assumptions, character, and implications of counterforce strategy, see the work of one of its major proponents: Schelling, *Arms and Influence* (New Haven, Conn., 1966), esp. pp. 24-26, 190-92, which refer specifically to McNamara's Ann Arbor speech.

16. McNamara's Annual Posture Statement, U.S., Congress, House, Committee on Appropriations, *Department of Defense Appropriations for Fiscal 1965, Hearings before a Subcommittee of the Committee on Appropriations,* 88th Cong., 2d sess., 4:27 (hereafter referred to as *DOD Appropriations for Fiscal 1965*).

17. In McNamara's words, the latter theory "would enable us, should we strike first, to so reduce Soviet retaliatory power that the damage it could do to the U.S. population and industry would be brought down to an 'acceptable' level, whatever that might be." Ibid., pp. 26, 27.

18. Statement by Robert McNamara in U.S., Congress, House, Committee on Appropriations, *Department of Defense Appropriations for*

Fiscal 1966, Hearings before a Subcommittee of the Committee on Appropriations, 89th Cong., 1st sess., 3:33-57, esp. pp. 33-44 (hereafter referred to as DOD *Appropriations for Fiscal 1966*).

19. Ibid., p. 34.

20. Ibid., pp. 34-36.

21. Ibid., p. 35.

22. Ibid., pp. 35-36; see also Adams, *Ballistic Missile Defense,* p. 214.

23. DOD *Appropriations for Fiscal 1965,* p. 261; DOD *Appropriations for Fiscal 1966,* p. 53.

24. The text of the San Francisco speech is reprinted in the *New York Times,* September 19, 1967, p. 18; U.S., Congress, House, Committee on Appropriations, *Department of Defense Appropriations for Fiscal 1969, Hearings before a Subcommittee of the Committee on Appropriations,* 90th Cong., 2d sess., 1968, 1:119-547 (hereafter referred to as DOD *Appropriations for Fiscal 1969*).

25. McNamara, *The Fiscal Years 1969-1973 Defense Program and the 1969 Defense Budget,* p. 47.

26. Ibid., pp. 48-49.

27. For further analysis of this organizational dilemma, see Dawson and Lucas, *Organizational Politics of Defense,* pp. 101-20.

28. Dawson, "Nuclear Proliferation and the Politics of ABM," p. 33.

29. Armacost, *The Politics of Weapons Innovation,* p. 292.

30. See virtually any of the congressional hearings on ABM in 1969 and 1970, e.g., U.S., Congress, Senate, Committee on Foreign Relations, *Strategic and Foreign Policy Implications of ABM Systems, Hearings before the Subcommittee on International Organization and Disarmament Affairs of the Committee on Foreign Relations,* 91st Cong., 1st sess., 1969, passim (hereafter referred to as *Strategic and Foreign Policy Implications of ABM Systems*).

CHAPTER 4

1. James Barr, "Nike-Zeus Decision Is Looming," *Missiles and Rockets* (July 6, 1959), pp. 24-25.

2. See the testimony of Roy Johnson, then director of ARPA, in DOD *Appropriations for Fiscal 1960,* 6:108-10; Horner, ibid., pp. 164-74.

3. See Ernest J. Yanarella, "On the Concept of the Military-Industrial Complex: Notes toward a Strategy of Liberation," *Bulletin of the Peace Studies Institute* (November 1972), pp. 33-38.

4. This term is borrowed from Tristram Coffin, who uses it to denote congressmen who maintain close relations with the military services through their reserve or retired military status; Coffin, *The Armed Society: Militarism in America* (Baltimore, Md., 1964), p. 183.

5. John W. Finney, "Army Aides Warn on Anti-ICBM Race," *New York Times,* February 18, 1971, p. 5; for the congressional speeches, see U.S., Congress, *Congressional Record,* 87th Cong., 1st sess., 1961, 107:1580, 1727, 2002, 2439, 3560, and 4425; the text of Flood's letter is reprinted in "Flood Sends M/R Zeus Report to Kennedy," *Missiles and Rockets* (March 6, 1961), p. 18; *Congressional Record,* 107:7412.

6. The committee testimony of General Arthur Trudeau and Assistant Secretary of the Navy James Wakelin bare the details of this trip; see U.S., Congress, House, Committee on Appropriations, *Department of Defense Appropriations for Fiscal 1962, Hearings before a Subcommittee of the Committee on Appropriations,* 87th Cong., 1st sess., 1961,

4:205, 397-99 (hereafter referred to as *DOD Appropriations for Fiscal 1962*).

7. Since the annual posture statement as released by the Defense Department prior to the committee meetings is not materially different from the statement as presented to the various committees and subcommittees which review the defense budget, the latter has been used exclusively in all citations.

8. Secretary McNamara's Posture Statement, *DOD Appropriations for Fiscal 1962*, p. 18.

9. Ibid., p. 17.

10. "Army Mounts Major Budget Fight for Acceleration of Zeus Project," *Aviation Week* (November 14, 1960), p. 27.

11. Ibid.

12. *DOD Appropriations for Fiscal 1962*, 4:159.

13. Ibid., pp. 160-61.

14. Announced by McNamara, ibid., 3:16, and reiterated in argumentation by Morse, ibid., 4:164.

15. Ibid., 3:193-94, 194-96, and U.S., Congress, Senate, Committee on Armed Services, *Military Procurement Authorization for Fiscal 1962, Hearings before the Committee on Armed Services*, 87th Cong., 1st sess., 1961, pp. 141-42.

16. *DOD Appropriations for Fiscal 1962*, 3:16.

17. Ibid., pp. 16-17.

18. Ibid., p. 40.

19. Ibid., pp. 43-44.

20. Ibid., pp. 112, 46.

21. Ibid., pp. 202-3, 74.

22. Ibid., pp. 74-75.

23. "Army Renews Drive for Zeus Anti-ICBM," *Aviation Week* (March 13, 1961), p. 82; see testimony of York and Ruina in *DOD Appropriations for Fiscal 1961*, esp. pp. 1065-66.

24. House, *DOD Appropriations for Fiscal 1962*, 4:13.

25. Ibid., pp. 13, 54.

26. Ibid., pp. 78-91.

27. Ibid., p. 79.

28. Ibid., pp. 78, 81.

29. James Fusca, "Future ICBM's Look Unstoppable," *Missiles and Rockets* (March 7, 1960), p. 12.

30. "Terminal ICBM Defense," *Aviation Week* (April 10, 1961), p. 26.

31. Disclosure of the TYPHOON Project came in Vice Admiral J. T. Hayward's testimony before the House Appropriations Subcommittee; see *DOD Appropriations for Fiscal 1961*, 6:401; on SAINT, see *DOD Appropriations for Fiscal 1962*, 4:13, 52, 55; FABMDS stands for Field Army Ballistic Missile Defense System.

32. *DOD Appropriations for Fiscal 1962*, 3:446-47, 486-87.

33. See Ruina's testimony, ibid., 4:81-82, 91, and Philip Klass, "Bambi ICBM Defense Concept Analyzed," *Aviation Week & Space Technology* (October 23, 1961), p. 82; testimony of Joseph Charkey, undersecretary of the air force, *DOD Appropriations for Fiscal 1962*, 3:447; "Army Renews Drive for Zeus Anti-ICBM," p. 82.

34. The inferential status of this statement has been taken as an article of faith or a universal given by some politicians and intellectuals.

35. The Soviets claimed at this time and later that they possessed an effective ABM system. For example, during 1961, Soviet Defense Chief

Marshal Malinovski claimed that the Soviet Union had hit upon a defense against ICBMs; and the following year, Premier Khrushchev boasted that his nation possessed an antimissile missile that "can hit a fly in outer space" (see the *New York Times,* October 24, 1961, p. 1, and July 17, 1962, p. 1). The significance of these allegations for our argument is small, however, since U.S. intelligence sources could not validate them, nor were they given much credence within the civilian scientific elite in the Defense Department (*New York Times,* October 24, 1961, p. 2, and July 17, 1962, p. 2). In addition, when the Russian leaders tried to tout the existence of an ABM, the fundamental response in R&D agencies in OSD, characteristically, was to hasten development of a new strategic offensive weapons concept–specifically, the idea of multiple targeted reentry vehicles. (See York's comments in *Race to Oblivion,* p. 179, and the speech of John S. Foster, which first publicly revealed the origin and existence of MIRV–*New York Times,* December 14, 1967, pp. 1, 18).

CHAPTER 5

1. U.S., Congress, House, Committee on Appropriations, *Department of Defense Appropriations for Fiscal 1964, Hearings before a Subcommittee of the Committee on Appropriations,* 88th Cong., 1st sess., 1963, 3:87-221, esp. pp. 125-26 (hereafter referred to as *DOD Appropriations for Fiscal 1964*).

2. Ibid., pp. 126, 168.

3. Ibid., p. 128.

4. Such a contest was eventually blocked by executive decision.

5. "Department of Defense Restricts Nike-Zeus Testing Information," *Aviation Week & Space Technology* (February 5, 1962), p. 32.

6. U.S., Congress, House, Committee on Appropriations, *Department of Defense Appropriations for Fiscal 1963, Hearings before a Subcommittee of the Committee on Appropriations,* 87th Cong., 2d sess., 1962, 2:46, 257, and 258 (hereafter referred to as *DOD Appropriations for Fiscal 1963*).

7. James Trainor, "Nike Zeus Looks Finished as a Weapon," *Missiles and Rockets* (April 2, 1962), pp. 15-16; *DOD Appropriations for Fiscal 1963,* pp. 334, 347-48. Flood did feel, however, that Mc-Namara had altered his position on the BMD possibilities "one hundred per cent" since 1961.

8. *DOD Appropriations for Fiscal 1963,* p. 348; Trainor, "Nike Zeus Looks Finished as a Weapon," p. 16.

9. John W. Finney, "Nike Zeus Intercepts a Missile Fired from U.S. over Pacific," *New York Times,* July 20, 1962, p. 1+; James Trainor, "DOD Says AICBM Is Feasible," *Missiles and Rockets* (December 24, 1962), pp. 14-15.

10. Trainor, "DOD Says AICBM Is Feasible," p. 14.

11. Dawson, "Nuclear Proliferation and the Politics of ABM," p. 1; Trainor, "DOD Says AICBM Is Feasible," p. 14.

12. Trainor, "DOD Says AICBM Is Feasible," p. 14.

13. Ibid., pp. 14-15.

14. Ibid., p. 15.

15. Ibid.

16. *DOD Appropriations for Fiscal 1964,* p. 110; for a summary of the origins and the basic rationale for the Five-Year Defense Plan, see Enthoven and Smith, *How Much Is Enough?,* pp. 48-53.

17. *DOD Appropriations for Fiscal 1964,* pp. 125, 126.

18. Ibid., p. 427.

19. Adams, "McNamara's ABM Policy, 1961-1967," p. 205. My analysis here owes much to this lucid and penetrating article.

20. *DOD Appropriations for Fiscal 1964*, pp. 438-40, 450, 451.

21. Ibid., p. 439; *DOD Appropriations for Fiscal 1966*, 3:34, 41, 43, 53; U.S., Congress, House, Committee on Appropriations, *Department of Defense Appropriations for Fiscal 1967, Hearings before a Subcommittee of the Committee on Appropriations*, 89th Cong., 2d sess., 1966, 1:87, 123 (hereafter referred to as *DOD Appropriations for Fiscal 1967*). Quoted by Dawson, "Nuclear Proliferation and the Politics of ABM," p. 13.

22. *DOD Appropriations for Fiscal 1964*, see pp. 450, 437, 451 (for quotation).

23. Ibid., 6:4.

24. Ibid., pp. 4, 10-11; U.S., Congress, Senate, Committee on Foreign Relations, *Nuclear Test Ban Treaty, Hearings before the Committee on Foreign Relations*, 88th Cong., 1st sess., 1963, p. 531 (hereafter referred to as *Nuclear Test Ban Treaty*).

25. *DOD Appropriations for Fiscal 1964*, 6:11, 105, 10; see also *Nuclear Test Ban Treaty*, p. 531.

26. *DOD Appropriations for Fiscal 1964*, 6:202-4.

27. Ibid., p. 204.

28. Ibid., pp. 211-12.

29. Ibid., p. 211. For a detailed examination of the radar design and specific components of the multiphased or multifunction radar, see James Trainor, "Zeus May Get Array Radar System," *Missiles and Rockets* (January 22, 1962), pp. 31-32, 42; *DOD Appropriations for Fiscal 1964*, 6:211, 207.

30. C. J. LeVan's "Statement on Anti-ICBM Program," *DOD Appropriations for Fiscal 1964*, p. 259.

31. Ibid., p. 270; "DOD Emphasizes Nike-X Anti-Missile," *Aviation Week & Space Technology* (March 11, 1963), p. 143.

32. *DOD Appropriations for Fiscal 1964*, 6:264, 270 (for quotation).

33. Ibid., pp. 270-71, 263.

34. Ibid., 2:131, 586-87.

35. Ibid., 1:435; 2:131, 314 (for quotation).

36. *Congressional Quarterly Weekly Report* (April 19, 1963), pp. 629-30, 639, and "Senate Rejects Nike-Zeus Production," *Aviation Week & Space Technology* (April 22, 1963), pp. 27, 127.

37. "Senate Rejects Nike-Zeus Production," p. 127.

38. Kennedy quoted by Schlesinger, *A Thousand Days*, p. 831; for a more general study of the policy formulation process during the debate over the Nuclear Test Ban Treaty (and one which does not focus on its implications for ABM), see Mary Milling Lepper's book, *Foreign Policy Formulation: A Case Study of the Nuclear Test Ban Treaty of 1963* (Columbus, Ohio, 1971).

39. U.S., Congress, Senate, *Report of the Committee on Foreign Relations: The Nuclear Test Ban Treaty, Exec. Rept. 3*, 88th Cong., 1st sess., 1963, p. 11 and passim.

40. Ibid., pp. 103, 162.

41. Ibid., pp. 103-4.

42. Ibid., pp. 217, 854, 570, 314-77, 543, 378, 852-53, 245-46.

43. Ibid., pp. 422, 424, 433, 437-40.

44. Ibid., pp. 613, 615, 637.

45. DOD *Appropriations for Fiscal 1964*, 1:126; *Nuclear Test Ban Treaty*, pp. 244-45, 139. McNamara's concession came only after extensive dodging.

46. See Adams, "McNamara's ABM Policy," pp. 207-11, for supporting material for this deduction; *Nuclear Test Ban Treaty*, pp. 174, 761-63.

47. See Freeman Dyson, "Defense against Ballistic Missiles," *Bulletin of the Atomic Scientists* (June 1964), p. 13; U.S., Congress, Senate, Committee on Armed Services, *Military Procurement Authorization for Fiscal 1964, Hearings before the Committee on Armed Services*, 88th Cong., 1st sess., 1963, p. 71.

48. I. F. Stone, "McGovern vs. Nixon on the Arms Race," *New York Review of Books* 19 (July 20, 1972):9, 10; and John Newhouse, *Cold Dawn: The Story of SALT* (New York, 1973), pp. 27, 73.

49. U.S., Congress, Senate, *ABM, MIRV, SALT, and the Nuclear Arms Race, Hearings before the Subcommittee on Arms Control, International Law and Organizations of the Committee on Foreign Relations*, 91st Cong., 2d sess., 1970, p. 59.

50. DOD *Appropriations for Fiscal 1964*, p. 110.

CHAPTER 6

1. DOD *Appropriations for Fiscal 1965*, 4:3-300, 187 (for quotation).

2. Ibid., p. 188.

3. Quoted by Adams, "McNamara's ABM Policy," p. 213; from DOD *Appropriations for Fiscal 1964*, p. 109.

4. U.S., Congress, Senate, Committee on Appropriations, *Department of Defense Appropriations for Fiscal 1965, Hearings before a Subcommittee of the Committee on Appropriations*, 88th Cong., 2d sess., 1964, p. 397.

5. Ibid., pp. 869-85, esp. pp. 882-83.

6. James Trainor, "Missile Site Radar Paces Nike-X," *Missiles and Rockets* (May 25, 1964), p. 14.

7. Ibid., p. 15.

8. James Trainor, "Nike-X Fate Keyed to DOD Study," *Missiles and Rockets* (May 18, 1964), pp. 14-15. The following year Trainor obtained information on results of the Betts Report; see "Study Aids Case for Nike-X," *Missiles and Rockets* (January 4, 1965), pp. 12-13.

9. Hanson Baldwin, "U.S. Missile Defense," *New York Times*, February 15, 1964, p. 8; Henry Tannern, "Soviet Parades Six New Rockets at Celebration," *New York Times*, November 8, 1964, pp. 1, 3.

10. Jerome Wiesner and Herbert York, "National Security and the Nuclear Test Ban," *Scientific American* 211 (October 1964):7-35.

11. Roswell Gilpatric, "Our Defense Needs," *Foreign Affairs* 42 (April 1964):368; Dyson, "Defense against Ballistic Missiles," p. 13.

12. Gilpin, *American Scientists and Nuclear Weapons Policy*. Also relevant are Robert Gilpin and Christopher Wright, eds., *Scientists and National Policy-making* (New York, 1964); Harold K. Jacobson and Eric Stein, *Diplomats, Scientists, and Politicians: The United States and the Nuclear Test Ban Negotiations* (Ann Arbor, 1966); and Dean Schooler, Jr., *Science, Scientists, and Public Policy* (New York, 1971). Some historical background to this period is provided by Stephane Groueff, *Manhattan Project* (Boston, 1967) and Alice Kimball Smith, *A Peril and a Hope: The Scientists' Movement in America, 1945-1957* (Chicago, 1965).

13. Gilpin, *American Scientists and Nuclear Weapons Policy*, p. 103.

14. Ibid., p. 105.

15. Ibid., p. 98. Undoubtedly, the leading spokesman of the finite containment school was J. Robert Oppenheimer.

16. Ibid., p. 155. Linus Pauling, Philip Morrison, and Harlow Shapley have been most closely identified with this segment of the scientific community.

17. Ibid., p. 157.

18. Investigations of the political involvement of scientists in some of these policy debates may be found in Warner Schilling, "The H-Bomb Decision: How to Decide without Actually Choosing," *Political Science Quarterly* 76 (March 1961):24-46; "The Hidden Struggle for the H-Bomb," *Fortune* 47 (May 1953):109-10, 230; Gilpin, *American Scientists and Nuclear Weapons Policy*, pp. 112-34; Lepper, *Foreign Policy Formulation*.

19. See his posture statement in DOD *Appropriations for Fiscal 1966*, 3:32-58 (quotations on pp. 43, 53).

20. Enthoven and Smith, *How Much Is Enough?*, pp. 177, 178.

21. Stewart Alsop, "His Business Is War," *Saturday Evening Post* (May 21, 1966), p. 31.

22. DOD *Appropriations for Fiscal 1966*, pp. 355, 626. For Wheeler's response to Mahon's query about JCS's position on the Nike-X, see ibid., p. 397.

23. Ibid., pp. 42-43.

24. Michael Getler, "New A-ICBM City Defense Studied," *Missiles and Rockets* (January 18, 1965), p. 13; DOD *Appropriations for Fiscal 1966*, 1:472. Cited by Adams, "McNamara's ABM Policy," p. 216.

25. See "Chinese Nuclear Threat Pushes Studies of Nike-X Options," *Missiles and Rockets* (May 31, 1965), p. 17.

26. "Decision Time Grows Shorter for Nike-X," *Aviation Week & Space Technology* (March 15, 1965), pp. 147-49; "Nike-X Go-Ahead Followed Fierce Struggle," *Aviation Week & Space Technology* (October 23, 1967), p. 75.

27. Jack Raymond, "New U.S. Delay Likely in Building Missile Defense," *New York Times*, December 1, 1965, p. 1; see also William Beecher, "Nike-X in the Balance," *Astronautics and Aeronautics* (December 1965), p. 5; "Viet Needs May Delay Nike-X Production," *Aviation Week & Space Technology* (October 4, 1965), p. 23.

28. DOD *Appropriations for Fiscal 1967*, 1:49, 62.

29. Ibid., pp. 50-51.

30. Ibid., p. 51.

31. Ibid., p. 62.

32. Ibid., 5:156, 1:531.

33. George C. Wilson, "Joint Chiefs Fear Soviet Technical Coup," *Aviation Week & Space Technology* (February 28, 1966), p. 16; Wilson, "Senate May Force New Anti-Missile Policy," *Aviation Week & Space Technology* (May 2, 1966), p. 28. Later in the year, as Wilson predicted, both the House and the Senate Armed Services committees voted unanimously to add supplementary funds for Nike-X advancement.

34. George C. Wilson, "House Seen Pushing Nike-X Acceleration," *Aviation Week & Space Technology* (June 6, 1966), pp. 30-31; Michael Getler, "McNamara Says Soviets Err on ABM," *Missiles and Rockets* (May 2, 1966), p. 12.

35. Ron Barnhart, "Bids Due Soon on New Nike-X Radar," *Missiles and Rockets* (May 30, 1966), p. 14; and "VHF ICBM Radars Planned," *Aviation Week & Space Technology* (May 30, 1966), p. 31.

36. Michael Getler, "U.S. Opting for New, Low-Cost ABM," *Technology Week* (June 20, 1966), pp. 14-15; *DOD Appropriations for Fiscal 1967,* 5:38-39.

37. On October 27, 1966, the Chinese announced that they had successfully test-flown a guided missile with a nuclear warhead; see Michael Getler, "Chinese Missile Shot Forcing Nike Choice," *Technology Week* (November 7, 1966), pp. 13-14, and Cecil Brownlow, "Nike-X Production Still in Doubt," *Aviation Week & Space Technology* (November 7, 1966), pp. 26-27. Robert Semple, Jr., "McNamara Hints Soviets Deploy Anti-missile Net," *New York Times,* November 11, 1966, p. 1, and Michael Getler, "Soviet ABM Deployment Expected in Year," *Technology Week* (November 21, 1966), pp. 10, 1.

38. John Finney, "Rusk Seeks Curb in Missiles Race," *New York Times,* December 22, 1966, pp. 1, 19.

CHAPTER 7

1. The text of the San Francisco speech may be found in the *New York Times,* September 19, 1967, p. 18. See also Robert J. Art and Kenneth N. Waltz, eds., *The Use of Force: International Politics and Foreign Policy* (Boston, 1971), pp. 503-15.

2. *Nuclear Test Ban Treaty,* p. 115; see also *New York Times,* August 2, 1963, p. 18; Armacost, *The Politics of Weapons Innovation,* p. 234.

3. See Richard Neustadt, *Presidential Power,* passim; Morton Halperin, "The Decision to Deploy the ABM: Bureaucratic and Domestic Politics in the Johnson Administration," *World Politics* 25 (October 1972):62-95.

4. See Getler, "Soviet ABM Deployment Expected in Year," p. 1.

5. Text of State of the Union Message, *New York Times,* January 11, 1967, p. 16; John Finney, "Johnson Backed on Missile Pact," *New York Times,* January 18, 1967, p. 2; Halperin, "The Decision to Deploy ABM," pp. 24-25.

6. See Herbert York, "Military Technology and National Security," *Scientific American* 221 (August 1969):17-29, esp. p. 18; and the testimony of Fink and Hornig in *Strategic and Foreign Policy Implications of ABM Systems,* pp. 51, 538-39.

7. York, "Military Technology and National Security," p. 18. As Newhouse recounts the meeting, there was at least one dissenter in the room, John Foster; but, according to Newhouse, McNamara studiously avoided asking Foster his opinion and his silence was taken as concurrence. See Newhouse, *Cold Dawn,* p. 89.

8. *Strategic and Foreign Policy Implications of ABM Systems,* p. 539.

9. I owe this insight to Morton Halperin, "The Decision to Deploy the ABM," p. 75.

10. Republican National Committee, *The Missile Defense Question: Is LBJ Right?* referred to by Ralph Lapp in *Arms beyond Doubt,* p. 48; U.S., Congress, House, Republican Policy Committee, *Statement on the Deployment of an Anti-Ballistic Missile System* (Washington, D.C., 1967).

11. Edward Jayne and Morton Halperin place great weight on the fact that Johnson and McNamara were unable at the Glassboro Con-

ference in mid-June 1967 to convince Kosygin of the urgency of setting a date for strategic arms limitation talks. Apparently, while McNamara and Johnson constantly emphasized in their discussions the destabilizing effects of ABM systems, Kosygin countered that such systems were defensive in nature and therefore unobjectionable. This unyielding stance toward the larger issue of initiating immediate talks on strategic weapons reductions led the president to conclude that there was little chance of negotiations beginning before his next budget message to Congress in January 1968. See Halperin, "The Decision to Deploy the ABM," p. 87, where Jayne's parallel interpretation is cited. See also Lyndon B. Johnson, *The Vantage Point: Perspectives of the Presidency, 1963-1969* (New York, 1971), pp. 483-85.

12. U.S., Congress, House, Committee on Appropriations, *Department of Defense Appropriations for Fiscal 1968, Hearings before a Subcommittee of the Committee on Appropriations,* 90th Cong., 1st sess., 1967, 2:156, 159 (hereafter referred to as *DOD Appropriations for Fiscal 1968).*

13. Ibid., pp. 159, 196-97.

14. Ibid., pp. 160, 169-70.

15. Ibid., p. 165.

16. Ibid., p. 162.

17. Ibid., pp. 163, 164.

18. Goulding, *Confirm or Deny,* p. 233.

19. *DOD Appropriations for Fiscal 1968,* pp. 167, 168.

20. Ibid., p. 168.

21. Ibid., pp. 196, 200, 205.

22. "Service Secretaries Support Area Defense Nike-X ABM," *Technology Week* (May 8, 1967), p. 15, and Getler, "Soviet ABM Deployment Expected in Year," p. 11, for a report of the reversal by Foster and Herzfeld. Supporting evidence concerning the changed attitudes of the civilian secretaries was documented in the DOD appropriations hearings of the House Armed Services Committee's Appropriations Subcommittee. Goulding, *Confirm or Deny,* p. 233.

23. *DOD Appropriations for Fiscal 1968,* pp. 636-55 (quotation on p. 643).

24. Ibid., pp. 643, 645.

25. Halperin, "The Decision to Deploy the ABM," p. 18.

26. *DOD Appropriations for Fiscal 1968,* pp. 176-79; "Service Secretaries Support Area Defense Nike-X ABM," p. 15.

27. *DOD Appropriations for Fiscal 1968,* pp. 177, 178.

28. Ibid., p. 178.

29. Ibid., p. 179.

30. Hedrick Smith, "McNamara Doubts Bombing in North Can End the War," *New York Times,* August 27, 1967, p. 1 (text, p. 4). For some significant insights and the essential background to this speech, see Townsend Hoopes, *The Limits of Intervention* (New York, 1969), pp. 75-91, and Goulding, *Confirm or Deny,* pp. 168-213.

31. Katherine Johnson, "Atomic Committee Report Spurs Renewed ABM Deployment Drive," *Aviation Week & Space Technology* (August 7, 1967), p. 23; Evert Clark, "Pastore Promises Fight in Congress to Obtain a Defense System," *New York Times,* September 10, 1967, pp. 1, 17; *DOD Appropriations for Fiscal 1968,* p. 7. Townsend Hoopes hypothesizes that Johnson's decision to deploy an ABM rested, in part, in his desire to relieve pressure from Senate hawks on his war policies; *The Limits of Intervention,* p. 84.

32. "McNamara to Get Red China/Nike-X Briefing," *Aerospace Technology* (August 14, 1967), p. 3; "A McNamara Switch on Nike-X?" *Aerospace Technology* (August 28, 1967); p. 3; see also Enthoven and Smith, *How Much Is Enough?*, pp. 53-58; John Finney, "Rusk Urges Speed on Missile Defense," *New York Times*, September 9, 1967, p. 1.

33. See the analysis of Phil Goulding, McNamara's assistant secretary for public affairs, in his book, *Confirm or Deny*, pp. 217-21, (p. 244 for quotation). See Resor's remarks in testimony, *DOD Appropriations for Fiscal 1969*, 1:592. McNamara was not successful in altering sufficiently the basic design of the Sentinel to check its growth potential. Thus the Joint Chiefs could assure its allies in Congress and elsewhere that the Sentinel system was simply the first installment in the construction of a heavier, anti-Soviet ABM shield. See Newhouse, *Cold Dawn*, p. 97.

CHAPTER 8

1. For a description of the bureaucratic maneuverings within the Johnson administration to work out a consensus on the American position, see John Newhouse, *Cold Dawn*, pp. 103-32.

2. William Beecher, "Sentinel Project Halted by Laird Pending Review," *New York Times*, February 7, 1969, pp. 1, 2.

3. John Finney, "Congressional Panel May Oppose Nixon If He Pushes for Sentinel Deployment," *New York Times*, February 16, 1969, p. 26; "Missile Hearing Slated," *New York Times*, March 1, 1969, p. 17.

4. See Jonathan Allen, *March 4: Scientists, Students, and Society* (Cambridge, Mass., 1970); John Finney, "Kennedy Accuses Pentagon of Pretense in Review of Sentinel," *New York Times*, February 20, 1969, p. 11.

5. Robert Semple, "Nixon for Limited Missile Plan to Protect U.S. Nuclear Bases; Faces Major Test in Congress," *New York Times*, March 15, 1969, pp. 1, 17; text, p. 16.

6. See Gabriel Almond's classic study, *The American People and Foreign Policy* (New York, 1960), esp. pp. 226-44. Also relevant here are Francis Rourke, "The Domestic Scene," in *America and the World: From the Truman Doctrine to Vietnam*, ed. Robert E. Osgood (Baltimore, Md., 1970), pp. 147-88; William Caspary, "The Mood Theory: A Study of Public Opinion and Foreign Policy," *American Political Science Review* 64 (June 1970):536-47; John E. Mueller, "Presidential Popularity from Truman to Johnson," *American Political Science Review* 64 (March 1970):18-34; and Sidney Verba et al., "Public Opinion and the War in Vietnam," *American Political Science Review* 61 (June 1967):317-33. For an excellent analysis which documents the dramatic decline in public support for defense spending in the general time period covered in this chapter, see Bruce M. Russett, "The Revolt of the Masses: Public Opinion on Military Expenditures," in *Peace, War, and Numbers*, ed. Bruce M. Russett (Beverly Hills, Calif., 1972), pp. 299-319.

7. Donald L. Zylstra, "Public Ignorant of A-ICBM Situation," *Missiles and Rockets* (August 16, 1965), p. 32. Well over a majority conceived of ABM deployment as an asset to national defense. Almond, *The American People and Foreign Policy*, pp. 139, 151, 229.

8. John Finney, "Halt of Sentinel Is Traced to a 10-Month-Old Memo," *New York Times*, February 9, 1969, pp. 1, 64.

9. Ibid., p. 64.

10. This trend in executive-legislative relationships has been ex-

plored most recently by Arthur Schlesinger, Jr., and Frances O. Wilcox; see Schlesinger, *The Imperial Presidency* (Boston, 1973), and Wilcox, *Congress, the Executive, and Foreign Policy* (New York, 1971).

11. Finney, "Halt of Sentinel Is Traced to a 10-Month-Old Memo," p. 64.

12. Ibid. See also John Finney, "Winds of Change in the Senate," *New Republic* (April 5, 1969), pp. 21-35.

13. Eileen Shanahan, "Conferees Clear Surtax and $6-Billion Fund Cuts," *New York Times*, May 9, 1968, pp. 1, 27.

14. U.S., Congress, Senate, Committee on Appropriations, *Department of Defense Appropriations for Fiscal 1969, Hearings before the Committee on Appropriations*, 90th Cong., 2d sess., 1968, 1:2719; Raymond Anderson, "Moscow Offers to Start Talks on Missile Curb," *New York Times*, June 28, 1968, pp. 1, 12; Peter Grose, "U.S. and Soviet Agree to Parleys on Limitation of Missile Systems," *New York Times*, July 2, 1968, pp. 1, 3.

15. Finney, "Halt to Sentinel Is Traced to a 10-Month-Old Memo," p. 64.

16. See John Finney's two articles, "Conflict Mounts on Sentinel Plan in 2 Senate Units," *New York Times*, March 16, 1969, pp. 1, 7, and "A Power Struggle between Two Fiefdoms," *New York Times*, March 30, 1969, p. 2E.

17. John Finney, "Senate Defeats a Move to Delay Sentinel System," *New York Times*, June 25, 1968, pp. 1, 16; Finney, "Senate Rejects Missile Delay," *New York Times*, October 3, 1968, pp. 1, 14.

18. U.S., Congress, Senate, *Congressional Record*, 90th Cong., 2d sess., 1968, 114:9638-50; see also Finney, "A Power Struggle between Two Fiefdoms."

19. Finney, "Senate Rejects Missile Delay," p. 1.

20. "Rivers Temporarily Blocks Sentinel Missile System in House," *New York Times*, February 6, 1969, p. 20.

21. Finney, "Conflict Mounts on Sentinel Plan in 2 Senate Units," p. 1, and Finney, "A Power Struggle between Two Fiefdoms."

22. For an insightful, but overdrawn, portrait of the domestic political features of the 1969-1970 ABM dispute, see Aaron Wildavsky, "The Politics of ABM," *Commentary* 48 (November 1969):55-63. "Two Committees in Congress Open Hearings in Move to Tighten Rein on Spending by Military," *New York Times*, June 4, 1969, p. 5. See also the relevant subcommittee hearings, including U.S., Congress, Joint Economic Committee, *Changing National Priorities, Hearings before the Subcommittee on Economy in Government of the Joint Economic Committee*, 91st Cong., 2d sess., vols. 1 and 2, 1970, and U.S., Congress, Joint Economic Committee, *The Acquisition of Weapons Systems, Hearings before the Subcommittee on Economy in Government of the Joint Economic Committee*, 90th Cong., 2d sess., 1970.

23. For a partial transcript of the proceedings of the Conference on the Military Budget and National Priorities, see Erwin Knoll and Judith Nies McFadden, eds., *American Militarism, 1970* (New York, 1969). See the counter defense budget offered in the "Report on Military Spending," submitted to the Members of Congress for Peace through Law by Its Committee on Spending, July 2, 1969.

24. John Finney, "Missile Debate Turns into a Battle of the Charts: Packard Disputed at Missile Inquiry," *New York Times*, March 27, 1969, pp. 1, 21; Finney, "Senate Panel with Film and Reports, Rest Case against ABM," *New York Times*, July 31, 1969, p. 8. The three

secret and critical studies were prepared by the Institute for Defense Analysis, the Aerospace Corporation, and ARPA.

25. John Finney, "ABM Debate Is Becoming a Political Struggle for the Votes of 3 or 4 Senators," *New York Times*, July 16, 1969, p. 14; Warren Weaver, Jr., "A Complete Ban on ABM Sought by Senator Smith," *New York Times*, August 6, 1969, pp. 1, 46; Weaver, "Nixon Missile Plan Wins in Senate by a 51-50 Vote; House Approval Likely," *New York Times*, August 7, 1969, pp. 1, 22.

26. While losing on ABM, the Senate foes of the Safeguard ABM system did manage to secure for Congress the right to audit independently major Pentagon contracts for weapons through the General Accounting Office. In succeeding controversies, Congress would use this source as a means of obtaining independent judgments on the military estimates of major weapons programs and as a check of the accuracy of Pentagon figures on the Soviet technological threat. See Warren Weaver, Jr., "Senate, 47 to 46, Asks for Review of Weapon Costs," *New York Times*, August 8, 1969, pp. 1, 12. See also Max Frankel, "The Missile Vote: Both Sides Can Claim a Victory," *New York Times*, August 7, 1969, p. 22. David Rosenbaum, "Nixon Vows Veto of Big Fund Bill as Inflationary," *New York Times*, December 19, 1969, p. 1.

27. See "Transcript," *New York Times*, January 31, 1970, p. 14; "Mansfield Decries Price of Expanded ABM Plan," *New York Times*, February 1, 1970, pp. 1, 44.

28. William Beecher, "Expansion of ABM to 3rd Missile Site Is Sought by Laird," *New York Times*, February 25, 1970, pp. 1, 30; John Finney, "Two Key Senators Express Doubts on Expanded ABM," *New York Times*, February 24, 1970, pp. 1, 11.

29. "Nixon's Report to Congress on Foreign Policy" [text: *United States Foreign Policy for the 1970's: A Strategy for Peace*], *New York Times*, February 19, 1970, esp. pp. 25 and 26. See also William Beecher, "Nixon Says Soviet Missile Buildup Raises Concern over Moscow's Intentions," ibid., p. 28. The "bargaining chip" argument was voiced with increasing frequency during these months by President Nixon, Kissinger, and other administration spokesmen; see John Finney, "President Warns U.S. Could Lose Arms Race Lead," *New York Times*, July 24, 1970, p. 2; and Gerard Smith's comments in his telegram to the Senate.

30. John Finney, "ABM Critics Say Pentagon Agrees," *New York Times*, August 1, 1970, p. 9. See also the comments by Herbert York and Jack Ruina in John Finney's article, "ABM Called Defense for Obsolete Missile Force," *New York Times*, July 17, 1969, p. 8. Finney, "ABM's Opponents Select Strategy," *New York Times*, July 31, 1970, p. 11.

31. John Finney, "3rd Site Approved for ABM System by Senate Panel," *New York Times*, June 18, 1970, pp. 1, 19.

32. John Finney, "Expansion of ABM Backed by Senate by 52-to-47 Vote," *New York Times*, August 13, 1970, pp. 1, 12; Finney, "Envoy's Message on ABM Clarified," *New York Times*, August 14, 1970, p. 2. As Fulbright recalled, Smith had said in February before the Senate Armed Services Committee: "I don't think I go as far as some people would who think you ought to go ahead faster with Safeguard to step up the bargaining advantage." In contrast, in his telegram he characterized Safeguard expansion as a "vital bargaining element." Finney, "Expansion of ABM Backed by Senate by 52-to-47 Vote," p. 12.

33. A somewhat attenuated and edited version of Wiesner's original

paper appears in his book *Where Science and Politics Meet* (New York, 1965), pp. 209-46.

34. See, e.g., Jerome Wiesner and Herbert York, "National Security and the Nuclear Test Ban"; York, "Military Technology and National Security"; George Rathjens, "The Dynamics of Arms Races," *Scientific American* 220 (April 1969):15-25; Rathjens and George Kistiakowsky, "The Limitation of Strategic Arms," *Scientific American* 222 (January 1970):19-29; and York, "ABM, MIRV, and the Arms Race," *Science* 169 (July 17, 1970):257-60.

35. Besides the most active leaders and lobbyists in this scientific group, the various Senate committees and subcommittees involved in investigating this dispute heard testimony from several other scientists who might be regarded as members of the finite containment school, including J. P. Ruina, Hans Bethe, Donald Hornig, and Richard Garwin. See *Strategic and Foreign Policy Implications of ABM Systems*, vols. 1 and 2, passim.

36. See Kistiakowsky's restatement of this argument, *ABM, MIRV, SALT, and the Nuclear Arms Race*, p. 391, and Wiesner, *Where Science and Politics Meet*, pp. 226-30.

37. Rathjens, "The Dynamics of the Arms Race," p. 23; Bethe, in *Strategic and Foreign Policy Implications of ABM Systems*, pp. 35-38.

38. See York, in *Strategic and Foreign Policy Implications of ABM Systems*, 1:78-79, and Jerome Wiesner, ibid., 2:488.

39. York, *Race to Oblivion*, pp. 149, 160-65. Belief in the emergence of a technological plateau was expressed by York as early as 1960; see *DOD Appropriations for Fiscal 1961*, p. 96.

40. George Rathjens, U.S., Congress, Joint Economic Committee, *The Economics of National Priorities, Hearings before the Subcommittee on Priorities and Economy in Government of the Joint Economic Committee*, 92d Cong., 1st sess., 1971, pp. 404-5.

41. F. A. Long, "The Impact of Anti-Ballistic Missile Deployment on the Uncertainties of Strategic Balance," in C. F. Barnaby and A. Boserup, eds., *Implications of Anti-Ballistic Missile Systems*, p. 121; see also Rathjens, "The Dynamics of the Arms Race," p. 24.

42. Herbert York, U.S., Congress, Senate, *Authorization for Military Procurement, Research and Development, Fiscal Year 1970, and Reserve Strength, Hearings before the Committee on Armed Services*, 91st Cong., 1st sess., 1969, p. 1119 (hereafter referred to as *Military Procurement, Research and Development, Fiscal 1970*). Kistiakowsky, in *Strategic and Foreign Policy Implications of ABM Systems*, 1:84.

43. York, *Race to Oblivion*, p. 180.

44. Abram Chayes, et al., "An Overview," *ABM: An Evaluation of the Decision to Deploy an Anti-Ballistic Missile System* (New York, 1969), pp. 52-53; York, in *ABM, MIRV, SALT, and the Nuclear Arms Race*, pp. 59-62; John Finney, "Air Force Orders MIRV Warheads," *New York Times*, June 27, 1969, pp. 1, 10; "U.S. Speeds Timetable for MIRV Deployment," *New York Times*, March 11, 1970, p. 35; "Air Force Deploys Multiple Warheads on Missiles," *New York Times*, June 20, 1970, p. 1. Two perceptive essays on the origins and history of MIRV technology are York, "The Origins of MIRV," *SIPRI Research Report* 9 (August 1973), and York, "Multiple-Warhead Missiles," *Scientific American* 224 (November 1973):18-27.

45. In *Military Procurement, Research and Development, Fiscal 1970*, pp. 1115-53. Of course, confrontations of spokesmen of the infinite containment school in this dispute were also staged by anti-

ABM chairmen for the opposite purpose. See the clash between Jerome Wiesner and Edward Teller at the Gore subcommittee hearings, *Strategic and Foreign Policy Implications of ABM Systems*, 2:485-533.

46. William Beecher, "U.S. Aide Believes Soviet Test MIRV," *New York Times*, August 6, 1969, p. 38. See Foster's testimony, U.S., Congress, House, Committee on Appropriations, *Department of Defense Appropriations for Fiscal 1971, Hearings before a Subcommittee of the Committee on Appropriations*, 91st Cong., 2d sess., 1970, 6:40 (hereafter referred to as *DOD Appropriations for Fiscal 1971*). See also U.S., Congress, House, Committee on Appropriations, *Department of Defense Appropriations for Fiscal 1972, Hearings before a Subcommittee of the Committee on Appropriations*, 92d Cong., 1st sess., 1971, 6:3-4. Compare these statements with the critical analysis by the GAO, "Comparison of Military Research and Development Expenditures of the United States and the Soviet Union," Study No. B-172553 (Washington, D.C., 1971), vols. 1 and 2.

47. The main representatives who appeared before various congressional subcommittees included Edward Teller, John S. Foster, William McMillan, Eugene Wigner, Albert Wohlstetter, and Charles Herzfeld. An important figure in the infinite containment school who did not testify is Harold Agnew, former director of the Weapons Division of the Los Alamos Scientific Laboratory.

48. See Teller's testimony, *Strategic and Foreign Policy Implications of ABM Systems*, 2:504, 511, 517, 523; also Harold Agnew, "Technological Innovation: A Necessary Deterrent or Provocation," *Air Force & Space Digest* (May 1967), esp. pp. 66, 170.

49. See Foster's remarks, *DOD Appropriations for Fiscal 1971*, pp. 5, 14, 16, 17.

50. See Eugene Wigner's chess metaphor in his testimony before the Subcommittee on International Organization and Disarmament Affairs, *Strategic and Foreign Policy Implications of ABM Systems*, 2:558. Also germane to this point is the overview of the battle between the California Group (infinite containment school) and the Cambridge Group (finite containment school) written by Hanson Baldwin, "The Great Missile Debate," *Reporter* (June 29, 1967), esp. pp. 23, 24.

51. Teller, in *Strategic and Foreign Policy Implications of ABM Systems*, 2:511, and Foster, *DOD Appropriations for Fiscal 1971*, pp. 16, 17.

52. The control school is excluded from this discussion because of its negligible role in the controversy. Aside from the largely individual campaign of George Wald to mobilize public opinion against the insanity of the arms race and its militarizing effects upon society, no person of note espousing the views of the control school in this debate could be identified. Even the Pugwash Conferences–early forums of the control school's views–have been transformed into scientific meetings largely dominated by representatives of the finite containment school. See George Wald, "A Generation in Search of a Future," in Allen, ed., *March 4*, pp. 106-15. For two other studies of the involvement of American scientists in public affairs, see Ann Hessing Cahn, "American Scientists and the ABM: A Case Study in Controversy," and David Nichols, "The Associational Interests of Groups of American Science," both in *Science and Public Affairs*, ed. Albert Teich (Cambridge, Mass., 1974), pp. 41-120, 123-70.

53. R. W. Apple, Jr., "Nixon Promises Arms Superiority over the Soviet," *New York Times*, October 25, 1968, pp. 1, 31.

54. "Text," *New York Times*, January 21, 1969, p. 21.

55. This reconstruction of the decision-making process is largely drawn from Robert Semple's lengthy account and relevant news articles which filled in the gaps; see Semple, "Nixon Staff Had Central Role in Missile Decision," *New York Times*, March 19, 1969, p. 22.

56. Phillips, *Ballistic Missile Defense*, p. 26; "Sentinel Is Renamed the Safeguard System," *New York Times*, March 21, 1969, p. 20.

57. Hedrick Smith, "Nixon Would Link Political Issues to Missile Talks," *New York Times*, January 29, 1969, pp. 1, 13, and "Transcript," ibid., p. 12; Richard M. Nixon, *U.S. Foreign Policy for the 1970's*, extracted in U.S. Arms Control and Disarmament Agency, *Documents on Disarmament, 1970* (Washington, D.C., 1971), p. 22; Nixon, *U.S. Foreign Policy for the 1970's: The Emerging Structure of Peace* (Washington, D.C., 1972), pp. 156-58.

58. Ibid., p. 157.

59. Because the Safeguard controversy from 1969 to 1970 took place largely within the realm of domestic politics, Laird's role was perhaps smaller than it might have been in other circumstances. The basic framework within which the decision was formulated was the National Security Council, rather than the Defense Department. A staunch defender of military superiority, Laird did not hesitate to defend enthusiastically the decision to deploy the Safeguard system. Laird, an astute student of American domestic politics, strove to foster a congenial environment in Congress for passage of Safeguard funding in these two years by inflating the Soviet strategic offensive threat to a point where he characterized it as moving toward a "first-strike capability." While he moved quickly upon taking office to dismantle some of the more politically offensive features of McNamara's organizational revolution in the Defense Department and to put his own imprint on the structure of the Pentagon, his actions in these respects had little bearing on the ABM debate. See, among others, John Finney, "Sentinel Backed by Laird as Vital to Thwart Soviet," *New York Times*, March 21, 1969, pp. 1, 20; William Beecher, "Laird Says Soviet Can Lead by 2 to 1 in Missiles by '75," *New York Times*, April 26, 1969, pp. 1, 17; Beecher, "Laird Says Soviet Speeds Up Threat," *New York Times*, January 8, 1970, pp. 1, 15; and Beecher, "Laird Cites Peril if Soviet Presses Missile Build-up," *New York Times*, February 21, 1970, pp. 1, 14. John Finney, "Nixon Tries the Soft Sell on a Closely Divided Senate," *New York Times*, June 1, 1969, p. E2.

60. Robert Semple, "Nixon, Defending Policy, Hits 'New Isolationists'; Pledges World Role," *New York Times*, June 5, 1969, pp. 1, 30; "Text," ibid., p. 30.

61. "Text," *New York Times*, p. 30, cited from former President Eisenhower's Farewell Address.

62. Phillips, *Ballistic Missile Defense*, p. 54. In succeeding years, President Nixon's efforts to diminish the role of scientists in executive policymaking would take the form of eliminating White House advisers for science and technology and thereby removing any significant and institutionalized science and technology presence in the inner circles of presidential decision-making. For a reflection upon this state of affairs by a concerned scientist and arms control advocate, see F. A. Long, "President Nixon's 1973 Reorganization Plan No. 4: Where Do Science and Technology Go Now?" *Science and Public Affairs: Bulletin of the Atomic Scientists* 29 (May 1973):5-8, 40-42.

63. John Finney, "Pentagon Drops Air Force Plans for Orbiting

Lab," *New York Times*, June 11, 1969, pp. 1, 11; William Beecher, "President Sets Up Panel to Explore Pentagon Reform," *New York Times*, July 1, 1969, pp. 1, 14; and for a perceptive evaluation of the panel's recommendations, see Raymond H. Dawson, "The Blue Ribbon Panel Report: Unification Orthodoxy Revisited and Revised," *Aerospace Historian* 18 (March 1971):4-11.

64. Letter by Jeremy J. Stone, *New York Times*, August 15, 1970, p. 24, and John Finney, "Government Now Wants ABM as a 'Bargaining Chip,'" *New York Times*, August 2, 1970, p. 2E.

65. Coral Bell, *Negotiation from Strength: A Study in the Politics of Power* (New York, 1963), esp. pp. 210-42.

66. E. W. Kenworthy, "Missile Vote Reassures Nixon on Political Strategy for 1972," *New York Times*, August 8, 1969, p. 12.

67. To date, the best and most informative history of SALT is undoubtedly Newhouse's *Cold Dawn*.

68. Foster's testimony, U.S., Congress, *Developments in Technical Capabilities for Detecting and Identifying Nuclear Weapons Tests, Hearings before the Joint Committee on Atomic Energy*, 88th Cong., 1st sess., 1963, pp. 435-39; U.S. Arms Control and Disarmament Agency, *Documents on Disarmament, 1963* (Washington, D.C., 1964), p. 567.

69. U.S. Arms Control and Disarmament Agency, *Documents on Disarmament, 1964* (Washington, D.C., 1965), p. 8.

70. John Finney, "Russians Agree to Talks on Curbing Missile Race, Offensive and Defensive," *New York Times*, March 3, 1967, pp. 1, 14; Johnson, *The Vantage Point*, pp. 484-85.

71. Nicolai Talensky, "Anti-Missile Systems and Disarmament," *International Affairs* (Moscow) 10 (1964):18; *Izvestia*, June 27, 1967, p. 1.

72. See Nixon, *U.S. Foreign Policy for the 1970's*, extracted in U.S. Arms Control and Disarmament Agency, *Documents on Disarmament, 1970*, pp. 27-30; William Beecher, "Some Officials See ABM Vote Spurring Arms Limitation Talks," *New York Times*, August 8, 1969, p. 12; Richard Halloran, "U.S.-Soviet Talks on Missiles Open Nov. 17 in Helsinki," *New York Times*, October 26, 1969, pp. 1, 20.

73. See the charts and analyses in *World Armaments and Disarmament: SIPRI Yearbook, 1972* (New York, 1972), pp. 1-22 (prepared by the Stockholm International Peace Research Institute).

74. Hedrick Smith, "U.S. and Soviet Sign Two Arms Accords to Limit Growth of Atomic Arsenals," *New York Times*, May 27, 1972, pp. 1, 8.

75. For the latest restatement of his position, see Brennan, "Strategic Alternatives: I," *New York Times*, May 24, 1971, p. 31, and "Strategic Alternatives: II," *New York Times*, May 25, 1971, p. 33.

76. The acceleration of the strategic arms race qualitatively (largely by the United States) and quantitatively (largely by the Soviet Union) during the SALT I negotiations is amply documented by the researchers at SIPRI—see *World Armaments and Disarmament*, pp. 1-22. Colin S. Gray, "Security through SALT?" *Behind the Headlines* 30 (April 1971):15, 16. Dieter Senghaas's term, examined in Senghaas, "Arms Race by Arms Control?" *Bulletin of Peace Proposals* 4 (1973):359-74.

CHAPTER 9

1. Ronald Reagan, "Announcement of Strategic Defense Initiative" [text of nationally televised speech], March 23, 1983. <http://www.townhall.com/hall_of_fame/reagan/speech/sdi.html>.

2. Frances FitzGerald, *Way out There in the Blue: Reagan, Star Wars, and the End of the Cold War* (New York: Simon and Schuster, 2000).

3. Two studies especially attuned to the rhetorical dimensions of Reagan's speech are Gordon R. Mitchell, *Strategic Deception: Rhetoric, Science and Politics in Missile Advocacy* (East Lansing, MI: Michigan State Univ. Press, 2000), esp. pp. 53-58; and Rebecca Bjork, *The Strategic Defense Initiative: Symbolic Containment of the Nuclear Threat* (New York: SUNY Press, 1992).

4. Reagan, March 23, 1983, speech.

5. Ibid.

6. Ibid.

7. Col. Daniel Smith (USA, ret.), "Chronology of U.S. National Missile Defense Programs." <http://www.cdi.org/hotspots/issuebrief/ch9/>.

8. See Ronald Reagan, "Presenting the Strategic Defense Initiative" (NSDD 172, May 30, 1985) in *National Security Decision Directives of the Reagan and Bush Administrations*, ed. Christopher Simpson (Boulder, Colo.: Westview Press, 1995), pp. 535-48.

9. See George Yang, "The Strategic Defense Initiative," *Daedalus* 114 (1985): 73-90, for a detailed summary of the Hoffman (and Fletcher) report. The Hoffman report can be found in U.S. Senate, Senate Foreign Relations Committee, *Strategic Defense and Anti-Satellite Weapons, Hearings*, 98th Cong., 2[d] sess., April 25, 1984.

10. Yang, "The Strategic Defense Initiative." Declassified sections of the Fletcher report are available in U.S. Senate, Senate Foreign Relations Committee, *Strategic Defense and Anti-Satellite Weapons, Hearings*, 98th Cong., 2d sess., April 25, 1984, pp. 94-175.

11. The OTA study is discussed in Janne E. Nolan, *Guardians of the Arsenal: The Politics of Nuclear Energy* (New York: Basic Books, 1989), pp. 204-5. For discussion of the Union of Concerned Scientists study crafted by Garwin and a response by astrophysicist and Star Wars supporter Robert Jastrow, as well as Garwin's rejoinder, see FitzGerald, *Way out There in the Blue*, pp. 246-47.

12. For a sampling of the issues and parameters of the SDI debate, including some of the key arguments offered by schools in the scientific community, see Arms Control Association, *Star Wars Quotes* (Washington, D.C.: Arms Control Association, July 1986); Steven Anzovin, *The Star Wars Debate* (New York: W. H. Wilson, 1986); and Phillip Boffey, William J. Broad, Leslie Gelb, Charles Mohr, and Holcomb B. Noble, *Claiming the Heavens: The New York Times Complete Guide to the Star Wars Debate* (New York: Times Books, 1988).

13. The issues and temper of the congressional debate can be assayed in former South Dakota senator Larry Pressler's book, *Star Wars: The Strategic Defense Initiative Debates in the Congress* (Westport, Conn.: Greenwood Press, 1986).

14. See my treatment of these arguments by McNamara in chapter 3.

15. Virtually all anti-SDI scientists and skeptical legislators and national security policymakers deployed this argument drawn from the McNamara heritage, though additional scientific studies continued to confirm its veracity. See, e.g., U.S. Cong., Office of Technology Assessment, *Strategic Defenses: Ballistic Missile Defense Technologies, Anti-Satellite Weapons, Countermeasures, and Arms Control* (Princeton, NJ: Princeton Univ. Press, 1986).

16. This issue was brought to light during one of the hearings on SDI and anti-satellite

weapons conducted by the Senate Foreign Relations Committee: U.S. Senate, Committee on Foreign Relations, *Strategic Defense and Anti-satellite Weapons, Hearing*, 98th Cong., 2d sess., April 25, 1984, pp. 69ff.

17. Mitchell, *Strategic Deception*, p. 69.

18. William J. Broad, *Teller's War* (New York: Simon and Schuster, 1985), 148-49.

19. Quoted in Tina Rosenberg, "The Authorized Version," *Atlantic Monthly*, February 1986, p. 26.

20. Guertner, "What is Proof?" in *The Search for Security in Space*, ed. Kenneth Luongo and W. Thomas Wander (Ithaca, N.Y.: Cornell Univ. Press, 1989), p. 191.

21. For analyses of Teller's role in generating the "Star Wars" idea and militantly lobbying for its realization as an operational weapons system, see FitzGerald, *Way out There in the Blue*, pp. 121, 127-29, 131-37, 210-11, and passim. For another reckoning of his influence, see William J. Broad's *Teller's War*.

22. FitzGerald, *Way out There in the Blue*, p. 16.

23. For the most complete and incisive treatment of the deceptive practices engaged in during these tests, see the analysis of Gordon Mitchell in *Strategic Deception*, pp. 60-63.

24. See, for example, the following reports: John Pike, "Strategic 'Deceptive' Initiative," *Arms Control Today* 23 (1993): 3-4; Tim Weiner, "Lies and Rigged 'Star Wars' Fooled the Kremlin, and Congress," *New York Times*, August 1993, p. A1+; and Jeffrey Smith, "3 'Star Wars' Tests Rigged, Aspin Says," *Washington Post*, September 1993, A19. In addition to Mitchell's treatment cited above, see FitzGerald's analysis—*Way out There in the Blue*, p. 489.

25. Donald Baucom, "Missile Defense Milestones, 1944-2000," Missile Defense Agency— <http://www.acq.osd.mil/bmdo/bmdolink/html/milstone.html>.

26. See FitzGerald, *Way out There in the Blue*, passim; former secretary of state George Schultz, *Turmoil and Triumph*, (New York: Charles Scribner's Sons, 1993); Paul Nitze with Ann N. Smith, *From Hiroshima to Glasnost: At the Center of Decisionmaking—a Memoir* (New York: Grove Weidenfeld, 1989); Colin Powell with Joseph E. Persico, *My American Journey* (New York: Random House, 1995); Michael Deaver, *Behind the Scenes* (New York: William Morrow, 1987); and James Baker, The *Politics of Diplomacy* (New York: G. P. Putnam's Sons, 1995).

27. See Mikhail Gorbachev, *Reykjavik: Results and Lessons* (Madison, Conn.: Sphinx Press, 1987); and Gorbachev, *Memoirs* (New York: Doubleday, 1995) for the Soviet leader's rendering of his political motives and intentions relating to the START process. I am persuaded by Frances FitzGerald's analysis and arguments regarding the utopian side of President Reagan's hopes and aspirations for significant strategic arms reductions—see her *Way out There in the Blue*, especially pp. 206, 207, 230, 363, and 354.

28. FitzGerald, esp. ch. 7. Indeed, internal conflicts, debates, and obtacles within the Reagan administration were so fierce that at one point, a Reagan National Security Council deputy remarked: "Even if the Soviets did not exist we might not get a START treaty because of disagreements on our side"—quoted in Strobe Talbott, *Master of the Game: Paul Nitze and the Nuclear Game* (New York: Alfred A. Knopf, 1988), p. 382.

29. Gorbachev, *Reykjavik: Results and Lessons;* and his *Memoirs*.

30. See Douglas Walker, *Congress and the Nuclear Freeze* (Amherst, Mass.: Univ. of Massachusetts Press, 1987).

31. See FitzGerald, *Way out There in the Blue*, and Talbott, *Master of the Game*, passim.

32. Despite the strenuous efforts of administrative spokespeople and scientific supporters of BMD to put a positive spin on technological developments and preliminary testing of the proposed anti-missile system components, the performance standards necessitated by the requirements of an impenetrable—or even mostly leakproof—shield were formidable and, given the developing state of the art of offensive weapons and countermeasures (ABM's Achilles' heel), nearly impossible.

33. See Gordon Mitchell's summary analysis and critical evaluation in his book, *Strate-*

gic Deception, pp. 87-94; and FitzGerald's like-minded assessment, *Way out There in the Blue*, pp. 472-76. For its most vociferous defenders, see Robert McFarlane, "Consider What Star Wars Accomplished," *New York Times*, August 24, 1993, p. A15; Zbigniew Brzezinski, "The Cold War and Its Aftermath," *Foreign Affairs* 71 (Fall 1992): 31-49; Jeane J. Kirkpatrick, "Beyond the Cold War," *Foreign Affairs* 69 (1989-90): 1-16; and Daniel Duedney and G. John Ikenberry, "Who Won the Cold War?" *Foreign Policy* 89 (Summer 1992): 123-38.

34. See John Pike, Bruce G. Blair, and Steven I. Schwartz, "Defending against the Bomb," in *Atomic Audit: The Costs and Consequences of U.S. Nuclear Weapons Since 1940*, ed. Steven I. Schwartz (Washington, D.C.: Brookings Institution Press, 1998), pp. 269-325; Edward Reiss, *The Strategic Defense Initiative* (Cambridge: Cambridge Univ. Press, 1992); and Joseph A. Camilleri, "The Cold War . . . and After: A New Period of Upheaval in World Politics," in *Why the Cold War Ended*, ed. Ralph Summy and Michael E. Salla (Westport, Conn.: Greenwood Press, 1995), pp. 233-47.

35. Quoted in Colin Powell, *My American Journey*, p. 375.

36. FitzGerald, *Way out There in the Blue*, pp. 468-73.

37. See "A History of SDIO and BMDO," at <http://tsi.simplenet.com/tsihtml/ sdio.html>; and US Naval Institute Military Database, "Brilliant Pebbles," at <http://www/ periscope1.comdemo/weapons/missrock/antiball/w0003565.html>; and Col. Daniel Smith, "Chronology of U.S. National Missile Defense Programs."

38. William Broad, *Teller's War*, pp. 265-66.

39. Ibid., pp. 253-55, and passim.

40. See my discussion, pp. 74-75, 90. In addition, see Herbert F. York, *Race to Oblivion*, pp. 131 and 143; and U.S. Rep. John Spratt (Dem. S.C.), "Ballistic Missile Defense and National Security," Remarks to the American Institute of Aeronautics and Astronautics, Monterey, Calif., January 20, 2000— <http://www.house.gov/spratt/news_archive/99_00/ s10624.htm>.

41. FitzGerald, *Way out There in the Blue*, pp. 482-83.

42. Ibid., p. 483.

43. Bruce A. MacDonald, "Falling Star: SDI's Troubled Seventh Year," *Arms Control Today*, September 1990, p. 8.

44. US Naval Institute Military Database, "Brilliant Pebbles."

45. U.S. Government Accounting Office, "Strategic Defense Initiative: Some Claims Overstated for Early Flight Tests of Interceptors" [GAO/NSIAD-92-282], September 1992 (Washington, D.C.: USGPO, 1992); and *New York Times*, June 2, 1992; and Seymour Hersh, "Missile Wars," *New Yorker*, September 20, 1994, pp. 86-99.

46. For critical assessments of the television coverage of the war, see Douglass Kellner, *The Persian Gulf TV War* (Boulder, Colo.: Westview Press, 1992); David Campbell, *Politics Without Principle: Sovereignty, Ethics and the Narratives of the Gulf War* (Boulder, Colo.: Lynne Reinner Publishers, 1993); and the essays in *Taken by Storm: The Media, Public Opinion and Foreign Policy in the Gulf War*, ed. W. Lance Bennett and David Paletz (Chicago: Univ. of Chicago Press, 1994).

47. See, e.g., Steven A. Hildreth, "Evaluation of U.S. Army Assessment of Patriot Antitactical Missile Effectiveness in the War against Iraq" [Report], U.S., House Committee on Operations, *Performance of the Patriot Missile in the Gulf War, Hearing*, 102d Cong., 2d sess., April 7, 1992 (Washington, D.C.: USGPO, 1992); and Marvin Feuerwerger, "Defense against Missiles: Patriot Lessons," *Orbis* 36 (1992): 581-88.

48. Mitchell, "The Rhetoric of Patriot Missile Accuracy in the 1991 Persian Gulf War," *Strategic Deception*, ch. 3; and see also David Hughes, "Success of Patriot System Shapes Debate on Future Antimissile Weapons," *Aviation Week & Space Technology*, April 22, 1991, pp. 90-91.

49. Theodore Postol, "Lessons of the Gulf War Experience with Patriot," *Interna-*

tional Security 16 (1991-92): 118-71; and Reuven Pelatzer, statement before the House Committee on Government Operations—U.S. House, Committee on Government Operations, *Performance of the Patriot Missile in the Gulf War, Hearing*, pp. 118-21.

50. Mitchell, "The Rhetoric of Patriot Missile Accuracy in the 1991 Persian Gulf War," pp. 142-48.

51. See GAO analyst Richard Davis in his statement before the House Committee on Government Operations—U.S. House, Committee on Government Operations, *Performance of the Patriot Missile in the Gulf War, Hearing*, esp. p. 98.

52. FitzGerald, *Way out There in the Blue*, p. 485.

53. *New York Times*, July 18, 1991, p. 1+.

54. FitzGerald, *Way out There in the Blue*, p. 487.

55. U.S. Government Accounting Office, "Strategic Defense Initiative: Some Claims Overstated for Early Flight Tests of Interceptors."

56. In addition to those cited earlier, see the extensive number of studies referenced throughout Mitchell's *Strategic Deception*.

57. Les Aspin, "The End of the Star Wars Era," News Brief, Office of the Assistant Secretary of Defense (Public Affairs), May 13, 1993. <http://www.fas.org/spp/offdocus/d93051.htm>.

58. Willis Stanley, "The Clinton Administration and Ballistic Missile Defense: a Chronology 1993 to 1998," National Institute for Public Policy, <http://www.nip.org/Adobe/Chronology.pdf>; and "Congress Approves Defense Bill, Cuts Back BMD Spending," *Arms Control Today*, December 1993, p. 24.

59. For background on theater BMD policy and systems, see Steven A. Hildreth, "Theater Ballistic Missile Defense Policy, Missions, and Current Status" [no. 95-585], Congressional Research Service, June 10, 1993 (Washington, D.C.: USGPO, 1993); and U.S. Department of Defense, Ballistic Missile Defense Organization, "National Missile Defense" [Fact Sheet JN-00-05], January 2000, <http://www.acq.osd.mil/bmdo/bmdolink/pdf/jn9905.pdf>. More generally, see Mitchell, "Whose Shoe Fits Best? Dubious Physics and Power Politics in the TMD Footprint Controversy," *Strategic Deception*, ch. 4.

60. See, e.g., Joseph Cirincione, Director, Non-Proliferation Project, Carnegie Endowment for Peace, "The Political and Strategic Imperatives of National Missile Defense." <http://www.ceip.org/files/publications/imperativesnmd.asp>.

61. Mitchell makes this cogent and perceptive point in *Strategic Deception*, p. 183.

62. I use these qualifications of the two major scientific schools because the end of the cold war and the assumptions and biases within these American schools of thought meant that the character of scientific debate and the forms it would take call for new ways of categorizing the divisions within the scientific community on political issues relating to war and peace.

63. Mitchell, *Strategic Deception*, p. 183.

64. See Robert Blackwill, "The ABM Treaty and Ballistic Missile Defense," Arms Control and the US-Soviet Relationship: Problems, Prospects and Prescriptions (New York: Council on Foreign Relations, 1996), pp. 37-47, esp. 42-43. <http://www.fas.org/spp/eprint/cfr_nc_4.htm>.

65. Ibid., pp. 209-215.

66. Gen. Larry Welch, Report of the Panel on Reducing Risk in Flight Test Programs, Federation of American Scientists, February 27, 1998—Government Accounting Office, "Issues Concerning Acquisition of THAAD Prototype System" [Report # GAOINSIAD-96-136], July 9, 1996 (Washington, D.C.: USGPO, 1996), <http://www.fas.org/spp/starwars/program/welch/>; and Joseph Cirincione, "The Persistence of the Missile Defense Illusion" (paper presented at the UNESCO Conference on Nuclear Disarmament, Safe Disposal of Nuclear Materials and New Weapons Development, Como, Italy, July 2-4, 1998), available at the Carnegie Endowment Web site: <http://www.ceip.org/programs/npp/ bmd.htm>.

67. Mitchell, *Strategic Deception*, p. 209.

68. U.S. GAO, Issues Concerning Acquisition of THAAD Prototype System," p. 10.

69. William D. Hartung and Michelle Ciarrocca, "Tangled Web: The Marketing of Missile Defense 1994-2000," May 2000, <http://www.worldpolicy.org/projects/arms/reports/tangled.htm>; and Steven A. Hildreth, "National Missile Defense: The Current Debate," [Issue Brief #96-441F, June 7, 1996] Congressional Research Service (Washington, D.C.: USGPO, 1996).

70. John Pike, "National Missile Defense," Federation of American Scientists, June 27, 2000. <http://www.fas.org/spp/starwars/program/nmd/>.

71. Ibid.

72. Rumsfeld Commission, Report of the Commission to Assess the Ballistic Missile Threat to the United States (Washington, D.C.: USGPO, 1998)— <http://www.house.gov/hasc/testimony/105thcongress/BMThreat.htm>. For divergent perspectives on the substance and recommendations of the report, see Richard L. Garwin, "The Rumsfeld Report—What We Did," *Bulletin of the Atomic Scientists* 54 (1998): 40-45; and Charles Pena and Barbara Conry, "National Missile Defense," *Policy Analysis* 337 (March 16, 1999): 5-6.

73. FitzGerald, *Way out There in the Blue*, p. 495.

74. William S. Cohen, Office of Assistant Secretary of Defense (Public Affairs), News Briefing, January 20, 1999. <http://www.fas.org/spp/starwars/program/news99/t01201999_t0120md.htm>.

75. John Isaacs, "Go Slow: The People Speak on Missile Defense," *Arms Control Today*, January/February 2000, <http://www.armscontrol.org/act/2000_01-02/jijf00.asp>; and FitzGerald, *Way out There in the Blue*, p. 499.

76. Donald Baucom, "Missile Defense Milestones, 1944-2000," (Washington, D.C.: BMDO, 2000). <http://www.acq.osd.mil/bmdo/bmdolink/html/milstone.html>.

77. For the text, see <http://www.cdi.org/hotspots/missiledefense/act.html>.

78. Baucom, "Missile Defense Milestones, 1944-2000."

79. <http://usinfo.state.gov/topical/pol/arms/nmd/nmdarch.htm>.

80. Col. Daniel Smith, "Chronology of U.S. National Missile Defense Programs."

81. Ibid.

82. Philip Coyle, "Missile Defense and Related Programs" [FY'99 Annual Report], Director, Operational Test & Evaluation Office Website—<http://www.dote.osd.mil/reports/FY99/index.html>.

83. Col. Daniel Smith, "Chronology of U.S. National Missile Defense Programs."

84. *New York Times*, September 2, 2000; and the revealing exchange between Senator Jon Kyl (Rep., AZ) and John Pike, Director, FAS Space Policy Project, in *Jim Lehrer News Hour* (PBS), "Missile Defense Politics" [transcript], September 1, 2000, <http://www.pbs.org/newshour/bb/military/july-dec00/nmd_9-01.html>.

85. Wade Boese, "Bush Assembles Pro-Missile Defense National Security Team," *Arms Control Today*, January/February 2001, <http://www.armscontrol.org/ACT/janfeb01/bushjanfeb01.htm>; and Jonathan Landay, "At Confirmation, Rumsfeld Promotes Missile Defense," *Philadelphia Inquirer*, January 12, 2001, <http://inq.philly.com/content/inquirer/2001/01/12/national/RUMSFELD/2.htm>.

86. George W. Bush, "Missile Defense" [text], National Defense University, Washington, D.C., May 1, 2001. <http://www.newsmax.com/archives/articles/2001/5/1/183500.shtml>.

87. See, for example, George Will, "What Is a 'Working' Weapon?" *Washington Post*, May 10, 2001, p. A31; and Thomas Shanker, "Missile Defenses Need More Tests, Senator Says," *New York Times*, June 1, 2001, <http://groups.yahoo.com/group/abolition-caucus/message/4832>; and more generally, Michael Gordon, "Military Analysis: Grand Plan, Few Details," *New York Times*, May 2, 2001, <http://www.nytimes.com/2001/05/02/world/02MILI.html>.

88. David E. Sanger and Thom Shanker, "U.S. Plans Offer to Russia to End ABM Treaty Dispute," *New York Times Online*, May 28, 2001, <http://dailynews.yahoo.com/htx/nyt/20010528/ts/u_s_plans_offer_to_russia_to_end_abm_treaty_dispute_1.html>; "Bush: Allies Have Say on Missile Shield Development," *Reuters News Service*, June 11, 2001, <http://dailynews.yahoo.com/htx/nm/20010611/pl/arms_bush_dc_1.html>; Martin Nesirky, "Russia Unconvinced on Missiles, U.S. Talks to Go On," *Reuters News Service*, May 11, 2001, <http://dailynews.yahoo.com/h/nm/20010511/ts/arms_use_russia_dc.html>; and Michael Wines, "Russia Continues to Oppose Scrapping ABM Treaty," *New York Times*, May 29, 2001, <http://www.nci.org/0new/bmd-nyt52901.htm>; and Paul Eckert, "China Rebuffs U.S. on Missile Shield," *Reuters News Service*, May 15, 2001, <http://www.space.com/news/spaceagencies/china_missile_defense_0010515_wg.html>.

89. Steven Mufsun and Walter Pincus, "Missile Defense Outstrips Technology." *Washington Post*, May 3, 2001, p. A16.

90. Robert Burns, "Pentagon Revives Reagan-Era Proposal," *AP Newsline*, July 17, 2001. <http://www.commondreams.org/headlines01/0717-04.htm>.

91. Robert Burns, "Military Chief Urges Space Weaponry," *Associated Press Newsline*, August 1, 2001. <http://elections.excite.com/news/ap/010801/15/space-weapons>.

92. Thomas E. Ricks and Walter Pincus, "Pentagon Plans Major Changes in U.S. Strategy," *Washington Post*, May 7, 2001, p. 1+.

93. Wade Boese, "Bush Meets Opposition to Missile Defense while in Europe," *Arms Control Today*, July/August 2001, <http://www.armscontrol.org/act/2001_07-08/bushtripjul_aug01.asp>; and Carter M. Yang, "Tough Sell: Bush Pitches Missile Plan to NATO," ABCNEWS.com, June 13, 2001, <http://abcnews.go.com/sections/politics/DailyNews/Bush_Europe010613.html>.

94. Martin Nesirky, "Russia Unconvinced on Missiles, U.S. Talks to Go On," <yahoo.com/h/nm/20010511/ts/arms_usa_rusia_dc.htm>; David Sanger and Thom Shanker, "U.S. Plans Offer to Russia to End ABM Treaty Dispute," *New York Times Online*, <http://www.nci.org/0new/bmd-nyt52801.htm>; and Michael Wines, "Russia Continues to Oppose Scrapping ABM Treaty," *New York Times*, May 29, 2001, <http://dailynews.yahoo.com/htx/nyt/20010529/wl/russia_continues_to_oppose_scrapping_abm_treaty_1/html>.

95. "Rumsfeld: Missile Defense Would Have Holes at First," *China Daily*, May 2, 2001, <http://www1.chinadaily.com.cn/news/2001-05-02/4088.html>; and Thomas L. Friedman's acerbic op/ed critique of the defense secretary's position, "Who's Crazy Here?" *New York Times*, May 15, 2001, <http://www.nytimes.com/2001/05/15/opinion/15FRIE.html>.

96. Sharon LaFraniere, "Rice Expects Russian Assent on U.S. Shield," *Washington Post*, July 27, 2001, p. A27.

97. Elain Monaghan, "Documents Show U.S. Expects to Violate ABM [Treaty] in Months," *Reuters News Service*, July 12, 2001, <http://www.commondreams.org/headlines01/0712-01.htm>; and Patricia Wilson, "Bush Says U.S. to Quit Arms Pact on 'Our Timetable,'" *New York Times Daily News*, August 23, 2001, <http://dailynews.yahoo.com/h/nm/20010823/ts/arms_usa_bush_dc_4.html>.

98. Jim Wolf, "U.S. Plans Missile Defense Test Sites in Alaska," *Reuters New Service*, July 10, 2001. <http://www.gn.apc.org/cndyorks/yspace/articles/bmd/alaskamdsites.htm>.

99. James Dao, "Pentagon to Seek Money for Testing Missile Defense," *New York Times Online*, July 10, 2001. <http://www.gn.apc.org/cndyorks/yspace/articles/bmd/moneyformdtest.htm>.

100. See John F. Tierney, "Pentagon Report Reveals Flaws in Missile Defense," boston.com, July 10, 2001; Charles Adinger, "U.S. Anti-Missile Test Aided by Beacon—Officials," *Reuters News Service*, July 28, 2001, <http://dailynews.yahoo.com/h/nm/20010727/ts/arms_usa_missile_dc_1.html>.

CONCLUSION

1. I am indebted to Rene Herrmann for this term and for his invaluable comments and suggested references relating to comparative American and Soviet R&D and deployment strategies. Especially valuable in situating my own work in this area was his paper "The Technological Environment of US-SU Antagonism and the Arms Race Concept" (prepared at the third annual National Security Education Seminar, Colorado Springs, Colo., Summer 1973). For additional sources dealing with U.S. long-range planning and weapons development policies, see Ernest J. Yanarella, "The 'Technological Imperative' and the Strategic Arms Race," *Peace and Change* 3 (Spring 1975): 15, n. 46.

2. See Art's *The TFX Controversy* for a case analysis of the technological problems and political woes to which TFX was heir.

3. As Ida Hoos has stated, "It is the technological approach to national security that has been deliberately and rationally chosen. The model devised by the Department of Defense experts has created in the minds of the bemused public the myth that there are technological solutions, even though the problems may be essentially political, economic, or social." Hoos, *Systems Analysis in Public Policy*, p. 56.

4. This term was also coined by Rene Herrmann, though the notion of an incremental acquisition strategy was first suggested as a category by Robert Perry et al., in "System Acquisition Strategies," RAND Report No. R-827-PR ARPA (Santa Monica, Calif., June 1971), p. 39. For additional materials on this style of technological planning, see Yanarella, "The 'Technological Imperative' and the Strategic Arms Race," p. 14, n. 38.

5. This belief often led American strategic planners to conclude mistakenly that the Soviets were one generation behind strategically.

6. This was the "Griffon" system, a forerunner of the Soviet Tallinn ABM system, as Johan Holst has pointed out—Holst, "Missile Defense, the Soviet Union, and the Arms Race," p. 151.

7. George Rathjens has made this point about the benefits the Soviets derive from being in second place technologically: "My . . . point on the relationship of output and input has to do with the difference between breaking new ground on the one hand and following someone else on the other. . . . It takes much less effort to keep up than it does to lead. The fact is that even if one does not know exactly how someone else has done something, there is nevertheless great advantage in simply knowing that it is possible. . . . We have, in effect, done much of their R&D for them." Joint Economic Committee, *The Economics of National Priorities*, pp. 404-5.

8. Johan Holst calls this an imitative rather than offsetting reaction on the part of the Soviets (Holst, "Missile Defense, the Soviet Union, and the Arms Race," pp. 163, 169).

9. Arnold Horelick and Myron Rush, *Strategic Power and Soviet Foreign Policy* (Chicago, 1966), passim.

10. In 1964 General Nicolai Talensky voiced the Soviet military establishment's position on ABM from this defense-minded tradition when he stated: "It is obvious that the creation of an effective anti-missile system merely serves to build up the security of the peaceable nonaggressive state. The creation of an effective anti-missile system enables the state to make its defense dependent chiefly on its own possibilities, and not on mutual deterrence, that is on the goodwill of the other side." Talensky, "Anti-Missile Systems and Disarmament," p. 18.

11. York, *Race to Oblivion*, p. 230.

12. Quoted by James Dick, "The Strategic Arms Race, 1957-1961," *Journal of Politics* 34 (November 1972): 1063, from a reference in Jacob Javits's essay, "Can President Nixon Stop the Arms?" *Saturday Review*, March 1, 1968, p. 16.

13. These are terms coined by German social theorist and philosopher Jurgen Habermas.

14. In this respect, civilian strategists like Donald Brennan, Johan Holst, and others

who supported deployment of ABM systems strategic and arms control reasons were far better "empiricists" than McNamara and his team of economic analysts. See Edgar Bottome, *The Balance of Terror* (Boston, 1971), passim.

15. Advanced by Colin S. Gray and Johan Holst—Gray, "Action and Reaction in the Nuclear Arms Race," *Military Review* 51 (August 1971): 19-20; and Holst, "Missile Defense, the Soviet Union, and the Arms Race," p. 174.

16. In this policy, the United States was apparently following the logical corollary to "action-reaction," namely, "inaction-reaction." If the "action-reaction" logic is correct, then, as Colin Gray observes, "it should follow that a conspicuous and unambiguous act of self-denial will meet with parallel responsive inaction from an adversary." Gray, "Action and Reaction in the Nuclear Arms Race," p. 22.

17. Cited by Holst, "Missile Defense, the Soviet Union, and the Arms Race," pp. 168-69.

18. Ibid., pp. 154-85.

19. See Tom Raum, "Talk of U.S. Isolationism Increasing," *Washington Post Online*, July 26, 2001, <http://www.washingtonpost.com/wp-dyn/articles/A57132-2001Jul26.html>; and Andrew Chang, "Why the World Community Attacks the U.S.," ABCNews.com, July 31, 2001, <http://abcnews.go.com/sections/world/DailyNews/world10731_protest.htm>.

20. Tuveson, *Redeemer Nation: The Idea of America's Millennial Role* (Chicago: Univ. of Chicago Press, 1968).

21. Frances FitzGerald, *City on a Hill: A Journey through Contemporary American Cultures* (New York: Simon and Schuster, 1988); and *Way out There in the Blue*.

22. For greater elaboration on the background and context of this symbolization, see Ernest J. Yanarella, *The Cross, the Plow and the Skyline: Contemporary Science Fiction and the Ecological Imagination* (Parkland, Fla.: Brown Walker Press, 2001), chapters 1 and 2.

23. John Winthrop, City Upon a Hill Sermon, 1630. <http://www.mtholyoke.edu/acad /intrel/winthrop.htm>.

24. Cited in Jim Lobe, "U.S. Anti-Europeanism Raises Its Hoary Head," *TerraViva On Line*, no. 52 (August/September 2001). <http://www.nscentre.org/monthly/opinion/opinion51_2.htm>.

25. See James Morone, "The Corrosive Politics of Virtue," *American Prospect* 76 (May/June 1996). <http:www.prospect.org/V7/26/morone-j.htm>.

26. Daryl Baskin, *American Pluralist Democracy: A Critique* (New York: VanNostrand Reinhold Co., 1971).

27. Louis Hartz, *The Liberal Tradition in America: An Interpretation of American Political Thought Since the Revolution* (New York: Harcourt, Brace, 1955).

28. See Lobe's "U.S. Anti-Europeanism Raises Its Hoary Head" for a cataloguing of right-wing criticism of European leaders' reactions to the Bush administration's moral lecturing and political consultations on global warming, racism, and missile defense.

29. It should be pointed out that the right-wing intellectual interpretation of this dialectic of isolationism and unilateralism foreswears Wilsonian internationalism and claims that it offers a third pathway to foreign and military policies—see Irving Kristol's "A Post-Wilsonian Foreign Policy," *On the Issues* [a monthly forum of opinion published by the American Enterprise Institute], August 1996, <http://www.aei.org/oti6856.htm>.

30. Charles Krauthammer, "The Bush Doctrine, ABM, Kyoto, and the New American Unilateralism," *Weekly Standard* 6 (June 4, 2001). <http:www.weeklystandard.com/magazine/mag_6_36_01/krauthammer_feat_6_36_01.asp>.

31. See Charles and Mary Beard, *America in Midpassage—Vol. I* (New York: The Macmillan Company, 1939).

32. I owe this insight to Frances FitzGerald (*Way out There in the Blue*, esp. p. 78) and her interview comments on the Bush missile defense announcement collected in Fiona Morgan, "Missile Defense Goes Global," Salon.com, May 2, 2001, <http://www.salon.com/politics/feature/2001/05/02/abm/print.htm>.

33. See, e.g., William Hartung and Michelle Ciarrocca, "Tangled Web: the Marketing of Missile Defense, 1994-2000," *World Policy Institute Special Brief*, May 2000. <http://www.worldpolicy.org/ projects/arms/reports/tangled.htm>.

34. William Martin explores the Christian right's disproportionate influence upon the Republican Party in his essay, "The Christian Right and American Foreign Policy," *Foreign Policy*, no. 114 (Spring 1999): 66-80.

35. David Shapiro, for example, in his book, *Neurotic Styles* (New York: Basic Books, 1972).

36. See Jonathan Schell's earlier articulation of this possibility and Gordon R. Mitchell's more recent provisional embrace of this idea: Schell, *The Abolition* (New York: Alfred A. Knopf, 1984); and Mitchell, *Strategic Deception*, pp. 282-83.

37. For a contrary view by the popularizer of the end-of-history thesis, see Francis Fukayama, *The End of History and the Last Man* (New York: The Free Press, 1992).

INDEX